READINGS IN EPISTEMOLOGY

from
Aquinas,
Bacon, Galileo, Descartes,
Locke, Berkeley, Hume,
Kant

by
VINCENT G. POTTER

Fordham University Press
New York
1993

Library of Congress Cataloging-in-Publication Data

Readings in epistemology : from Aquinas, Bacon, Galileo, Descartes,
    Locke, Berkeley, Hume, Kant / introduction and selection by
    Vincent G. Potter. — 2nd ed. rev.
            p.   cm.
    Includes bibliographical references.
    ISBN 0-8232-1493-1. — ISBN 0-8232-1492-3 (pbk.)
    1. Knowledge, Theory of.   I. Potter, Vincent G.
    BD161.R342   1993
    121—dc20   92-45079
                                                         CIP

Printed in the United States of America

To

MY TEACHERS

who taught me to read
the great philosophers
respectfully
but critically

CONTENTS

PREFACE

THIS COLLECTION OF READINGS was gathered to fulfill the requirements of a specific course taught at Fordham College, namely, a
core course, required of all sophomores, in epistemology. The
aims of the course were not only to acquaint the students with the
major issues in the philosophy of knowledge, but also to introduce them to that period of European philosophical thought
known as the Enlightenment. The authors presented here are
mainly from the British Empiricists, with the exceptions of
Descartes, "Father of modern philosophy," and Kant, the great
critical synthesizer. This in no way implies that the great
Rationalists of the period (Spinoza and Leibniz) are not important. The choice represents a preference for what can be covered
in the limited time available within a single semester. In some
ways the British Empiricists are easier for beginners to grasp; they
have a peculiar inner logic of development (from Locke to
Berkeley to Hume); and, finally, they have had great influence on
so much of contemporary Anglo-American philosophy (for better
or for worse!).

I wish to thank Dr. Vincent Colapietro, my colleague in the
Fordham Department of Philosophy, for his helpful suggestions
in selecting texts to be included in this volume. Besides certain
passages from Locke, Hume, and Kant, he recommended including something from Aquinas, Bacon, and Galileo. The short piece
from Aquinas included in the Appendix makes an important
point about the nature of signs as they function in cognition:
namely, that they are not usually what is known but that by
which or in which something is known. And this is in contrast to
what seem to be the representationalist views of some
Enlightenment thinkers. The excerpts from Galileo and Bacon
introduce the influence of empirical science in shaping the
Enlightenment and also make the famous distinction between
primary and secondary sensibles which plays such an important
role in Locke.

I have added no footnotes and have provided Study
Questions at the end of each selection simply to help focus the
students' attention on the main ideas of each section. The
Introduction attempts to situate these philosophers in the broader

historical context of Europe from the sixteenth through the eighteenth centuries. At the beginning of each author's selections, there is a brief biographical sketch and a very brief list of suggested readings. The teacher no doubt has his own preferred references adapted to the group he is teaching. Finally, I have provided no critical commentary or evaluation, with the exception of some brief and very general remarks concerning (erroneous) assumptions which the Rationalists and Empiricists of the period held in common. I leave further elaboration (or contradiction) to the teacher. Again, more specific criticism is best left to each one's own particular emphasis and point of view.

In the situation in which these readings are a supplement to a regular course in epistemology, the teacher may find that covering them all is too much for this or that particular group. At Fordham the faculty decided that this course should include at least Descartes, Hume, and Kant.

VINCENT G. POTTER
Fordham University

INTRODUCTION

THE PERIOD FROM DESCARTES TO KANT (from the end of the sixteenth to the end of the eighteenth centuries) is sometimes called the "classical" period of modern European philosophy. It extends from the close of the Renaissance through the Age of the Enlightenment. Usually the Enlightenment is said to have taken place in the eighteenth century. With the exception of Descartes (who died in 1650), each of the philosophers included in our readings lived during the eighteenth century and all (including Descartes) had decisive influence on the Enlightenment.

Whether one ultimately judges the name "enlightenment" to be accurate, whimsical, or ironic will depend upon one's judgment about that period's contribution to the advancement of culture, politics, and society. More generally, the philosopher must ask whether and to what extent the new "light" advanced wisdom and mankind's love of it. In any case, regardless of what history or historians or we ourselves may think of that era, those who lived during it considered themselves "enlightened" (by what and by whom needs to be considered later) and "liberated" (from what and for what might also bear consideration).

During those two hundred years, Modern European philosophy was formed. Descartes is usually credited with beginning the "modern" philosophical movement of which the Enlightenment schools of Rationalism and Empiricism are the major expression. What the differences between these schools were will become evident in the course of our reading. What may slip by unnoticed is what their similarities were—their common assumptions, substantive and methodological.

Rationalism reigned chiefly on the Continent; Empiricism prospered in the British Isles. Perhaps the best-known proponents of Rationalism were Descartes, Spinoza, and Leibniz, while Empiricism found its champions in Locke, Berkeley, and Hume. Kant attempted to synthesize the best traits of both schools of the Enlightenment. His synthesis is known as "transcendental philosophy," perhaps the best philosophical thought of that period. However that may be, Kant's work was certainly the transition to nineteenth-century German Idealism (Fichte, Schelling, and Hegel).

First, then, what was the "Enlightenment"? As a result of the rebirth of culture (the "Renaissance") which took place mainly in Italy through the rediscovery of Classical civilization, man and things human became the center of attention. With that came a conviction about the competence of human reason for handling human affairs and for solving human problems. The tremendous success of the new science and the advances in technology held out hope for unlimited progress. With science came an awareness of method for dealing with any problematic situation. This disciplined use of reason brought "light" where previously there had been only the darkness of superstition and the blindness of *a priori* opinion. Reason, then, was considered to be the "light of the world." The only difficulty was to find the correct method for using it. So Descartes and Bacon, each in different ways, tried to construct a method or *organum*. Leibniz dreamed of a universal calculus, while Hume sought the universal laws of thinking.

Besides the rise of modern science, which had so decisive an effect on Enlightenment thinking, consider what had happened to Europe politically, socially, and economically by the end of the sixteenth century and what was happening during the seventeenth and eighteenth centuries. These events both shaped and were shaped by the ideas of the Enlightenment. In the first place, Europe had just come through a religious revolution (the Reformation) which fragmented Christianity both on the Continent and in England. A series of bloody religious wars were fought which not only left the Church as an institution considerably weaker but made for her bitter and lasting enemies.

This religious rebellion, coupled with the discovery of the power of scientific reasoning, made many feel that they had been freed from the superstition of religion in general and from the repression of thought by the institutional Church in particular. Not all the Enlightenment's leaders were non-believers, but many of them were anticlerical. A good many more adopted a "natural" religion or a religion congenial to science and reason as they understood them. Hence many became deists of one sort or another.

This religious fragmentation fueled the flames of rivalry between the various kingdoms of Europe in that it effectively ended any notion of the Holy Roman Empire or of the papacy as political arbiter between Christian sovereigns. Political fragmentation in Europe was well on its way. The political ambitions of the various kingdoms were further advanced by the newfound wealth coming in from the "new world" colonies. Nationalism was not very far away, a sort of international "individualism" fostered by the Enlightenment.

The monarchy itself came under fire when the so-called "divine right" of kings was challenged by Robert Bellarmine (against the English king James I in 1607, and against Gallicanism in 1610), and by John Locke (in his first treatise on government in 1690), in favor of some sort of theory whereby the power of governing is vested in the people. Then, in England, the "Glorious Revolution" of 1688 also weakened the power of the monarchy. In any case, absolute monarchy had begun its slide toward the bloody events of the French Revolution.

Along with attacks on established arrangements for both Church and State came a beginning of the decline of the hereditary aristocracy. Not least among the developments which weakened it as a political and social institution was the tremendous rise in commerce due to trade with various colonies. The source of wealth was beginning to shift from landholdings to shares in trading companies and to retail know-how. More and more emphasis was being placed on individual initiative and even on ruthlessness in the trading of goods. Capitalism was in the making. Whether as a result of this rise in the importance of commerce or as its cause, individuals were beginning to replace the collectivity in the thinking and even in the legislation of the eighteenth century. This spirit of free trade and of individual worth, of "liberty, equality, fraternity," brought the Enlightenment to its climax in the American and French Revolutions.

As historians have pointed out, European institutions changed as a result of a change of ideas—a change of outlook on the world. In the new outlook, change was preferred to stability; this world became more important than the next; scientific method and research were considered better than an appeal to authority or to metaphysics; and finally the paradigm of knowing was the scientific use of reason.

The philosophers during this period are generally classified as either Rationalist or Empiricist. They are considered to be

Rationalist if their ideal of knowing was the deductive model captured in mathematics (e.g., Descartes) and if they considered intellect in its clear and distinct ideas to be the only reliable source of certain knowledge. These ideas were generally thought to be innate and to arise in consciousness on the occasion of sense experience. The senses of themselves were unreliable and so not a source of our knowing. Those philosophers were considered to be Empiricist if their ideal of knowing was the inductive method of the physical sciences (e.g., Francis Bacon) and if they thought that all our ideas, howsoever abstract, came through the senses. Not only were the senses reliable sources of knowledge, they were the only sources. There were no innate ideas.

Different as these approaches to philosophy are, Rationalism and Empiricism during this period still had many assumptions in common. In the first place, both assumed that complex "ideas" could be broken down, without loss, into simple ones, and that, conversely, complex ideas could be reconstructed out of their simple constituents. This principle is sometimes called "reductionism" according to which some phenomenon "x" is analyzed into its parts and is then said to be "nothing but" those parts. This led eventually to positing an atomistic world of simple absolutes, intrinsically unrelated among themselves (except through mental association, as in Hume's criticism of causality).

Again, the common assumption of reductionism implied the common methodological assumption of Analysis and Synthesis. Something was understood if and only if it had been analyzed into its simple parts and then reconstituted in its complexity.

Further, the Enlightenment philosophers, whether Rationalist or Empiricist, assumed that *what* we know are "ideas," that is, some sort of psychic representation of reality. (It is because of this assumption that I have included the Appendix selection from Aquinas [*Summa theologiae*, q. 85, a. 2].) The difference between Rationalist and Empiricist was merely in what kind of psychic representation to make fundamental: sense impressions for the Empiricists; clear and distinct ideas (innate intellectual contents) for the Rationalists. For both schools this assumption led to immanentism (knowledge is a state of the subject) and to the "problem of the bridge" (how to "get outside" one's mind).

Finally, most of the Enlightenment philosophers assumed that to know is to be certain. They were haunted by the search for cer-titude, to the point that Hume was driven to a form of skepticism. Certainty for these philosophers meant "impossibility of error"; hence a proposition was certain if and only if its denial implied a contradiction, whether logical or performatory. This standard for the certitude which characterizes knowledge was so high and so stringent that most of what we would ordinarily say "we know" we would not know but merely believe. This connection between certitude and knowledge is multiply vulnerable. I leave it to the reader to find the weaknesses. I will only suggest the following points as typical: (1) although it is no doubt true that if I know that-p, then I have a right to be certain about that-p; (2) but to exercise my right to be certain about that-p, I must know that I know that-p; is this always and necessarily the case? (3) being certain that-p does not guarantee that-p is true and hence does not guarantee that I know that-p; and (4) is knowing that-p a state of mind at all? Does it exhibit some characteristic (say, overwhelm-ing conviction) available to introspection by which knowing is recognized?

These are some of the more obvious and more important (and, in my opinion, erroneous) assumptions which classical Rationalism and Empiricism shared. As one goes through the fol-lowing readings, others may emerge. When these common assumptions are made explicit, it becomes clear that it is not so much a case of our choosing between rival schools as a case of rejecting the entire approach to philosophy based on such assumptions.

The English version of St. Thomas is that generally known as The Dominican Translation of St. Thomas, revised and corrected by Anton C. Pegis in Volume I of his edition of *The Basic Writings of Saint Thomas Aquinas*, published by Random House in 1945. The selection from Galileo is taken from Stillman Drake's *Discoveries and Opinions of Galileo* (1957), as reprinted in Richard H. Popkin's *The Philosophy of the Sixteenth and Seventeenth Centuries* published by The Free Press in 1966. The passages from Bacon's *Novum Organum* are from J. Devey's edition published by Collier in 1902.

The translation of Descartes' *A Discourse on Method* (1637) and *The Meditations on the First Philosophy* (1641) is by John Veitch, first published in 1850. The text of Locke is from *An Essay Concerning Human Understanding* (1690) as found in A. C. Fraser's 1894 edition, published in two volumes by The Clarendon Press, Oxford. The text of Berkeley's *A Treatise Concerning the Principles of Human Knowledge* (1710) follows Fraser's 1871 edition, *The Works of George Berkeley, D.D.* (Oxford: Clarendon Press). The text of Hume's *Enquiry Concerning Human Understanding* (1748) follows the text of 1777 published in 1826. Finally, the translation of Kant's *Prolegomena to Any Future Metaphysics* (1783) is by Paul Carus; the selections from the *Critique of Pure Reason* are from Norman Kemp Smith's translation (London: Macmillan, 1918), while that of "What is Enlightenment" is by Ted Humphrey in *Perpetual Peace and Other Essays* published by Hackett in 1983.

Readings in Epistemology

1

Francis Bacon

(1561–1626)

FRANCIS BACON WAS BORN in London in 1561. His father, Sir Nicholas Bacon, was Lord Keeper of the Great Seal under Elizabeth I. He attended Trinity College, Cambridge, from 1573 to 1575. The following year he enrolled at Gray's Inn to study law but in fact spent much of his time in France with the English ambassador. It was only after his father's death in 1579 that he studied law seriously and eventually became a member of Parliament.

With the accession of James I to the throne in 1603 Bacon was favored by the court and was knighted. During the following years he held a number of important positions including Solicitor General, Attorney General, Lord Keeper of the Great Seal, and Lord Chancellor. In consequence he was also raised in rank among the nobility, being made Baron Verulam in 1618 and Viscount St. Albans in 1621.

Bacon was accused of taking bribes and was found guilty. He lost all his offices and went into retirement to write and pursue scientific work. He died in 1626.

During his Cambridge days Bacon acquired a great distaste for the Aristotelianism of his day. He considered it without any real fruit and full of useless argument. His best-known work, *Novum Organum* (1620), both criticized the Aristotelian way of doing things and proposed a new method better suited to scientific investigation, the inductive method. The duties of his public life seriously impeded his scientific projects. Nonetheless, he managed to produce several works: his Essays in 1597, and his *Of the Proficiency and Advancement of Learning* in 1605. He was also working on a plan for a utopia which would be a center for scientific research. This work was published in 1627 and entitled *New Atlantis*.

Bacon's *Novum Organum* was only one part of a great work he had planned which was to be called the *Great Instauration of Human Control in the Universe*. This work was to have had six parts: (1) The Division of the Sciences; (2) The New Organon; (3) The Phenomena of the Universe; (4) The Ladder of the Intellect; (5) The Forerunners or Anticipations of the New Philosophy; and (6) The New Philosophy or Active Science. Bacon finished part one and wrote portions of parts two and three. The rest remained only in the planning stage.

In general, Bacon's anti-Aristotelian position looked to formulating a method of discovery which would expand human knowledge rather than simply expound and explicitate what was already known. This is the inductive procedure in contrast to the deductive.

Bacon's attempt at formulating a logic of discovery seems crude to us and is full of errors. Still it was a pioneering attempt to formulate the experimental mindset being introduced by the "new" science. Bacon's understanding of inductive generalization is still influenced by Aristotelianism insofar as he thought that through induction one reached forms in things which grounded our certitude of those general-izations. Bacon had no idea of statistical generalization. Hence his work is of more historical than philosophical interest today. For all that, he is an essential figure for understanding the modern mind.

SUGGESTED READING

Anderson, F. H. *The Philosophy of Francis Bacon*. Chicago: The University of Chicago Press, 1948.

Collins, J. *A History of Modern European Philosophy*. Milwaukee: Bruce, 1956.

Copleston, F., S.J. *A History of Philosophy*. III. *Ockham to Suarez*. Westminster, Md.: Newman, 1953.

From

Novum Organum
or
True Suggestions for the Interpretation of Nature

Preface

They who have presumed to dogmatize on nature, as on some well investigated subject, either from self-conceit or arrogance, and in the professorial style, have inflicted the greatest injury on philosophy and learning. For they have tended to stifle and interrupt inquiry exactly in proportion as they have prevailed in bringing others to their opinion: and their own activity has not counterbalanced the mischief they have occasioned by corrupting and destroying that of others. They again who have entered upon a contrary course, and asserted that nothing whatever can be known, whether they have fallen into this opinion from their hatred of the ancient sophists, or from the hesitation of their minds, or from an exuberance of learning, have certainly adduced reasons for it which are by no means contemptible. They have not, however, derived their opinion from true sources, and hurried on by their zeal and some affection, have certainly exceeded due moderation. But the more ancient Greeks (whose writings have perished), held a more prudent mean, between the arrogance of dogmatism, and the despair of scepticism; and though too frequently intermingling complaints and indignation at the difficulty of inquiry, and the obscurity of things, and champing, as it were, the bit, have still persisted in pressing their point, and pursuing their intercourse with nature; thinking, as it seems, that the better method was not to dispute upon the very point of the possibility of anything being known, but to put it to the test of experience. Yet they themselves, by only employing the power of the understanding, have not adopted a fixed rule, but have laid their whole stress upon intense meditation, and a continual exercise and perpetual agitation of the mind.

Our method, though difficult in its operation, is easily
explained. It consists in determining the degrees of certainty,
while we, as it were, restore the senses to their former rank, but
generally reject that operation of the mind which follows close
upon the senses, and open and establish a new and certain course
for the mind from the first actual perceptions of the senses themselves. This, no doubt, was the view taken by those who have
assigned so to much logic; showing clearly thereby that they
sought some support for the mind, and suspected its natural and
spontaneous mode of action. But this is now employed too late as
a remedy, when all is clearly lost, and after the mind, by the daily
habit and intercourse of life, has come prepossessed with corrupt-
ed doctrines, and filled with the vainest idols. The art of logic
therefore being (as we have mentioned), too late a precaution,
and in no way remedying the matter, has tended more to confirm
errors, than to disclose truth. Our only remaining hope and salva-
tion is to begin the whole labor of the mind again; not leaving it
to itself, but directing it perpetually from the very first, and
attaining our end as it were by mechanical aid. If men, for
instance, had attempted mechanical labors with the hands alone,
and without the power and aid of instruments, as they have not
hesitated to carry on the labors of their understanding with the
unaided efforts of their mind, they would have been able to move
and overcome but little, though they had exerted their utmost
and united powers. And just to pause awhile on this comparison,
and look into it as a mirror; let us ask, if any obelisk of a remarkable size were perchance required to be moved, for the purpose of
gracing a triumph or any similar pageant, and men were to
attempt it with their bare hands, would not any sober spectator
avow it to be an act of the greatest madness? And if they should
increase the number of workmen, and imagine that they could
thus succeed, would he not think so still more? But if they chose
to make a selection, and to remove the weak, and only employ
the strong and vigorous, thinking by this means, at any rate, to
achieve their object, would he not say that they were more fondly
deranged? Nay, if not content with this, they were to determine
on consulting the athletic art, and were to give orders for all to
appear with their hands, arms, and muscles regularly oiled and
prepared, would he not exclaim that they were taking pains to

rave by method and design? Yet men are hurried on with the same senseless energy and useless combination in intellectual matters, as long as they expect great results either from the number and agreement, or the excellence and acuteness of their wits; or even strengthen their minds with logic, which may be considered as an athletic preparation, but yet do not desist (if we rightly consider the matter) from applying their own understandings merely with all this zeal and effort. While nothing is more clear, than that in every great work executed by the hand of man without machines or implements, it is impossible for the strength of individuals to be increased, or for that of the multitude to combine.

Having premised so much, we lay down two points on which we would admonish mankind, lest they should fail to see or to observe them. The first of these is, that it is our good fortune (as we consider it), for the sake of extinguishing and removing contradiction and irritation of mind, to leave the honour and reverence due to the ancients untouched and undiminished, so that we can perform our intended work, and yet enjoy the benefit of our respectful moderation. For if we should profess to offer something better than the ancients, and yet should pursue the same course as they have done, we would never, by any artifice, contrive to avoid the imputation of having engaged in a contest or rivalry as to our respective wits, excellencies, or talents; which, though neither inadmissible or new (for why should we not blame and point out anything that is imperfectly discovered or laid down by them, of our own right, a right common to all?), yet however just and allowable, would perhaps be scarcely an equal match, on account of the disproportion of our strength. But since our present plan leads us to open an entirely different course to the understanding, and one unattempted and unknown to them, the case is altered. There is an end to party zeal, and we only take upon ourselves the character of a guide, which requires a moderate share of authority and good fortune, rather than talents and excellence. The first admonition relates to persons, the next to things.

We make no attempt to disturb the system of philosophy that now prevails, or any other which may or will exist, either more correct or more complete. For we deny not that the received system of philosophy, and others of a similar nature, encourage discussion, embellish harangues, are employed, and are of service on the duties of the professor, and the affairs of civil life. Nay, we openly express and declare that the philosophy we offer will not be very useful in such respects. It is not obvious, nor to be understood in a cursory view, nor does it flatter the mind in its preconceived notions, nor will it descend to the level of the generality of mankind unless by its advantages and effects.

Let there exist then (and may it be of advantage to both), two sources, and two distributions of learning, and in like manner two tribes, and as it were kindred families of contemplators or philosophers, without any hostility or alienation between them; but rather allied and united by mutual assistance. Let there be in short one method of cultivating the sciences, and another of discovering them. And as for those who prefer and more readily receive the former, on account of their haste or from motives arising from their ordinary life, or because they are unable from weakness of mind to comprehend and embrace the other (which must necessarily be the case with by far the greater number), let us wish that they may prosper as they desire in their undertaking, and attain what they pursue. But if any individual desire, and is anxious not merely to adhere to, and make use of present discoveries, but to penetrate still further, and not to overcome his adversaries in disputes, but nature by labor, not in short to give elegant and specious opinions, but to know to a certainty and demonstration, let him, as a true son of science (if such be his wish), join with us; that when he has left the antechambers of nature trodden by the multitude, an entrance may at last be discovered to her inner apartments. And in order to be better understood, and to render our meaning more familiar by assigning determinate names, we have accustomed ourselves to call the one method the anticipation of the mind, and the other the interpretation of nature.

We have still one request left. We have at least reflected and taken pains in order to render our propositions not only true, but of easy and familiar access to men's minds, however wonderfully prepossessed and limited. Yet it is but just that we should obtain this favour from mankind (especially in so great a restoration of learning and the sciences) that whosoever may be desirous of forming any determination upon an opinion of this our work either from his own perception, or the crown of authorities, or the forms of demonstrations, he will not expect to be able to do so in a cursory manner, and while attending to other matters; but in order to have a thorough knowledge of the subject, will himself by degrees attempt the course which we describe and maintain; will be accustomed to the subtlety of things which is manifested by experience; and will correct the depraved and deeply rooted habits of his mind by a seasonable, and, as it were, just hesitation: and then, finally (if he will), use his judgement when he had begun to be master of himself.

Aphorisms—Book I
On the Interpretation of Nature
and the Empire of Man

I. Man, as the minister and interpreter of nature, does and understands as much as his observations on the order of nature, either with regard to things or the mind, permit him, and neither knows nor is capable of more.

II. The unassisted hand and the understanding left to itself possess but little power. Effects are produced by the means of instruments and helps, which the understanding requires no less than the hand; and as instruments either promote or regulate the motion of the hand, so those that are applied to the mind prompt or protect the understanding.

III. Knowledge and human power are synonymous, since the ignorance of the cause frustrates the effect; for nature is only subdued by submission, and that which in contemplative philosophy corresponds with the cause in practical science becomes the rule.

IV. Man while operating can only apply or withdraw natural bodies; nature internally performs the rest.

V. Those who become practically versed in nature are, the mechanic, the mathematician, the physician, the alchemist, and the *magician*, but all (as matters now stand) with faint efforts and meagre success.

VI. It would be madness and inconsistency to suppose that things which have never yet been performed can be performed without employing some hitherto untried means.

VII. The creations of the mind and hand appear very numerous, if we judge by books and manufactures; but all that variety consists of an excessive refinement, and of deductions from a few well known matters—*not of a number of axioms.*

VIII. Even the effects already discovered are due to chance and experiment rather than to the sciences; for our present sciences are nothing more than peculiar arrangements of matters already discovered, and not methods for discovery or plans for new operations.

IX. The sole cause and root of almost every defect in the sciences is this, that while we falsely admire and extol the powers of the human mind, we do not search for its real helps.

X. The subtlety of nature is far beyond that of sense or of the understanding: so that the specious meditations, speculations, and theories of mankind are but a kind of insanity, only there is no one to stand by and observe it.

*   *   *

XX. The understanding when left to itself proceeds by the same way as that which it would have adopted under the guidance of logic, namely, the first; for the mind is fond of starting off to generalities, that it may avoid labor, and after dwelling a little on a subject is fatigued by experiment. But those evils are augmented by logic, for the sake of the ostentation of dispute.

XXI. The understanding, when left to itself in a man of a steady, patient, and reflecting disposition (especially when unimpeded by received doctrines), makes some attempt in the right way, but with little effect, since the understanding, undirected and unassisted, is unequal to and unfit for the task of vanquishing the obscurity of things.

XXII. Each of these two ways begins from the senses and particulars, and ends in the greatest generalities. But they are immeasurably different; for the one merely touches cursorily the limits of experiment and particulars, while the other runs duly and regularly through them—the one from the very outset lays down some abstract and useless generalities, the other gradually rises to those principles which are really the most common in nature.

XXIII. There is no small difference between the idols of the human mind and the ideas of the Divine mind—that is to say, between certain idle dogmas and the real stamp and impression of created objects, as they are found in nature.

* * *

XXXIX. Four species of idols beset the human mind, to which (for distinction's sake) we have assigned names, calling the first Idols of the Tribe, the second Idols of the Den, the Third Idols of the Market, the fourth Idols of the Theatre.

* * *

XLI. The idols of the tribe are inherent in human nature and the very tribe or race of man; for man's sense is falsely asserted to be the standard of things; on the contrary, all the perceptions both of the senses and the mind bear reference to man and not to the universe, and the human mind resembles those uneven mirrors which impart their own properties to different objects, from which rays are emitted and distort and disfigure them.

XLII. The idols of the den are those of each individual; for everybody (in addition to the errors common to the race of man) has his own individual den or cavern, which intercepts and corrupts the light of nature, either from his own peculiar and singular disposition, or from his education and intercourse with others, or from his reading, and the authority acquired by those whom he reverences and admires, or from the different impressions produced on the mind, as it happens to be preoccupied and predisposed, or equable and tranquil, and the like; so that the spirit of man (according to its several dispositions), is variable, confused, and as it were actuated by chance; and Heraclitus said well that men search for knowledge in lesser worlds, and not in the greater or common world.

XLIII. There are also idols formed by the reciprocal intercourse and society of man with man, which we call idols of the market, from the commerce and association of men with each other; for men converse by means of language, but words are formed at the will of the generality, and there arises from a bad and unapt formation of words a wonderful obstruction to the mind. Nor can the definitions and explanations with which learned men are wont to guard and protect themselves in some instances afford a complete remedy—words still manifestly force the understanding, throw everything into confusion, and lead mankind into vain and innumerable controversies and fallacies.

XLIV. Lastly, there are idols which have crept into men's minds from the various dogmas of peculiar systems of philosophy, and also from the perverted rules of demonstration, and these we denominate idols of the theatre: for we regard all the systems of philosophy hitherto received or imagined, as so many plays brought out and performed, creating fictitious and theatrical worlds. Nor do we speak only of the present systems, or of the philosophy and sects of the ancients, since numerous other plays of a similar nature can be still composed and made to agree with each other, the causes of the most opposite errors being generally the same. Nor, again, do we allude merely to general systems, but also to many elements and axioms of sciences which have become inveterate by tradition, implicit credence, and neglect. We must, however, discuss each species of idols more fully and distinctly in order to guard the human understanding against them.

* * *

XCV. Those who have treated of the sciences have been either empirics or dogmatical. The former like ants only heap up and use their store, the latter like spiders spin out their own webs. The bee, a mean between both, extracts matter from the flowers of the garden and the field, but works and fashions it by its own efforts. The true labour of philosophy resembles hers, for it neither relies entirely or principally on the powers of the mind, nor yet lays up in the memory the matter afforded by the experiments of natural history and mechnanics in its raw state, but changes and works it in the understanding. We have good reason, therefore, to derive hope from a closer and purer alliance of these faculties (the experimental and rational) than has yet been attempted.

Study Questions

Preface

1. What group of thinkers has, in Bacon's opinion, inflicted the greatest injury on philosophy and learning?

2. What other group does Bacon oppose to this first?

3. What is Bacon's own position concerning these two groups?

4. What does Bacon say about his own attitude toward the ancients? How are we to interpret his remarks in this connection?

5. What two sources and "two distributions" does Bacon distinguish in the Preface?

Aphorisms: Book I

1. What, according to Bacon, is humanity's role in relation to nature?

2. What comparison does Bacon make between the hand and the understanding?

3. With what does Bacon identify knowledge? Explain.

4. What four "species of idols beset the human mind"? Explain each.

5. Explain the analogy Bacon constructs to distinguish three kinds of investigators? Which of the three does he himself endorse?

2

Galileo Galilei
(1564–1642)

GALILEO WAS BORN in the town of Pisa in the year 1564. He entered the university there in 1581 to become a physician but became so enamored of mathematics and physical science that he decided to follow that direction instead.

He was a professor at the University of Pisa from 1589 to 1591 and at the University of Padua from 1592 to 1610. During the latter period he came to know very well the Aristotelian physics and scientific methodology being taught at Padua.

In 1610 Galileo left Padua for Florence where he became mathematician and philosopher to the Grand Duke of Tuscany. It was also a decisive year in his life since it was then that he learned about the invention of the telescope (in the Netherlands) and set about constructing an even more powerful one for himself. Galileo began observing the moon and the planets, and reported his empirical findings in *The Sidereal Message* (1610), which concluded that the moon was made of the same material as the earth (something which the Aristotelians would not accept since they considered the heavenly bodies to be in some sense "divine" and in any case made up of a "fifth essence" other than the normal earth, water, fire, and air). He also began openly to profess the views of Copernicus concerning the revolution of the earth and the other planets around the sun (while, of course, the Aristotelians taught that the sun and other heavenly bodies revolved around the earth—the Ptolemaic theory).

Although the heliocentric position of Copernicus seems a view ordinary to us, it was a very radical position indeed in the early seventeenth century. Galileo was told by the Holy Office in Rome that he may not hold the heliocentric theory as *demonstrated* truth. It could be held as an *hypothesis* for which demonstration could be sought, but until such time as it was demonstrated, Galileo was asked to promise that he would not teach or disseminate the new theory. Galileo gave his word, returned to Florence, and in 1623 published two important pieces supporting the Copernican views. The first (contained in this collection of readings) was *The Assayer*; and the second, the *Dialogue on the Two Main Systems of the World* (the Copernican and the Ptolemaic).

Galileo was summoned to Rome to answer for having broken his promise. In 1633 he recanted, was condemned by the Inquisition, and put under house arrest, where he lived out his days in comfortable circumstances, receiving distinguished visitors (among whom were Thomas Hobbes and John Milton) and continuing to write. His most important work during this period was *Discourses and Mathematical Demonstrations Concerning Two New Sciences* (1638). He died in 1642 totally blind but continuing to work.

Perhaps Galileo's most important and lasting contribution to Western scientific thought is not so much his support of the heliocentric hypothesis as his underlining in no uncertain terms the fundamental differences between Aristotelian science and "modern" science. Those differences are to be found in their respective notions of *demonstration* and *method*. The modern methods were more inductive and empirical, giving greater place to probability than to rigorous deductive certitude, and putting emphasis on a logic of *discovery* rather than on a logic of *exposition*. It would take centuries before a statistical understanding of physical laws would receive widespread acceptance even among scientists.

SUGGESTED READING

Butterfield, H. *The Origins of Modern Science, 1300-1800.* London: Bell, 1955.

Collins, J. *A History of Modern European Philosophy.* Milwaukee: Bruce, 1956.

Copleston, F., S.J. *A History of Philosophy.* III. *Ockham to Suarez.* Westminster, Md.: Newman, 1953.

From

The Assayer

A Letter
to the Illustrious and Very Reverend
Don Virginio Cesarini

*   *   *

It now remains for me to tell Your Excellency, as I promised, some thoughts of mine about the proposition "motion is the cause of heat," and to show in what sense this may be true. But first I must consider what it is that we call heat, as I suspect that people in general have a concept of this which is very remote from the truth. For they believe that heat is a real phenomenon, or property, or quality, which actually resides in the material by which we feel ourselves warmed. Now I say that whenever I conceive any material or corporeal substance, I immediately feel the need to think of it as bounded, and as having this or that shape; as being large or small in relation to other things, and in some specific place at any given time; as being in motion or at rest; as touching or not touching some other body; and as being one in number, or few, or many. From these conditions I cannot separate such a substance by any stretch of my imagination. But that it must be white or red, bitter or sweet, noisy or silent and of sweet or foul odor, my mind does not feel compelled to bring in as necessry accompaniments. Without the senses as our guides, reason or imagination unaided would probably never arrive at qualities like these. Hence I think that tastes, odors, colors, and so on are no more than mere names so far as the object in which we place them is concerned, and that they reside only in the consciousness. Hence if the living creature were removed, all these qualities would be wiped away and annihilated. But since we have imposed upon them special names, distinct from those of the other and real qualities mentioned previously, we wish to believe that they really exist as actually different from those.

I may be able to make my notion clearer by means of some

examples. I move my hand first over a marble statue and then over a living man. As to the effect flowing from my hand, this is the same with regard to both objects and my hand; it consists of the primary phenomena of motion and touch, for which we have no further names. But the live body which receives these operations feels different sensations according to the various places touched. When touched upon the soles of the feet, for example, or under the knee or armpit, it feels in addition to the common sensation of touch a sensation on which we have imposed a special name, "tickling." This sensation belongs to us and not to the hand. Anyone would make a serious error if he said that the hand, in addition to the properties of moving and touching, possessed another faculty of "tickling," as if tickling were a phenomenon that resided in the hand that tickled. A piece of paper or a feather drawn lightly over any part of our bodies performs intrinsically the same operations of moving and touching, but by touching the eye, the nose, or the upper lip it excites in us an almost intolerable titillation, even though elsewhere it is scarcely felt. This titillation belongs entirely to us and not to the feather; if the live and sensitive body were removed it would remain no more than a mere word. I believe that no more solid an existence belongs to many qualities which we have come to attribute to physical bodies—tastes, odors, colors, and many more.

A body which is solid and, so to speak, quite material, when moved in contact with any part of my person produces in me the sensation we call touch. This, though it exists over my entire body, seems to reside principally in the palms of the hands and in the finger tips, by whose means we sense the most minute differences in texture that are not easily distinguished by other parts of our bodies. Some of these sensations are more pleasant to us than others. . . . The sense of touch is more material than the other senses; and, as it arises from the solidity of matter, it seems to be related to the earthly element.

Perhaps the origin of two other senses lies in the fact that there are bodies which constantly dissolve into minute particles, some of which are heavier than air and descend, while others are lighter and rise up. The former may strike upon a certain part of our bodies that is much more sensitive than the skin, which does not feel the invasion of such subtle matter. This is the upper surface of the tongue; here the tiny particles are received, and mixing with and penetrating its moisture, they give rise to tastes, which are sweet or unsavory according to the various shapes, numbers, and speeds of the particles. And those minute particles which rise up may enter by our nostrils and strike upon some small protuberances which are the instrument of smelling; here likewise their touch and passage is received to our like or dislike according as they have this or that shape, are fast or slow, and are numerous or few. The tongue and nasal passages are providently arranged for these things, as the one extends from below to receive descending particles, and the other is adapted to those which ascend. Perhaps the excitation of tastes may be given a certain analogy to fluids, which descend through air, and odors to fires, which ascend.

Then there remains the air itself, an element available for sounds, which come to us indifferently from below, above, and all sides—for we reside in the air and its movements displace it equally in all directions. The location of the ear is most fittingly accommodated to all positions in space. Sounds are made and heard by us when the air—without any special property of "sonority" or "transonority"—is ruffled by a rapid tremor into very minute waves and moves certain cartilages of a tympanum in our ear. External means capable of thus ruffling the air are very numerous, but for the most part they may be reduced to the trembling of some body which pushes the air and disturbs it. Waves are propagated very rapidly in this way, and high tones are produced by frequent waves and low tones by sparse ones.

To excite in us tastes, odors, and sounds I believe that nothing is required in external bodies except shapes, numbers, and slow or rapid movements. I think that if ears, tongues, and noses were removed, shapes and numbers and motions would remain, but not odors or tastes or sounds. The latter, I believe, are nothing more than names when separated from living beings, just as tickling and titillation are nothing but names in the absence of such things as noses and armpits. And as these four senses are related to the four elements, so I believe that vision, the sense eminent above all others in the proportion of the finite to the infinite, the temporal to the instantaneous, the quantitative to the indivisible, the illuminated to the obscure—that vision, I say, is related to light itself. But of this sensation and the things pertaining to it I pretend to understand but little; and since even a long time would not suffice to explain that trifle, or even to hint at an explanation, I pass this over in silence.

*   *   *

STUDY QUESTIONS

1. What is the point of Galileo's discussion of "what we call heat"?

2. What criterion does Galileo use for distinguishing the shape, size, place, motion and rest, etc. of a corporeal substance from its taste, odor, color, etc.?

3. How does Galileo use the example of "tickling" to illustrate his point?

4. Discuss Galileo's treatment of taste, odors, and sounds.

5. What general conclusion does Galileo draw concerning what Locke later will call "secondary sense qualities," that is, tastes, odors, sounds, etc.?

3

René Descartes
(1596–1650)

RENÉ DESCARTES, son of a councilor of the Brittany parliament, was born on March 31, 1596, at La Haye, Touraine, France. From 1606 to 1614 he attended the Jesuit college of La Flèche, where he studied humanities (grammar, history, poetry, and rhetoric), philosophy (logic, philosophy of nature, metaphysics, and ethics), and mathematics. He was particularly taken by this last because of its certainty, and he used it as an ideal or model in working out his own philosophical method. Descartes continued his studies at the University of Poitiers, where he received both a baccalaureate and a licentiate in law. He also studied a little medicine.

After his university studies, Descartes decided to see the world at first hand; so he joined the army of Maurice of Nassau, in which he served in the Netherlands until 1619. Mustered out, he went to Germany and joined the army of Maximilian of Bavaria, which service took him near the town of Ulm. There he began to consider restructuring all of philosophy according to mathematical method and thereby achieve a perfect unity of the sciences. On the night of November 10, 1619, Descartes had three consecutive dreams which he interpreted to be a sign of his mission to seek truth by reason. In gratitude for this enlightenment, he vowed to make a pilgrimage to the shrine of Our Lady at Loreto in Italy which he fulfilled in 1623 on his way to Rome.

Descartes lived in Paris for a few years, but found the city too distracting and in 1628 retired to Holland where he lived until 1649. In that year he went to Sweden to give Queen Christina philosophical instructions. He died there on February 11, 1650.

By 1627-1628, while Descartes was still living in Paris, the primary lines of his philosophy were set in his mind. At about this same time he had written down the main features of his method in *Rules for the Direction of the Mind*, which was circulated in manuscript form but not published until 1701. Descartes was working on a theory of the physical world much like Copernicus' when in 1633 Galileo was condemned by the Holy Office in Rome. Hence the surviving portions of those works, *The World* or *Treatise on Light*, were not published until after Descartes' death. In 1637 his *Discourse on Method* appeared and in 1641 his *Meditations on First Philosophy*. In 1644 he put his system into textbook form (*Principles of Philosophy*) in the hope that it would be adopted by Jesuit schools (which did not happen). Finally, in his later years, Descartes became more and more interested in moral philosophy and in 1649 wrote a treatise on *The Passions of the Soul*.

Descartes is known as the "Father of Modern Philosophy." This is so for a number of reasons. First, Descartes attempted consciously to break away from the decadent Scholasticism of the Renaissance and to "start over." This new beginning put great emphasis on method—a characteristic of "modern" philosophy. Second, Descartes in large part set the problems and technical language of "modern" philosophy. Subsequent discussion was always in terms of the Cartesian set of concerns—whether to support his views or to attack them. Third, Descartes gave "modern" philosophy its "subjective" turn, that is, brought the role of the subject in knowing explicitly to the fore. There is something ironic in all this since the "Father of Modern Philosophy" turns out to have been, in spirit at least, a conservative reactionary relative to the skepticism and moral libertinism of his day. Indeed, it was to combat skeptics and atheists that Descartes developed his *Method*. It is an irony of history that he ushered in the "Enlightenment," a period of "freethinking" whose outcome was precisely skepticism and, for many, atheism.

As you read the following selections keep in mind these themes: (1) to know is to be certain, in the sense that all doubt is *impossible*; (2) the self is known in a special, privileged way, that is, by intuition which is certain; (3) the senses are not trustworthy in themselves and so knowledge of the physical world is indirect; (4) intuition and demonstration are the only sources of knowledge.

SUGGESTED READING

Collins, J. *A History of Modern European Philosophy*. Milwaukee: Bruce, 1956.

Copleston, F., S.J. *A History of Philosophy*. IV. *Descartes to Leibniz*. Westminster, Md.: Newman, 1960.

Descartes: A Collection of Critical Essays. Ed. W. Doney. Garden City, N.Y.: Doubleday Anchor, 1967.

Katz, J. J. *Cogitations: A Study of the Cogito in Relation to the Philosophy of Logic and Language and a Study of Them in Relation to the Cogito*. New York: Oxford University Press, 1986.

From

A Discourse on Method

Part I

Good Sense is, of all things among men, the most equally distributed; for everyone thinks himself so abundantly provided with it, that even those who are the most difficult to satisfy in everything else, do not usually desire a larger measure of this quality than they already possess. And in this it is not likely that all are mistaken: the conviction is rather to be held as testifying that the power of judging aright and of distinguishing Truth from Error, which is properly what is called good sense or reason, is by nature equal in all men; and that the diversity of our opinions, consequently, does not arise from some being endowed with a larger share of reason than others, but solely from this, that we conduct our thoughts along different ways, and do not fix our attention on the same objects. For to be possessed of a vigorous mind is not enough; the prime requisite is rightly to apply it. The greatest minds, as they are capable of the highest excellences, are open likewise to the greatest aberrations; and those who travel very slowly may yet make far greater progress, provided they keep always to the straight road, than those who, while they run, forsake it.

For myself, I have never fancied my mind to be in any respect more perfect than those of the generality; on the contrary, I have often wished that I were equal to some others in promptitude of thought, or in clearness and distinctness of imagination, or in fulness and readiness of memory. And besides these, I know of no other qualities that contribute to the perfection of the mind; for as to the Reason or Sense, inasmuch as it is that alone which constitutes us men, and distinguishes us from the brutes, I am disposed to believe that it is to be found complete in each individual; and on this point to adopt the common opinion of philosophers, who say that the difference of greater and less holds only for the *accidents*, and not among the *forms* or *natures of individuals* of the same *species*.

I will not hesitate, however, to avow my belief that it has been my singular good fortune to have very early in life fallen in with certain tracks which have conducted me to considerations and maxims, of which I have formed a Method that gives me the means, as I think, of gradually augmenting my knowledge, and of raising it by little and little to the highest point which the mediocrity of my talents and the brief duration of my life will permit me to reach. For I have already reaped from it such fruits that, although I have been accustomed to think lowly enough of myself, and although when I look with the eye of a philosopher at the varied courses and pursuits of mankind at large, I find scarcely one which does not appear vain and useless, I nevertheless derive the highest satisfaction from the progress I conceive myself to have already made in the search after truth, and cannot help entertaining such expectations of the future as to believe that if, among the occupations of men as men, there is any one really excellent and important, it is that which I have chosen.

After all, it is possible I may be mistaken; and it is but a little copper and glass, perhaps, that I take for gold and diamonds. I know how very liable we are to delusion in what relates to ourselves, and also how much the judgment of our friends are to be suspected when given in our favor. But I shall endeavor in this discourse to describe the paths I have followed, and to delineate my life as in a picture, in order that each one may be able to judge of them for himself, and that in the general opinion entertained of them, as gathered from current report, I myself may have a new help towards instruction to be added to those I have been in the habit of employing.

My present design, then, is not to teach the Method which each ought to follow for the right conduct of his reason, but solely to describe the way in which I have endeavored to conduct my own. They who set themselves to give precepts must of course regard themselves as possessed of greater skill than those to whom they prescribe; and if they err in the slightest particular, they subject themselves to censure. But as this Tract is put forth merely as a history, or, if you will, as a tale, in which, amid some examples worthy of imitation, there will be found, perhaps, as many more which it were advisable not to follow, I hope it will prove useful to some without being hurtful to any, and that my openness will find some favor with all.

* * *

Part II

* * *

. . . I cannot in any degree approve of those restless and busy meddlers who, called neither by birth nor fortune to take part in the management of public affairs, are yet always projecting reforms; and if I thought that this Tract contained aught which might justify the suspicion that I was the victim of such folly, I would by no means permit its publication. I have never contemplated anything higher than the reformation of my own opinions, and basing them on a foundation wholly my own. And although my satisfaction with my work has led me to present here a draft of it, I do not by any means therefore recommend to everyone else to make a similar attempt. Those whom God has endowed with a large measure of genius will entertain, perhaps, designs still more exalted; but for the many I am much afraid lest even the present undertaking be more than they can safely venture to imitate. The single design to strip one's self of all past beliefs is one that ought not to be taken by everyone. The majority of men is composed of two classes, for neither of which would this be at all a befitting resolution: in the *first* place, of those who with more than a due confidence in their own powers, are precipitate in their judgments and want the patience requisite for orderly and circumspect thinking; whence it happens, that if men of this class once take the liberty to doubt of their accustomed opinions, and quit the beaten highway, they will never be able to thread the byway that would lead them by a shorter course, and will lose themselves and continue to wander for life; in the *second* place, of those who, possessed of sufficient sense or modesty to determine that there are others who excel them in the power of discriminating between truth and error, and by whom they may be instructed, ought rather to content themselves with the opinions of such than trust for more correct to their own Reason.

For my own part, I should doubtless have belonged to the latter class, had I received instruction from but one master, or had I never known the diversities of opinion that from time immemorial have prevailed among men of the greatest learning. But I had become aware, even so early as during my college life, that no opinion, however absurd and incredible, can be imagined, which has not been maintained by some one of the philosophers; and afterwards in the course of my travels I remarked that all those whose opinions are decidedly repugnant to ours are not on that account barbarians and savages, but on the contrary that many of these nations make an equally good, if not a better, use of their reason than we do. I took into account also the very different character which a person brought up from infancy in France or Germany exhibits, from that which, with the same mind originally, this individual would have possessed had he lived always among the Chinese or with savages, and the circumstance that in dress itself the fashion, which pleased us ten years ago and which may again, perhaps, be received into favor before ten years have gone, appears to us at this moment extravagant and ridiculous. I was thus led to infer that the ground of our opinions is far more custom and example than any certain knowledge. And, finally, although such be the ground of our opinions, I remarked that a plurality of suffrages is no guarantee of truth where it is at all of difficult discovery, as in such cases it is much more likely that it will be found by one than by many. I could, however, select from the crowd no one whose opinions seemed worthy of preference, and thus I found myself constrained, as it were, to use my own Reason in the conduct of my life.

But like one walking alone and in the dark, I resolved to proceed so slowly and with such circumspection, that if I did not advance far, I would at least guard against falling. I did not even choose to dismiss summarily any of the opinions that had crept into my belief without having been introduced by Reason, but first of all took sufficient time carefully to satisfy myself of the general nature of the task I was setting myself, and ascertain the true Method by which to arrive at the knowledge of whatever lay within the compass of my powers.

Among the branches of Philosophy, I had, at an earlier period, given some attention to logic, and among those of the Mathematics to Geometrical Analysis and Algebra—three arts or Sciences which ought, as I conceived, to contribute something to my design. But, on examination, I found that, as for logic, its syllogisms and the majority of its other precepts are of avail rather in the communication of what we already know, or ever as the Art of Lully, in speaking without judgment of things of which we are ignorant, than in the investigation of the unknown; and although this science contains indeed a number of correct and very excellent precepts, there are, nevertheless, so many others, and these either injurious or superfluous, mingled with the former, that it is almost quite as difficult to effect a severance of the true from the false as it is to extract a Diana or a Minerva from a rough block of marble. Then as to the Analysis of the ancients and the Algebra of the moderns, besides that they embrace only matters highly abstract, and, to appearance, of no use, the former is so exclusively restricted to the consideration of figures, that it can exercise the Understanding only on condition of greatly fatiguing the Imagination; and, in the latter, there is so complete a subjection to certain rules and formulas, that there results an art full of confusion and obscurity calculated to embarrass, instead of a science fitted to cultivate the mind. By these considerations I was induced to seek some other Method which would comprise the advantages of the three and be exempt from their defects. And as a multitude of laws often only hampers justice, so that a state is best governed when, with few laws, these are rigidly administered; in like manner, instead of the great number of precepts of which logic is composed, I believed that the four following would prove perfectly sufficient for me, provided I took the firm and unwavering resolution never in a single instance to fail in observing them.

The *first* was never to accept anything for true which I did not clearly know to be such; that is to say, carefully to avoid precipitancy and prejudice, and to comprise nothing more in my judgment than what was presented to my mind so clearly and distinctly as to exclude all ground of doubt.

The *second*, to divide each of the difficulties under examination into as many parts as possible, and as might be necessary for its adequate solution.

The *third*, to conduct my thoughts in such order that, by commencing with objects the simplest and easiest to know, I might ascend by little and little, and, as it were, step by step, to the knowledge of the more complex; assigning in thought a certain order even to those objects which in their own nature do not stand in a relation of antecedence and sequence.

And the *last*, in every case to make enumerations so complete, and reviews so general, that I might be assured that nothing was omitted.

The long chains of simple and easy reasonings by means of which geometers are accustomed to reach the conclusions of their most difficult demonstrations, had led me to imagine that all things, to the knowledge of which man is competent, are mutually connected in the same way, and that there is nothing so far removed from us as to be beyond our reach, or so hidden that we cannot discover it, provided only we abstain from accepting the false for the true, and always preserve in our thoughts the order necessary for the deduction of one truth from another. And I had little difficulty in determining the objects with which it was necessary to commence, for I was already persuaded that it must be with the simplest and easiest to know, and, considering that of all those who have hitherto sought truth in the Sciences, the mathematicians alone have been able to find any demonstrations, that is, any certain and evident reasons, I did not doubt but that such must have been the rule of their investigations. I resolved to commence, therefore, with the examination of the simplest objects, not anticipating, however, from this any other advantage than that to be found in accustoming my mind to the love and nourishment of truth, and to a distaste for all such reasonings as were unsound. But I had no intention on that account of attempting to master all the particular Sciences commonly denominated Mathematics: but observing that, however different their objects, they all agree in considering only the various relations or proportions subsisting among those objects, I thought it best for my purpose to consider these proportions in the most general form possible, without referring them to any objects in particular, except such as would most facilitate the knowledge of them, and without by any means restricting them to these, that afterwards I might thus be the better able to apply them to every other class of objects to which they are legitimately applicable. Perceiving further, that in order to understand these relations I should sometimes have to consider them one by one, and sometimes only to bear them in mind, or embrace them in the aggregate, I thought that, in order the better to consider them individually, I should view them as subsisting between straight lines, than which I could find no objects more simple, or capable of being more distinctly represented to my imagination and senses; and on the other hand, that in order to retain them in the memory, or embrace an aggregate of many, I should express them by certain characters the briefest possible. In this way I believed that I could borrow all that was best both in Geometrical Analysis and in Algebra, and correct all the defects of the one by help of the other.

* * *

Part IV

I am in doubt as to the propriety of making my first meditations . . . matter of discourse; for these are so metaphysical, and so uncommon as not, perhaps, to be acceptable to every one. And yet, that it may be determined whether the foundations that I have laid are sufficiently secure, I find myself in a measure constrained to advert to them. I had long before remarked that, in relation to   practice, it is sometimes necessary to adopt, as if above doubt, opinions which we discern to be highly uncertain, as has been already said; but as I then desired to give my attention solely to the search after truth, I thought that a procedure exactly the opposite was called for, and that I ought to reject as absolutely false all opinions in regard to which I could suppose the least ground for doubt, in order to ascertain whether after that there remained aught in my belief that was wholly indubitable. Accordingly, seeing that our senses sometimes deceive us, I was willing to suppose that there existed nothing really such as they presented to us; and because some men err in reasoning, and fall into paralogisms, even on the simplest matter of Geometry, I, convinced that I was as open to error as any other, rejected as false all the reasonings I had hitherto taken for demonstrations; and finally, when I considered that the very same thoughts (presentations) which we experience when awake may also be experienced when we are asleep, while there is at that time not one of them true, I supposed that all the objects (presentations) that had ever entered into my mind when awake, had in them no more truth than the illusions of my dreams. But immediately upon this I observed that, whilst I thus wished to think that all was false, it was absolutely necessary that I, who thus thought, should be somewhat; and as I observed that this truth, *I think, hence I am*, was so certain and of such evidence, that no ground of doubt, however extravagant, could be alleged by the Sceptics capable of shaking it, I concluded that I might, without scruple, accept it as the first principle of the Philosophy of which I was in search.

In the next place, I attentively examined what I was, and as I observed that I could suppose that I had no body, and that there was no world nor any place in which I might be; but that I could not therefore suppose that I was not; and that, on the contrary, from the very circumstance that I thought to doubt of the truth of other things, it most clearly and certainly followed that I was, while, on the other hand, if I had only ceased to think, although all the other objects which I had ever imagined had been in reality existent, I would have had no reason to believe that I existed; I thence concluded that I was a substance whose whole essence or nature consists only in thinking, and which, that it may exist, has need of no place, nor is dependent on any material thing; so that "I," that is to say, the mind by which I am what I am, is wholly distinct from the body, and is even more easily known than the latter, and is such, that although the latter were not, it would still continue to be all that it is.

After this I inquired in general into what is essential to the truth and certainty of a proposition; for since I had discovered one which I knew to be true, I thought that I must likewise be able to discover the ground of this certitude. And as I observed that in the words *I think, hence I am*, there is nothing at all which gives me assurance of their truth beyond this, that I see very clearly that in order to think it is necessary to exist, I concluded that I might take, as a general rule, the principle, that all the things which we very clearly and distinctly conceive are true, only observing, however, that there is some difficulty in rightly determining the objects which we distinctly conceive.

In the next place, from reflecting on the circumstance that I doubted, and that consequently my being was not wholly perfect, (for I clearly saw that it was a greater perfection to know than to doubt,) I was led to inquire whence I had learned to think of something more perfect than myself; and I clearly recognized that I must hold this notion from some Nature which in reality was more perfect. As for the thoughts of many other objects external to me, as of the sky, the earth, light, heat, and a thousand more, I was less at a loss to know whence these came; for since I remarked in them nothing which seemed to render them superior to myself, I could believe that, if these were true, they were dependencies on my own nature, in so far as it possessed a certain perfection, and, if they were false, that I held them from nothing, that is to say, that they were in me because of a certain imperfection of my nature. But this could not be the case with the idea of a Nature more perfect than myself; for to receive it from nothing was a thing manifestly impossible; and, because it is not less repugnant that the more perfect should be an effect of, and dependence on the less perfect, than that something should proceed from nothing, it was equally impossible that I could hold it from myself; accordingly, it but remained that it had been placed in me by a Nature which was in reality more perfect than mine, and which even possessed within itself all the perfections of which I could form any idea; that is to say, in a single word, which was God. And to this I added that, since I knew some perfections which I did not possess, I was not the only being in existence, (I will here, with your permission, freely use the terms of the schools); but, on the contrary, that there was of necessity some other more perfect Being upon whom I was dependent, and from whom I had received all that I possessed; for if I had existed alone, and independently of every other being, so as to have had from myself all the perfection, however little, which I actually possessed, I should have been able, for the same reason, to have had from myself the whole remainder of perfection, of the want of which I was conscious, and thus could of myself have become infinite, eternal, immutable, omniscient, all-powerful, and, in fine, have possessed all the perfections which I could recognize in God. For in order to know the nature of God (whose existence has been established by the preceding reasonings), as far as my own nature permitted, I had only to consider in reference to all the properties of which I found in my mind some idea, whether their possession was a mark of perfection; and was assured that no one which indicated any imperfection was in him, and that none of the rest was awanting. Thus I perceived that doubt, inconstancy, sadness, and such like, could not be found in God, since I myself would have been happy to be free of them. Besides, I had ideas of many sensible and corporeal things; for although I might suppose that I was dreaming, and that all which I saw or imagined was false, I could not, nevertheless, deny that the ideas were in reality in my thoughts. But, because I had already very clearly recognized in myself that the intelligent nature is distinct from the corporeal, and as I observed that all composition is an evidence of dependency, and that a state of dependency is manifestly a state of imperfection, I therefore determined that it could not be a perfection in God to be compounded of these two natures, and that consequently he was not so compounded; but that if there were any bodies in the world, or even any intelligences, or other natures that were not wholly perfect, their existence depended on his power in such a way that they could not subsist without him for a single moment.

I was disposed straightway to search for other truths; and when I had represented to myself the object of the geometers, which I conceived to be a continuous body, or a space indefinitely extended in length, breadth, and height or depth, divisible into divers parts which admit of different figures and sizes, and of being moved or transposed in all manner of ways, (for all this the geometers suppose to be in the object they contemplate,) I went over some of their simplest demonstrations. And, in the first place, I observed, that the great certitude which by common consent is accorded to these demonstrations, is founded solely upon this, that they are clearly conceived in accordance with the rules I have already laid down. In the next place, I perceived that there was nothing at all in these demonstrations which could assure me of the existence of their object: thus, for example, supposing a triangle to be given, I distinctly perceived that its three angles were necessarily equal to two right angles, but I did not on that account perceive anything which could assure me that any triangle existed: while, on the contrary, recurring to the examination of the idea of a Perfect Being, I found that the existence of the Being was comprised in the idea in the same way that the equality of its three angles to two right angles is comprised in the idea of a triangle, or as in the idea of a sphere, the equidistance of all points on its surface from the center, or even still more clearly; and that consequently it is at least as certain that God, who is this Perfect Being, is, or exists, as any demonstration of geometry can be.

But the reason which leads many to persuade themselves that there is a difficulty in knowing this truth, and even in knowing what their mind really is, is that they never raise their thoughts above sensible objects, and are so accustomed to consider nothing except by way of imagination, which is a mode of thinking limited to material objects, that all that is not imaginable seems to them not intelligible. The truth of this is sufficiently manifest from the single circumstance, that the philosophers of the Schools accept as a maxim that there is nothing in the Understanding which was not previously in the Senses, in which however it is certain that the ideas of God and of the soul have never been; and it appears to me that they who make use of their imagination to comprehend these ideas do exactly the same thing as if, in order to hear sounds or smell odors, they strove to avail themselves of their eyes; unless indeed that there is this difference, that the sense of sight does not afford us an inferior assurance to those of smell or hearing; in place of which, neither our imagination nor our senses can give us assurance of anything unless our Understanding intervene.

Finally, if there be still persons who are not sufficiently persuaded of the existence of God and of the soul, by the reasons I have adduced, I am desirous that they should know that all the other propositions, of the truth of which they deem themselves perhaps more assured, as that we have a body, and that there exist stars and an earth, and such like, are less certain; for, although we have a moral assurance of these things, which is so strong that there is an appearance of extravagance in doubting of their existence, yet at the same time no one, unless his intellect is impaired, can deny, when the question relates to a metaphysical certitude, that there is sufficient reason to exclude entire assurance, in the observation that when asleep we can in the same way imagine ourselves possessed of another body and that we see other stars and another earth, when there is nothing of the kind.

For how do we know that the thoughts which occur in dreaming are false rather than those others which we experience when awake, since the former are often not less vivid and distinct than the latter? And though men of the highest genius study this question as long as they please, I do not believe that they will be able to give any reason which can be sufficient to remove this doubt, unless they presuppose the existence of God. For, in the first place, even the principle which I have already taken as a rule, viz., that all the things which we clearly and distinctly conceive are true, is certain only because God is or exists, and because he is a Perfect Being; and because all that we possess is derived from him: whence it follows that our ideas or notions, which to the extent of their clearness and distinctness are real, and proceed from God, must to that extent be true. Accordingly, whereas we not unfrequently have ideas or notions in which some falsity is contained, this can only be the case with such as are to some extent confused and obscure, and in this proceed from nothing, (participate of negation), that is, exist in us thus confused because we are not wholly perfect. And it is evident that it is not less repugnant that falsity or imperfection, in so far as it is imperfection, should proceed from God, than the truth or perfection should proceed from nothing. But if we did not know that all which we possess of real and true proceeds from a Perfect and Infinite Being, however clear and distinct our ideas might be, we should have no ground on that account for the assurance that they possessed the perfection of being true.

But after the knowledge of God and of the soul has rendered us certain of this rule, we can easily understand that the truth of the thoughts we experience when awake, ought not in the slightest degree to be called in question on account of the illusions of our dreams. For if it happened that an individual, even when asleep, had some very distinct idea, as, for example, if a geometer should discover some new demonstration, the circumstance of his being asleep would not militate against its truth; and as for the most ordinary error of our dreams, which consists in their representing to us various objects in the same way as our external senses, this is not prejudicial, since it leads us very properly to suspect the truth of the ideas of sense; for we are not unfrequently deceived in the same manner when awake; as when persons in the jaundice see all objects yellow, or when the stars or bodies at a great distance appear to us much smaller than they are. For, in fine, whether awake or asleep, we ought never to allow ourselves to be persuaded of the truth of anything unless on the evidence of our Reason. And it must be noted that I say of our Reason, and not of our imagination or of our senses: thus, for example, although we very clearly see the sun, we ought not therefore to determine that it is only of the size which our sense of sight presents; and we may very distinctly imagine the head of a lion joined to the body of a goat, without being therefore shut up to the conclusion that a Chimera exists; for it is not a dictate of Reason that what we thus see or imagine is in reality existent; but it plainly tells us that all our ideas or notions contain in them some truth; for otherwise it could not be that God, who is wholly perfect and veracious, should have placed them in us. And because our reasonings are never so clear and so complete during sleep as when we are awake, although sometimes the acts of our imagination are then as lively and distinct, if not more so than in our waking moments, Reason further dictates that, since all our thoughts cannot be true because of our partial imperfection, those possessing truth must infallibly be found in the experience of our waking moments rather than in that of our dreams.

STUDY QUESTIONS

Part I

1. What did Descartes call "the power of judging aright and of distinguishing Truth from Error"? *good sense / reason*

2. Did Descartes consider this power of judging to be by nature equal or unequal in all men? Why did he hold this? *equal*
*we do not apply
attention to bjs.*

3. What according to Descartes causes diversity of opinion? *attention o bjs.*

4. To what does Descartes attribute his own progress in the search for truth?

5. What precisely is Descartes' purpose in writing the *Discourse*?

Part II

1. Does Descartes recommend to all that they follow his Method? *No*

2. What according to Descartes are the two types of the majority of

men? Should these follow his Method?

3. What two events in the life of Descartes convinced him that most of our opinions are based on custom and example rather than on certain knowledge?

4. To what decision did the discovery that most of our opinions are based on custom and example lead Descartes?

5. What three "arts or sciences" did Descartes, at first, think would help him carry out his decision?

6. What shortcomings did Descartes find in these "arts and sciences," the discovery of which led him to work out a new method?

7. What are the four precepts of Descartes' Method?

Part IV

1. How did Descartes resolve to treat whatever was in any way open to doubt?

2. What truth did Descartes discover to be absolutely indubitable?

3. What did Descartes conclude to be the "whole essence or nature" of the "I"? How does he argue this point?

4. According to Descartes what is the ground of the certitude concerning the "Cogito ergo sum" (I think therefore I am)?

5. What did Descartes conclude about his own being from the very fact that he doubted?

6. How does Descartes argue from the idea of a "Nature more perfect than himself" to the existence of God?

7. Why according to Descartes are the demonstrations of geometry so certain?

8. How according to Descartes do the ideas of geometry differ from the idea of a Perfect Being?

9. According to Descartes, why are many persuaded that it is difficult to know God or to know what their mind is?

10. Why, according to Descartes, are other truths less certain than the existence of God and of the soul?

11. Why, according to Descartes, must the existence of God be presupposed if doubt is to be removed?

From

Meditations on the First Philosophy

Meditation II

On The Nature of the Human Mind: And that It Is More Easily Known than the Body

The Meditation of yesterday has filled my mind with so many doubts, that it is no longer in my power to forget them. Nor do I see, meanwhile, any principle on which they can be resolved; and, just as if I had fallen all of a sudden into very deep water, I am so greatly disconcerted as to be made unable either to plant my feet firmly on the bottom or sustain myself by swimming on the surface. I will, nevertheless, make an effort, and try anew the same path on which I had entered yesterday, that is, proceed by casting aside all that admits of the slightest doubt, not less than if I had discovered it to be absolutely false; and I will continue always in this track until I shall find something that is certain, or at least, if I can do nothing more, until I shall know with certainty that there is nothing certain. Archimedes, that he might transport the entire globe from the place it occupied to another, demanded only a point that was firm and immovable; so also, I shall be entitled to entertain the highest expectations, if I am fortunate enough to discover only one thing that is certain and indubitable.

I suppose, accordingly, that all the things which I see are false (fictitious); I believe that none of those objects which my fallacious memory represents ever existed; I suppose that I possess no senses; I believe that body, figure, extension, motion, and place are merely fictions of my mind. What is there, then, that can be esteemed true? Perhaps this only, that there is absolutely nothing certain.

But how do I know that there is not something different altogether from the objects I have now enumerated, of which it is impossible to entertain the slightest doubt? Is there not a God, or some being, by whatever name I may designate him, who causes these thoughts to arise in my mind? But why suppose such a being, for it may be I myself am capable of producing them? Am I, then, at least not something? But I before denied that I possessed senses or a body; I hesitate, however, for what follows from that? Am I so dependent on the body and the senses that without these I cannot exist? But I had the persuasion that there was absolutely nothing in the world, that there was no sky and no earth, neither minds nor bodies; was I not, therefore, at the same time, persuaded that I did not exist? Far from it; I assuredly existed, since I was persuaded. But there is I know not what being, who is possessed at once of the highest power and the deepest cunning, who is constantly employing all his ingenuity in deceiving me. Doubtless, then, I exist, since I am deceived; and, let him deceive me as he may, he can never bring it about that I am nothing, so long as I shall be conscious that I am something. So that it must, in fine, be maintained, all things being maturely and carefully considered, that this proposition (*pronunciatum*) I am, I exist, is necessarily true each time it is expressed by me, or conceived in my mind.

But I do not yet know with sufficient clearness what I am, though assured that I am; and hence, in the next place, I must take care, lest perchance I inconsiderately substitute some other object in room of what is properly myself, and thus wander from the truth, even in that knowledge (cognition) which I hold to be of all others the most certain and evident. For this reason, I will now consider anew what I formerly believed myself to be, before I entered on the present train of thought; and of my previous opinion I will retrench all that can in the least be invalidated by the grounds of doubt I have adduced, in order that there may at length remain nothing but what is certain and indubitable. What then did I formerly think I was? Undoubtedly I judged that I was a man. But what is a man? Shall I say a rational animal? Assuredly not; for it would be necessary forthwith to inquire into what is meant by animal, and what by rational, and thus, from a single question, I should insensibly glide into others, and these more difficult than the first; nor do I now possess enough of leisure to warrant me in wasting my time amid subtleties of this sort. I prefer here to attend to the thoughts that sprung up of themselves in my mind, and were inspired by my own nature alone, when I applied myself to the consideration of what I was. In the first place, then, I thought that I possessed a countenance, hands, arms, and all the fabric of members that appear in a corpse, and which I called by the name of body. It further occurred to me that I was nourished, that I walked, perceived, and thought, and all those actions I referred to the soul; but what the soul itself was I either did not stay to consider, or, if I did, I imagined that it was some thing extremely rare and subtle, like wind, or flame, or ether, spread through my grosser parts. As regarded the body, I did not even doubt of its nature, but thought I distinctly knew it, and if I had wished to describe it according to the notions I then entertained, I should have explained myself in this manner: By body I understand all that can be terminated by a certain figure; that can be comprised in a certain place, and so fill a certain space as therefrom to exclude every other body; that can be perceived either by touch, sight, hearing, taste, or smell; that can be moved in different ways, not indeed of itself, but by something foreign to it by which it is touched [and from which it receives the impression]; for the power of self-motion, as likewise that of perceiving and thinking, I held as by no means pertaining to the nature of body; on the contrary, I was somewhat astonished to find such faculties existing in some bodies.

But [as to myself, what can I now say that I am], since I suppose there exists an extremely powerful, and, if I may so speak, malignant being, whose whole endeavors are directed towards deceiving me? Can I affirm that I possess any one of all those attributes of which I have lately spoken as belonging to the nature of body? After attentively considering them in my own mind, I find none of them that can properly be said to belong to myself. To recount them were idle and tedious. Let us pass, then, to the attributes of the soul. The first mentioned were the powers of nutrition and walking; but, if it be true that I have no body, it is true likewise that I am capable of neither walking nor being nourished. Perception is another attribute of the soul; but perception too is impossible without the body: besides, I have frequently, during sleep, believed that I perceived objects which I afterwards observed I did not in reality perceive. Thinking is another attribute of the soul; and here I discover what properly belongs to myself. This alone is inseparable from me. I am—I exist: this is certain; but how often? As often as I think; for perhaps it would even happen, if I should wholly cease to think, that I should at the same time altogether cease to be. I now admit nothing that is not necessarily true: I am therefore, precisely speaking, only a thinking thing, that is, a mind (*mens sive animus*), understanding, or reason,—terms whose signification was before unknown to me. I am, however, a real thing, and really existent; but what thing? The answer was, a thinking thing. The question now arises, am I aught else besides? I will stimulate my imagination with a view to discover whether I am not still something more than a thinking being. Now it is plain I am not the assemblage of members called the human body; I am not a thin and penetrating air diffused through all these members, or wind, or flame, or vapor, or breath, or of any of all the things I can imagine; for I supposed that all these were not, and, without changing the supposition, I find that I still feel assured of my existence.

But it is true, perhaps, that those very things which I suppose to be non-existent, because they are unknown to me, are not in truth different from myself whom I know. This is a point I cannot determine, and do not now enter into any dispute regarding it. I can only judge of things known to me: I am conscious that I exist, and I who know that I exist inquire into what I am. It is, however, perfectly certain that the knowledge of my existence, thus precisely taken, is not dependent on things, the existence of which is as yet unknown to me: and consequently it is not dependent on any of the things I can feign in imagination. Moreover, the phrase itself, I frame an image (*effingo*), reminds me of my error; for I should in truth frame one if I were to imagine myself to be anything, since to imagine is nothing more than to contemplate the figure or image of a corporeal thing; but I already know that I exist, and that it is possible at the same time that all those images, and in general all that relates to the nature of body, are merely dreams [or chimeras]. From this I discover that it is not more reasonable to say, I will excite my imagination that I may know more distinctly what I am, than to express myself as follows: I am now awake, and perceive something real; but because my perception is not sufficiently clear, I will of express purpose go to sleep that my dreams may represent to me the object of my perception with more truth and clearness. And, therefore, I know that nothing of all that I can embrace in imagination belongs to the knowledge which I have of myself, and that there is need to recall with the utmost care the mind from this mode of thinking, that it may be able to know its own nature with perfect distinctness.

But what, then, am I? A thinking thing, it has been said. But what is a thinking thing? It is a thing that doubts, understands, [conceives], affirms, denies, wills, refuses, that imagines also, and perceives. Assuredly it is not little, if all these properties belong to my nature. But why should they not belong to it? Am I not that very being who now doubts of almost everything; who, for all that, understands and conceives certain things; who affirms one alone as true, and denies the others; who desires to know more of them, and does not wish to be deceived; who imagines many things, sometimes even despite his will; and is likewise percipient of many, as if through the medium of the senses. Is there nothing of all this as true as that I am, even although I should be always dreaming, and although he who gave me being employed all his ingenuity to deceive me? Is there also any one of these attributes that can be properly distinguished from my thought, or that can be said to be separate from myself? For it is of itself so evident that it is I who doubt, I who understand, and I who desire, that it is here unnecessary to add anything by way of rendering it more clear. And I am as certainly the same being who imagines; for, although it may be (as I before supposed) that nothing I imagine is true, still the power of imagination does not cease really to exist in me and to form part of my thoughts. In fine, I am the same being who perceives, that is, who apprehends certain objects as by the organs of sense, since, in truth, I see light, hear a noise, and feel heat. But it will be said that these presentations are false, and that I am dreaming. Let it be so. At all events it is certain that I seem to see light, hear a noise, and feel heat; this cannot be false, and this is what in me is properly called perceiving (*sentire*), which is nothing else than thinking. From this I begin to know what I am with somewhat greater clearness and distinctness than heretofore.

But, nevertheless, it still seems to me, and I cannot help believing, that corporeal things, whose images are formed by thought, [which fall under the senses], and are examined by the same, are known with much greater distinctness than that I know not what part of myself which is not imaginable; although, in truth, it may seem strange to say that I know and comprehend with greater distinctness things whose existence appears to me doubtful, that are unknown, and do not belong to me, than others of whose reality I am persuaded, that are known to me, and appertain to my proper nature; in a word, than myself. But I see clearly what is the state of the case. My mind is apt to wander, and will not yet submit to be restrained within the limits of truth. Let us therefore leave the mind to itself once more, and, according to it every kind of liberty, [permit it to consider the objects that appear to it from without], in order that, having afterwards withdrawn it from these gently and opportunely, [and fixed it on the consideration of its being and the properties it finds in itself], it may then be the more easily controlled.

Let us now accordingly consider the objects that are commonly thought to be [the most easily, and likewise] the most distinctly known, viz., the bodies we touch and see; not, indeed, bodies in general, for these general notions are usually somewhat more confused, but one body in particular. Take, for example, this piece of wax; it is quite fresh, having been but recently taken from the beehive; it has not yet lost the sweetness of the honey it contained; it still retains somewhat of the odor of the flowers from which it was gathered; its color, figure, size, are apparent (to the sight); it is hard, cold, easily handled; and sounds when struck upon by the finger. In fine, all that contributes to make a body as distinctly known as possible, is found in the one before us. But, while I am speaking, let it be placed near the fire—what remains of the taste exhales, the smell evaporates, the color changes, its figure is destroyed, its size increases, it becomes liquid, it grows hot, it can hardly be handled, and, although struck upon, it emits no sound. Does the same wax remain after the change? It must be admitted that it does remain; no one doubts it, or judges otherwise. What, then, was it I knew with so much distinctness in the piece of wax? Assuredly, it could be nothing of all I observed by means of the senses, since all the things that fell under taste, smell, sight, touch, and hearing are changed, and yet the same wax remains. It was perhaps what I now think, viz., that this wax was neither the sweetness of honey, the pleasant odor of flowers, the whiteness, the figure, nor the sound, but only a body that a little before appeared to me conspicuous under these forms, and which is now perceived under others. But, to speak precisely, what is it that I imagine when I think of it in this way? Let it be attentively considered, and, retrenching all that does not belong to the wax, let us see what remains. There certainly remains nothing, except some thing extended, flexible, and movable. But what is meant by flexible and movable? Is it not that I imagine that the piece of wax, being round, is capable of becoming square, or of passing from a square into a triangular figure? Assuredly such is not the case, because I conceive that it admits of an infinity of similar changes; and I am, moreover, unable to encompass this infinity by imagination, and consequently this conception which I have of the wax is not the product of the faculty of imagination. But what now is this extension? Is it not also unknown? For it becomes greater when the wax is melted, greater when it is boiled, and greater still when the heat increases; and I should not conceive [clearly and] according to truth, the wax as it is, if I did not suppose that the piece we are considering admitted even of a wider variety of extension than I ever imagined. I must, therefore, admit that I cannot even comprehend by imagination what the piece of wax is, and that it is the mind alone (*mens*, Lat., *entendement*, F.) which perceives it. I speak of one piece in particular; for, as to wax in general, this is still more evident. But what is the piece of wax that can be perceived only by the [understanding of] mind? It is certainly the same which I see, touch, imagine; and, in fine, it is the same which, from the beginning, I believed it to be. But (and this it is of moment to observe) the perception of it is neither an act of sight, of touch, nor or imagination, and never was either of these, although it might formerly seem so, but is simply an intuition (*inspectio*) of the mind, which may be imperfect and confused, as it formerly was, or very clear and distinct, as it is at present, according as the attention is more or less directed to the elements which it contains, and of which it is composed.

But, meanwhile, I feel greatly astonished when I observe [the weakness of my mind, and] its proneness to error. For although, without at all giving expression to what I think, I consider all this in my own mind, words yet occasionally impede my progress, and I am almost led into error by the terms of ordinary language.

We say, for example, that we see the same wax when it is before us, and not that we judge it to be the same from its retaining the same color and figure: whence I should forthwith be disposed to conclude that the wax is known by the act of sight, and not by the intuition of the mind alone, were it not for the analogous instance of human beings passing on in the street below, as observed from a window. In this case I do not fail to say that I see the men themselves, just as I say that I see the wax; and yet what do I see from the window beyond hats and cloaks that might cover artificial machines, whose motions might be determined by springs? But I judge that there are human beings from these appearances, and thus I comprehend, by the faculty of judgment alone which is in the mind, what I believed I saw with my eyes.

The man who makes it his aim to rise to knowledge superior to the common, ought to be ashamed to seek occasions of doubting from the vulgar forms of speech: instead, therefore, of doing this, I shall proceed with the matter in hand, and inquire whether I had a clear and more perfect perception of the piece of wax when I first saw it, and when I thought I knew it by means of the external sense itself, or, at all events, by the common sense (*sensus communis*), as it is called, that is, by the imaginative faculty; or whether I rather apprehend it more clearly at present, after having examined with greater care, both what it is, and in what way it can be known. I would certainly be ridiculous to entertain any doubt on this point. For what, in that first perception, was there distinct? What did I perceive which any animal might not have perceived? But when I distinguish the wax from its exterior forms, and when, as if I had stripped it of its vestments, I consider it quite naked, it is certain, although some error may still be found in my judgment, that I cannot, nevertheless, thus apprehend it without possessing a human mind.

But, finally, what shall I say of the mind itself, that is, of myself? For as yet I do not admit that I am anything but mind. What, then! I who seem to possess so distinct an apprehension of the piece of wax,—do I not know myself, both with greater truth and certitude, and also much more distinctly and clearly? For if I judge that the wax exists because I see it, it assuredly follows, much more evidently, that I myself am or exist, for the same reason: for it is possible that what I see may not in truth be wax, and that I do not even possess eyes with which to see anything; but it cannot be that when I see, or, which comes to the same thing, when I think I see, I myself who think am nothing. So likewise, if I judge that the wax exists because I touch it, it will still also follow that I am; and if I determine that my imagination, or any other cause, whatever it be, persuades me of the existence of the wax, I will still draw the same conclusion. And what is here remarked of the piece of wax, is applicable to all other things that are external to me. And further, if the [notion or] perception of wax appeared to me more precise and distinct, after that not only sight and touch, but many other causes besides, rendered it manifest to my apprehension, with how much greater distinctness must I now know myself, since all the reasons that contribute to the knowledge of the nature of wax, or of any body whatever, manifest still better the nature of my mind? And there are besides so many other things in the mind itself that contribute to the illustration of its nature, that those dependent on the body, to which I have referred, scarcely merit to be taken into account.

But, in conclusion, I find I have insensibly reverted to the point desired; for, since it is now manifest to me that bodies themselves are not properly perceived by the senses nor by the faculty of imagination, but by the intellect alone; and since they are not perceived because they are seen and touched, but only because they are understood [or rightly comprehended by thought], I readily discover that there is nothing more easily or more clearly apprehended than my own mind. But because it is difficult to rid one's self so promptly of an opinion to which one has long been accustomed, it will be desirable to tarry for some time at this stage, that, by long continued meditation, I may more deeply impress upon my memory this new knowledge.

* * *

Meditation VI

On the Existence of Material Things, and of the Real Distinction Between the Mind and Body of Man

There now only remains the inquiry as to whether material things exist. With regard to this question, I at least know with certainty that such things may exist, in as far as they constitute the object of the pure mathematics, since, regarding them in this aspect, I can conceive them clearly and distinctly. For there can be no doubt that God possesses the power of producing all the objects I am able distinctly to conceive, and I never considered anything impossible to him, unless when I experienced a contradiction in the attempt to conceive it aright. Further, the faculty of imagination which I possess, and of which I am conscious that I make use when I apply myself to the consideration of material things, is sufficient to persuade me of their existence: for, when I attentively consider what imagination is, I find that it is simply a certain application of the cognitive faculty (*facultas cognoscitiva*) to a body which is immediately present to it, and which therefore exists.

And to render this quite clear, I remark, in the first place, the difference that subsists between imagination and pure intellection [or conception]. For example, when I imagine a triangle I not only conceive (*intelligo*) that it is a figure comprehended by three lines, but at the same time also I look upon (*intueor*) these three lines as present by the power and internal application of my mind (*acie mentis*), and this is what I call imagining. But if I desire to think of a chiliogon, I indeed rightly conceive that it is a figure composed of a thousand sides, as easily as I conceive that a triangle is a figure composed of only three sides; but I cannot imagine the thousand sides of a chiliogon as I do the three sides of a triangle, nor, so to speak, view them as present [with the eyes of my mind]. And although, in accordance with the habit I have of always imagining something when I think of corporeal things, it may happen that, in conceiving a chiliogon, I confusedly represent some figure to myself, yet it is quite evident that this is not a chiliogon, since it in no wise differs from that which I would represent to myself, if I were to think of a myriogon, or any other figure of many sides; nor would this representation be of any use in discovering and unfolding the properties that constitute the difference between a chiliogon and other polygons. But if the question turns on a pentagon, it is quite true that I can conceive its figure, as well as that of a chiliogon, without the aid of imagination; but I can likewise imagine it by applying the attention of my mind to its five sides, and at the same time to the area which they contain. Thus I observe that a special effort of mind is necessary to the act of imagination, which is not required to conceiving or understanding (*ad intelligendum*); and this special exertion of mind clearly shows the difference between imagination and pure intellection (*imaginatio et intellectio pura*). I remark, besides, that this power of imagination which I possess, in as far as it differs from the power of conceiving, is in no way necessary to my [nature or] essence, that is, to the essence of my mind; for although I did not possess it, I should still remain the same that I now am, from which it seems we may conclude that it depends on something different from the mind. And I easily understand that, if some body exists, with which my mind is so conjoined and united as to be able, as it were, to consider it when it chooses, it may thus imagine corporeal objects; so that this mode of thinking differs from pure intellection only in this respect, that the mind in conceiving turns in some way upon itself, and considers some one of the ideas it possesses within itself; but in imagining it turns toward the body, and contemplates in it some object conformed to the idea which it either of itself conceived or apprehended by sense. I easily understand, I say, that imagination may be thus formed, if it is true that there are bodies; and because I find no other obvious mode of explaining it, I thence, with probability, conjecture that they exist, but only with probability; and although I carefully examine all things, nevertheless I do not find that, from the distinct idea of corporeal nature I have in my imagination, I can necessarily infer the existence of any body.

But I am accustomed to imagine many other objects besides that corporeal nature which is the object of the pure mathematics, as, for example, colors, sounds, tastes, pain, and the like, although with less distinctness; and, inasmuch as I perceive these objects much better by the senses, through the medium of which and of memory, they seem to have reached the imagination, believe that, in order the more advantageously to examine them, it is proper I should at the same time examine what sense perception is, and inquire whether from those ideas that are apprehended by this mode of thinking (consciousness), I cannot obtain a certain proof of the existence of corporeal objects.

And, in the first place, I will recall to my mind the things I have hitherto held as true, because perceived by the senses, and the foundations upon which my belief in their truth rested; I will in the second place, examine what afterwards constrained me to doubt of them; and, finally, I will consider what of them I ought now to believe.

Firstly, then, I perceived that I had a head, hands, feet, and other members composing that body which I considered as part, or perhaps even as a whole, of myself. I perceived further, that that body was placed among many others, by which it was capable of being affected in diverse ways, both beneficial and hurtful; and what was beneficial I remarked by a certain sensation of pleasure, and what was hurtful by a sensation of pain. And, besides this pleasure and pain, I was likewise conscious of hunger, thirst and other appetites, as well as certain corporeal inclinations towards joy, sadness, anger, and similar passions. And, out of myself, besides the extension, figure, and motions of bodies, I likewise perceived in them hardness, heat, and the other tactile qualities, and, in addition, light, colors, odors, tastes, and sounds, the variety of which gave me the means of distinguishing the sky, the earth, the sea, and generally all the other bodies, from one another. And certainly, considering the ideas of all these qualities, which were presented to my mind, and which alone I properly and immediately perceived, it was not without reason that I thought I perceived certain objects wholly different from my thought, namely, bodies from which those ideas proceeded; for I was conscious that the ideas were presented to me without my consent being required, so that I could not perceive any object, however desirous I might be, unless it were present to the organ of sense; and it was wholly out of my power not to perceive it when it was thus present. And because the ideas I perceived by the senses were much more lively and clear, and even, in their own way, more distinct than any of those I could of myself frame by meditation, or which I found impressed on my memory, it seemed that they could not have proceeded from myself, and must therefore have been caused in me by some other objects; and as of those objects I had no knowledge beyond what the ideas themselves gave me, nothing was so likely to occur to my mind as the supposition that the objects were similar to the ideas which they caused. And because I recollected also that I had formerly trusted to the senses, rather than to reason, and that the ideas which I myself had formed were not so clear as those I perceived by sense, and that they were even for the most part composed of parts of the latter, I was readily persuaded that I had no idea in my intellect which had not formerly passed through the senses. Nor was I altogether wrong in likewise believing that that body which, by a special right, I called my own, pertained to me more properly and strictly than any of the others; for in truth, I could never be separated from it as from other bodies: I felt in it and on account of it all my appetites and affections, and in fine I was affected in its parts by pain and the titillation of pleasure, and not in the parts of the other bodies that were separated from it. But when I inquired into the reason why, from this I know not what sensation of pain, sadness of mind should follow, and why from the sensation of pleasure joy should arise, or why this indescribable twitching of the stomach, which I call hunger, should put me in mind of taking food, and the parchedness of the throat of drink, and so in other cases, I was unable to give any explanation, unless that I was so taught by nature; for there is assuredly no affinity, at least none that I am able to comprehend, between this irritation of the stomach and the desire of food, any more than between the perception of an object that causes pain and the consciousness of sadness which springs from the perception. And in the same way it seemed to me that all the other judgments I had formed regarding the objects of sense, were dictates of nature; because I remarked that those judgments were formed in me, before I had leisure to weigh and consider the reasons that might constrain me to form them.

But, afterwards, a wide experience by degrees sapped the faith I had reposed in my senses; for I frequently observed that towers, which at a distance seemed round, appeared square when more closely viewed, and that colossal figures, raised on the summits of these towers, looked like small statues, when viewed from the bottom of them; and, in other instances without number, I also discovered errors in judgments founded on the external senses; and not only in those founded on the external, but even in those that rested on the internal senses; for is there aught more internal than pain? And yet I have sometimes been informed by parties whose arm or leg had been amputated, that they still occasionally seemed to feel pain in that part of the body which they had lost,—a circumstance that led me to think that I could not be quite certain even that any one of my members was affected when I felt pain in it. And to these grounds of doubt I shortly afterwards also added two others of very wide generality: the first of them was that I believed I never perceived anything when awake which I could not occasionally think I also perceived when asleep, and as I do not believe that the ideas I seem to perceive in my sleep proceed from objects external to me, I did not any more observe any ground for believing this of such as I seem to perceive when awake; the second was that since I was as yet ignorant of the author of my being, or at least supposed myself to be so, I saw nothing to prevent my having been so constituted by nature as that I should be deceived even in matters that appeared to me to possess the greatest truth. And, with respect to the grounds on which I had before been persuaded of the existence of sensible objects, I had no great difficulty in finding suitable answers to them; for as nature seemed to incline me to many things from which reason made me averse, I thought that I ought not to confide much in its teachings. And although the perceptions of the senses were not dependent on my will, I did not think that I ought on that ground to conclude that they proceeded from things different from myself, since perhaps there be found in me some faculty, though hitherto unknown to me, which produced them.

But now that I begin to know myself better, and to discover more clearly the author of my being, I do not, indeed, think that I ought rashly to admit all which the senses seem to teach, nor, on the other hand, is my conviction that I ought to doubt in general of their teachings.

And, firstly, because I know that all which I clearly and distinctly conceive can be produced by God exactly as I conceive it, it is sufficient that I am able clearly and distinctly to conceive one thing apart from another, in order to be certain that the one is different from the other, seeing that they may at least be made to exist separately, by the omnipotence of God; and it matters not by what power this separation is made, in order to be compelled to judge them different; and, therefore, merely because I know with certitude that I exist, and because, in the meantime, I do not observe aught that necessarily belongs to my nature or essence beyond my being a thinking thing, I rightly conclude that my essence consists only in my being a thinking thing [or substance whose whole essence or nature is merely thinking]. And although I may, or rather, as I will shortly say, although I certainly do possess a body with which I am very closely conjoined; nevertheless, because, on the one hand, I have a clear and distinct idea of myself, in as far as I am only a thinking and unextended thing, and as, on the other hand, I possess a distinct idea of body, in as far as it is only an extended and unthinking thing, it is certain that I [that is, my mind, by which I am what I am], is entirely and truly distinct from my body, and may exist without it.

Moreover, I find in myself diverse faculties of thinking that have each their special mode: for example, I find that I possess the faculties of imagining and perceiving, without which I can indeed clearly and distinctly conceive myself as entire, but I cannot reciprocally conceive them without conceiving myself, that is to say, without an intelligent substance in which they reside, for [in the notion we have of them, or to use the terms of the schools] in their formal concept, they comprise some sort of intellection; whence I perceive that they are distinct from myself as modes are from things. I remark likewise certain other faculties, as the power of changing place, of assuming diverse figures, and the like, that cannot be conceived and cannot therefore exist, any more than the preceding, apart from a substance in which they inhere. It is very evident, however, that these faculties, if they really exist, must belong to some corporeal or extended substance, since in their clear and distinct concept there is contained some sort of extension, but no intellection at all. Farther, I cannot doubt but that there is in me a certain passive faculty of perception, that is, of receiving and taking knowledge of the ideas of sensible things; but this would be useless to me, if there did not also exist in me, or in some other thing, another active faculty capable of forming and producing those ideas. But this active faculty cannot be in me [in as far as I am not a thinking thing], seeing that it does not presuppose thought, and also that those ideas are frequently produced in my mind without my contributing to it in any way, and even frequently contrary to my will. This faculty therefore must exist in some substance different from me, in which all the objective reality of the ideas that are produced by this faculty, is contained formally or eminently, as I before remarked; and this substance is either a body, that is to say, a corporeal nature in which is contained formally [and in effect] all that is objectively [and by representation] in those ideas; or it is God himself, or some other creature, of a rank superior to body, in which the same is contained eminently. But as God is no deceiver, it is manifest that he does not of himself and immediately communicate those ideas to me, nor even by the intervention of any creature in which their objective reality is not formally, but only eminently, contained. For as he has given me no faculty whereby I can discover this to be the case, but, on the contrary, a very strong inclination to believe that those ideas arise from corporeal objects, I do not see how he could be vindicated from the charge of deceit, if in truth they proceeded from any other source, or were produced by other causes than corporeal things: and accordingly it must be concluded that corporeal objects exist. Nevertheless they are not perhaps exactly such as we perceive by the senses for their comprehension by the senses is, in many instances, very obscure and confused; but it is at least necessary to admit that all which I clearly and distinctly conceive as in them, that is, generally speaking, all that is comprehended in the object of speculative geometry, really exists external to me.

But with respect to other things which are either only particular, as, for example, that the sun is of such a size and figure, etc., or are conceived with less clearness and distinctness, as light, sound, pain, and the like, although they are highly dubious and uncertain, nevertheless on the ground alone that God is no deceiver, and that consequently he had permitted no falsity in my opinions which he has not likewise given me a faculty of correcting, I think I may with safety conclude that I possess in myself the means of arriving at the truth. And, in the first place, it cannot be doubted that in each of the dictates of nature there is some truth: for by nature, considered in general, I now understand nothing more than God himself, or the order and disposition established by God in created things; and by my nature in particular I understand the assemblage of all that God has given me.

But there is nothing which that nature teaches me more expressly [or more sensibly] than that I have a body which is ill affected when I feel pain, and stands in need of food and drink when I experience the sensations of hunger and thirst, etc. And therefore I ought not to doubt but that there is some truth in these informations.

Nature likewise teaches me by these sensations of pain, hunger, thirst, etc., that I am not only lodged in my body as a pilot in a vessel, but that I am besides so intimately conjoined, and as it were intermixed with it, that my mind and body compose a certain unity. For if this were not the case, I should not feel pain when my body is hurt, seeing I am merely a thinking thing, but should perceive the wound by the understanding alone, just as a pilot perceives by sight when any part of his vessel is damaged: and when my body has need of food or drink, I should have a clear knowledge of this, and not be made aware of it by the confused sensations of hunger and thirst: for, in truth, all these sensations of hunger, thirst, pain, etc., are nothing more than certain confused modes of thinking, arising from the union and apparent fusion of mind and body.

Besides this, nature teaches me that my own body is surrounded by many other bodies, some of which I have to seek after, and others to shun. And indeed, as I perceive different sorts of colors, sounds, odors, tastes, heat, hardness, etc., I safely conclude that there are in the bodies from which the diverse perceptions of the senses proceed, certain varieties corresponding to them, although, perhaps, not in reality like them; and since, among these diverse perceptions of the senses, some are agreeable, and others disagreeable, there can be no doubt that my body, or rather my entire self, in as far as I am composed of body and mind, may be variously affected, both beneficially and hurtfully, by surrounding bodies.

But there are many other beliefs which, though seemingly the teaching of nature, are not in reality so, but which obtain a place in my mind through a habit of judging inconsiderately of things. It may thus easily happen that such judgments shall contain error: thus, for example, the opinion I have that all space in which there is nothing to affect [or make an impression on] my senses is void; that in a hot body there is something in every respect similar to the idea of heat in my mind; that in a white or green body there is the same whiteness or greenness which I perceive; that in a bitter or sweet body there is the same taste, and so in other instances; that the stars, towers, and all distant bodies, are of the same size and figure as they appear to our eyes, etc. But that I may avoid everything like indistinctness of conception, I must accurately define what I properly understand by being taught by nature. For nature is here taken in a narrower sense than when it signifies the sum of all the things which God has given me; seeing that in that meaning the notion comprehends much that belongs only to the mind [to which I am not here to be understood as referring when I use the term nature]; as, for example, the notion I have of the truth, that what is done cannot be undone, and all the other truths I discern by the natural light [without the aid of the body]; and seeing that it comprehends likewise much besides that belongs only to the body, and is not here any more contained under the name nature, as the quality of heaviness, and the like, of which I do not speak,—the term being reserved exclusively to designate the things which God has given to me as a being composed of mind and body. But nature, taking the term in the sense explained, teaches me to shun what causes in me the sensation of pain, and to pursue what affords me the sensation of pleasure, and other things of this sort; but I do not discover that it teaches me, in addition to this, from these diverse perceptions of the senses, to draw any conclusions respecting external objects without a previous [careful and mature] consideration of them by the mind; for it is, as appears to me, the office of the mind alone, and not of the composite whole of mind and body, to discern the truth in those matters. Thus, although the impression a star makes on my eye is not larger than that from the flame of a candle, I do not, nevertheless, experience any real or positive impulse determining me to believe that the star is not greater than the flame; the true account of the matter being merely that I have so judged from my youth without any rational ground. And, though on approaching the fire I feel heat, and even pain on approaching it too closely, I have, however, from this no ground for holding that something resembling the heat I feel is in the fire, any more than that there is something similar to the pain; all that I have ground for believing is, that there is something in it, whatever it may be, which excites in me those sensations of heat or pain. So also, although there are spaces in which I find nothing to excite and affect my senses, I must not therefore conclude that those spaces contain in them no body; for I see that in this, as in many other similar matters, I have been accustomed to pervert the order of nature, because these perceptions of the senses, although given me by nature merely to signify to the mind what things are beneficial and hurtful to the composite whole of which it is a part, and being sufficiently clear and distinct for that purpose, are nevertheless used by me as infallible rules by which to determine immediately the essence of the bodies that exist out of me, of which they can of course afford me only the most obscure and confused knowledge.

STUDY QUESTIONS

Meditation II

1. What is the role of Descartes' "evil genius" in his meditations?
2. What is Descartes' strategy for determining what he is?
3. What does Descartes understand by "body"?
4. According to Descartes what attribute alone is inseparable from himself?
5. Why does Descartes conclude that "nothing of all that I can embrace in imagination belongs to the knowledge which I have of myself"?
6. How does Descartes handle "perhaps I am dreaming"?
7. What is Descartes' analysis of the piece of wax and what precisely is he trying to show?
8. What does Descartes *know* about the piece of wax and by what faculty?
9. To what is Descartes referring when he says, "I am almost led into error by the terms of ordinary language"?
10. What is the point of Descartes' rhetorical question, "I who seem to possess so distinct an apprehension of the piece of wax,—do I know

myself, both with greater truth and certitude, and also much more distinctly and clearly?"

Meditation VI

1. What persuades Descartes that he at least knows with certainty that things *may* exist?

2. Why is the faculty of imagination sufficient to persuade him (almost) of the existence of material things?

3. What, according to Descartes, is the difference between imagination and pure intellection?

4. On what else besides mind does imagination depend and how does this make the existence of bodies probable?

5. What reasons does Descartes give for his confidence in sense perception?

6. What reasons does Descartes give for doubting what is given in sense perception?

7. What is Descartes' implied criterion for possibility and for separability?

8. What argument does Descartes give for the distinctness and separability of mind and body?

9. What is Descartes' criterion for determining whether something is a substance or a mode?

10. How does Descartes apply the distinction of substance and mode to mind and to body?

11. How does Descartes argue that sense perception is not a mode of mind but rather of something else (body or God)?

12. What does Descartes mean by the distinction "formally or virtually" and to what does he apply it?

13. What precisely is Descartes' argument to prove the existence of corporeal objects?

14. What does Descartes understand by "nature" in general?

15. What does "nature" teach Descartes?

4

John Locke
(1632–1704)

JOHN LOCKE, son of a country attorney, was born in Wrington, near Bristol, England in 1632. From 1646 to 1652 he attended Westminster School in London where he received a strict Puritan education. In 1652 he entered Christ Church, Oxford where he took his Bachelor's and Master's degrees. In 1659 he was elected to a senior studentship which he held until 1684. He lectured in Greek, and was a Reader in Rhetoric and Censor of Moral Philosophy.

Like many others of his day, Locke developed a great distaste for the Scholastic Aristotelianism of the Renaissance. In this he agreed with Descartes which he read privately, had a great deal to do with stirring his interest in philosophy (even though Locke was anti-Cartesian). Besides developing his interest in philosophy, Locke, while at Oxford, worked with the famous chemist Robert Boyle. He put his knowledge of science to use in obtaining a medical degree (1674).

In 1667 Locke entered the service of Lord Ashley, Earl of Shaftesbury, as medical adviser and tutor to the Earl's son. Shaftesbury became Lord Chancellor in 1672 and appointed Locke secretary for the Presentation of Benefices (ecclesiastical positions) and then secretary to the Council of Trade and Plantations (which dealt with colonial trade). A reversal of Shaftesbury's political fortunes and his own ill health forced Locke to retire first to Oxford and then to France, where he remained from 1675 to 1680. On his return to England he re-entered Shaftesbury's service but again was forced into retirement in Holland for plotting against James II. In 1688, when William of Orange ascended England's throne, Locke returned to London where he held various posts (including Commissioner of Trade) until his death in 1704.

Locke's principal philosophical work is his *Essay Concerning Human Understanding*, which, although written in 1671, was not published until 1690. In that year also Locke's *Two Treatises of Civil Government* appeared, the first attacking the "divine right of kings" advocated by Sir Robert Filmer, and the second justifying the revolution of 1688 which had put William on the throne. Other writings of his are extant but have not had the influence of the *Essay* and *Two Treatises*.

In the *Essay* Locke sets out to make an inventory of our "ideas"—

their kinds and origins. He is sometimes said, therefore, to be a pioneer empirical psychologist, although present psychological method would not look kindly upon "introspection." Locke is an epistemological realist in intent; that is, he believes that we truly and objectively know the external world of physical objects through our senses. His analysis of perception, however, puts this realistic stance in jeopardy since it is phenomenalistic (*what* we know through the senses are not physical objects themselves but our ideas of them). Locke also accepts the assumption that all "ideas" can be reduced to simples (ideational atoms, as it were), a position found in Descartes (the clear and distinct idea). Look for these themes as you read.

Suggested Reading

Collins, J. *A History of Modern European Philosophy.* Milwaukee: Bruce, 1956.

Copleston, F., s.j. *A History of Philosophy.* Vol. V. *Hobbes to Hume.* Westminster, Md.: Newman, 1964.

Cranston, M. *John Locke: A Biography.* New York: Oxford University Press, 1985.

Locke and Berkeley: A Collection of Critical Essays. Edd. C. B. Martin and D. M. Armstrong. Garden City, N.Y.: Doubleday Anchor, 1968.

From

An Essay Concerning Human Understanding

Book II: Of Ideas

CHAPTER I

OF IDEAS IN GENERAL, AND THEIR ORIGINAL

Idea Is the Object of Thinking.

1. Every man being conscious to himself that he thinks, and that which his mind is applied about whilst thinking being the *ideas* that are there, it is past doubt that men have in their minds several ideas, such as are those expressed by the words *whiteness, hardness, sweetness, thinking, motion, man, elephant, army, drunkenness*, and others: it is in the first place then to be inquired, *How he comes by them*?

I know it is a received doctrine, that men have native ideas and original characters stamped upon their minds in their very first being. This opinion I have at large examined already; and, I suppose, what I have said in the foregoing book will be much more easily admitted, when I have shown whence the understanding may get all the ideas it has, and by what ways and degrees they may come into the mind; for which I shall appeal to everyone's own observation and experience.

All Ideas Come from Sensation or Reflection.

2. Let us then suppose the mind to be, as we say, white paper, void of all characters, without any ideas:—How comes it to be furnished? Whence comes it by that vast store, which the busy and boundless fancy of man has painted on it with an almost endless variety? Whence has it all the *materials* of reason and knowledge? To this I answer, in one word, from EXPERIENCE. In

that all our knowledge is founded, and from that it ultimately derives itself. Our observation, employed either about external sensible objects, or about the internal operations of our minds, perceived and reflected on by ourselves, is that which supplies our understandings with all the *materials* of thinking. These two are the fountains of knowledge, from whence all the ideas we have, or can naturally have, do spring.

The Object of Sensation: One Source of Ideas.

3. First, our senses, conversant about particular sensible objects, do convey into the mind several distinct perceptions of things, according to those various ways wherein those objects do affect them; and thus we come by those *ideas* we have of *yellow, white, heat, cold, soft, hard, bitter, sweet,* and all those which we call sensible qualities; which when I say the senses convey into the mind, I mean, they from external objects convey into the mind what produces there those perceptions. This great source of most of the ideas we have, depending wholly upon our senses, and derived by them to the understanding, I call SENSATION.

The Operation of Our Minds: The Other Source of Them.

4. Secondly, the other fountain, from which experience furnishes the understanding with ideas, is the perception of the operations of our own mind within us, as it is employed about the ideas it has got; which operations when the soul comes to reflect on and consider, do furnish the understanding with another set of ideas which could not be had from things without; and such are *perception, thinking, doubting, believing, reasoning, knowing, willing,* and all the different actings of our own minds; which we, being conscious of, and observing in ourselves, do from these receive into our understandings as distinct ideas, as we do from the bodies affecting our senses. This source of ideas every man has wholly in himself; and though it be not sense as having nothing to do with external objects, yet it is very like it, and might properly enough be called *internal sense.* But as I call the other sensation, so I call this REFLECTION, the ideas it affords being such only as the mind gets by reflecting on its own operations within itself. By reflection, then, in the following part of this discourse, I

would be understood to mean that notice which the mind takes of its own operations, and the manner of them, by reason whereof there come to be ideas of these operations in the understanding. These two, I say, viz., external material things as the object of SENSATION, and the operations of our own minds within as the objects of REFLECTION, are, to me, the only originals from whence all our ideas take their beginnings. The term *operations* here, I use in a large sense, as comprehending not barely the actions of the mind about its ideas, but some sort of passions arising sometimes from them, such as is the satisfaction or uneasiness arising from any thought.

All Our Ideas Are of the One or the Other of These.

5. The understanding seems to me not to have the least glimmering of any ideas which it doth not receive from one of these two. *External objects* furnish the mind with the ideas of sensible qualities, which are all those different perceptions they produce in us; and *the mind* furnishes the understanding with ideas of its own operations.

These, when we have taken a full survey of them, and their several modes, [combinations, and relations] we shall find to contain all our whole stock of ideas; and that we have nothing in our minds which did not come in one of these two ways. Let anyone examine his own thoughts, and thoroughly search into his understanding, and then let him tell me, whether all the original ideas he has there, are any other than of the objects of his senses, or of the operations of his mind considered as objects of his reflection; and how great a mass of knowledge soever he imagines to be lodged there, he will, upon taking a strict view, see that he has not any idea in his mind but what one of these two have imprinted; though perhaps with infinite variety compounded and enlarged by the understanding, as we shall see hereafter.

Observable in Children.

6. He that attentively considers the state of a child at his first coming into the world, will have little reason to think him stored with plenty of ideas that are to be the matter of his future knowledge. It is *by degrees* he comes to be furnished with them; and

though the ideas of obvious and familiar qualities imprint them-selves before the memory begins to keep a register of time or order, yet it is often so late before some unusual qualities come in the way, that there are few men that cannot recollect the begin-ning of their acquaintance with them; and if it were worth while, no doubt a child might be so ordered as to have but a very few even of the ordinary ideas till he were grown up to a man. But all that are born into the world being surrounded with bodies that perpetually and diversely affect them, variety of ideas, whether care be taken about it or not, are imprinted on the minds of chil-dren. Light and colours are busy at hand everywhere when the eye is but open; sounds and some tangible qualities fail not to solicit their proper senses; and force an entrance into the mind; but yet I think it will be granted easily, that if a child were kept in a place where he never saw any other but black and white till he were a man, he would have no more ideas of scarlet or green than he that from his childhood never tasted an oyster or a pineapple has of those particular relishes.

Men Are Differently Furnished with These According to the Different Objects They Converse with.

7. Men then come to be furnished with fewer or more simple ideas from without, according as the objects they converse with afford greater or less variety; and from the operations of their minds within, according as they more or less reflect on them. For, though he that contemplates the operations of his mind cannot but have plain and clear ideas of them; yet, unless he turn his thoughts that way, and considers them *attentively*, he will no more have clear and distinct ideas of all the operations of his mind, and all that may be observed therein, than he will have all the particu-lar ideas of any landscape, or of the parts and motions of a clock, who will not turn his eyes to it, and with attention heed all the parts of it. The picture, or the clock may be so placed, that they may come in his way every day; but yet he will have a confused idea of all the parts they are made of, till he applies himself with attention to consider them each in particular.

Ideas of Reflection Later, Because They Need Attention.

8. And hence we see the reason why it is pretty late before most children get ideas of the operations of their own minds; and some have not any very clear or perfect ideas of the greatest part of them all their lives; because, though they pass there continually, yet like floating visions, they make not deep impressions enough to leave in their mind, clear, distinct, lasting ideas, till the understanding turns inward upon itself, reflects on its own operations, and makes them the objects of its own contemplation. Children, [when they come first into it, are surrounded with a world of new things, which, by a constant solicitation of their senses, draw the mind constantly to them; forward to take notice of new, and apt to be delighted with the variety of changing objects. Thus the first years are usually employed and diverted in looking abroad. Men's business in them is to acquaint themselves with what is to be found without;] and so, growing up in a constant attention to outward sensations, seldom make any considerable reflection on what passes within them till they have come to be of riper years; and some scarce ever at all.

The Soul Begins To Have Ideas When It Begins To Perceive.

9. To ask, at what *time* a man has first any ideas, is to ask when he begins to perceive; *having ideas*, and *perception*, being the same thing. I know it is an opinion, that the soul always thinks; and that it has the actual perception of ideas in itself constantly, as long as it exists; and that actual thinking is as inseparable from the soul, as actual extension is from the body: which if true, to inquire after the beginning of a man's ideas is the same as to inquire after the beginning of his soul. For by this account, soul and its ideas, as body and its extension, will begin to exist both at the same time.

The Soul Thinks Not Always; for This Wants Proofs.

10. But whether the soul be supposed to exist antecedent to, or coeval with, or some time after, the first rudiments or organization, or the beginnings of life in the body, I leave to be disputed by those who have better thought of the matter. I confess myself

to have one of those dull souls that doth not perceive itself always to contemplate ideas; nor can conceive it any more necessary for the soul always to think, than for the body always to move: the perception of ideas being, as I conceive, to the soul, what motion is to the body: not its essence, but one of its operations; and, therefore, though thinking be supposed never so much the proper action of the soul, yet it is not necessary to suppose that it should be always thinking, always in action. That, perhaps, is the privilege of the infinite Author and Preserver of all things, "who never slumbers nor sleeps"; but it is not competent to any finite being, at least not to the soul of man. We know certainly, by experience, that we *sometimes* think; and thence draw this infallible consequence—that there is something in us that has a power to think. But whether that substance *perpetually* thinks, or no, we can be no further assured than experience informs us. For to say that actual thinking is essential to the soul, and inseparable from it, is to beg what is in question, and not to prove it by reason; which is necessary to be done, if it be not a self-evident proposition. But whether this—that "the soul always thinks," be a self-evident proposition, that everybody assents to on first hearing, I appeal to mankind. [It is doubted whether I thought all last night, or no; the question being about a matter of fact, it is begging it to bring as a proof for it an hypothesis which is the very thing in dispute; by which one may prove anything; and it is but supposing that all watches, whilst the balance beats, think, and it is sufficiently proved, and past doubt, that my watch thought all last night. But he that would not deceive himself ought to build his hypothesis on matter of fact, and make it out by sensible experience, and not presume on matter of fact because of his hypothesis; that is, because he supposes it to be so; which way of proving amounts to this—that I must necessarily think all last night, because another supposes I always think, though I myself cannot perceive that I always do so.

But men in love with their opinions may not only suppose what is in question, but allege wrong matter of fact. How else could anyone make it an inference of mine, that a thing is not, because we are not sensible of it in our sleep? I do not say, there is no *soul* in a man because he is not sensible of it in his sleep; but I do say, he cannot *think* at any time, waking or sleeping, without being sensible of it. Our being sensible of it is not necessary to anything but to our thoughts; and to them it is, and to them it will always be, necessary, till we can think without being conscious of it.]

It Is Not Always Conscious of It.

11. I grant that the soul in a waking man is never without thought, because it is the condition of being awake; but whether sleeping without dreaming be not an affection of the whole man, mind as well as body, may be worth a waking man's consideration; it being hard to conceive that anything should think and not be conscious of it. If the soul doth think in a sleeping man without being conscious of it, I ask, whether, during such thinking, it has any pleasure or pain, or be capable of happiness or misery? I am sure the man is not, no more than the bed or earth he lies on. For to be happy or miserable without being conscious of it, seems to me utterly inconsistent and impossible. Or if it be possible that the *soul* can, whilst the body is sleeping, have its thinking, enjoyments, and concerns, its pleasures and pains, apart, which the *man* is not conscious of, nor partakes in, it is certain that Socrates asleep and Socrates awake is not the same person; but his soul when he sleeps, and Socrates the man, consisting of body and soul, when he is waking, are two persons; since waking Socrates has no knowledge of, or concernment for that happiness or misery of his soul, which it enjoys alone by itself whilst he sleeps, without perceiving anything of it, no more than he has for the happiness or misery of a man in the Indies, whom he knows not. For if we take wholly away all consciousness of our actions and sensations, especially of pleasure and pain, and the concernment that accompanies it, it will be hard to know wherein to place personal identity.

* * *

CHAPTER II

OF SIMPLE IDEAS

Uncompounded Appearances.

1. The better to understand the nature, manner, and extent of our knowledge, one thing is carefully to be observed concerning the ideas we have; and that is, that some of them are *simple* and some *complex*.

Though the qualities that affect our senses are, in the things themselves, so united and blended that there is no separation, no distance between them; yet it is plain the ideas they produce in the mind enter by the senses simple and unmixed. For though the sight and touch often take in from the same object, at the same time, different ideas—as a man sees at once motion and colour, the hand feels softness and warmth in the same piece of wax—yet the simple ideas thus united in the same subject are perfectly distinct as those that come in by different senses; the coldness and hardness which a man feels in a piece of ice being as distinct ideas in the mind as the smell and whiteness of a lily, or as the taste of sugar and smell of a rose: and there is nothing can be plainer to a man than the clear and distinct perception he has of those simple ideas; which, being each in itself uncompounded, contains in it nothing but *one uniform appearance or conception in the mind*, and is not distinguishable into different ideas.

The Mind Can Neither Make Nor Destroy Them.

2. These simple ideas, the materials of all our knowledge, are suggested and furnished to the mind only by those two ways above mentioned, viz., sensation and reflection. When the understanding is once stored with these simple ideas, it has the power to repeat, compare, and unite them, even to an almost infinite variety, and so can make at pleasure new complex ideas. But it is not in the power of the most exalted wit or enlarged understanding, by any quickness or variety of thought, to *invent* or *frame* one new simple idea in the mind, not taken in by the ways before mentioned; nor can any force of the understanding *destroy* those that are there: the dominion of man in this little world of his

understanding, being much what the same as it is in the great world of visible things; wherein his power, however managed by art and skill, reaches no farther than to compound and divide the materials that are made to his hand but can do nothing towards the making the least particle of new matter, or destroying one atom of what is already in being. The same inability will everyone find in himself, who shall go about to fashion in his understanding one simple idea not received in by his senses from external objects, or by reflection from the operations of his own mind about them. I would have anyone try to fancy any taste which had never affected his palate, or frame the idea of a scent he had never smelt; and when he can do this, I will also conclude that a blind man hath *ideas* of colours, and a deaf man true, distinct notions of sounds.

Only the Qualities that Affect the Senses Are Imaginable.

3. This is the reason why, though we cannot believe it impossible to God to make a creature with other organs, and more ways to convey into the understanding the notice of corporeal things than those five as they are usually counted, which He has given to man—yet I think it is not possible for any *man* to imagine any other qualities in bodies, howsoever constituted, whereby they can be taken notice of, besides sounds, tastes, smells, visible and tangible qualities. And had mankind been made but with four senses, the qualities then which are the objects of the fifth sense had been as far from our notice, imagination, and conception, as now any belonging to a sixth, seventh, or eighth sense can possibly be; which, whether yet some other creatures, in some other parts of this vast and stupendous universe, may not have, will be a great presumption to deny. He that will not set himself proudly at the top of all things, but will consider the immensity of this fabric, and the great variety that is to be found in this little and inconsiderable part of it which he has to do with, may be apt to think, that in other mansions of it there may be other and different intelligible beings, of whose faculties he has little knowledge or apprehension, as a worm shut up in one drawer of a cabinet hath of the senses or understanding of a man; such variety and excellency being suitable to the wisdom and power of the Maker. I have here followed the common opinion of man's having but

five senses, though perhaps there may be justly counted more; but either supposition serves equally to my present purpose.

*   *   *

Chapter VIII

Some Farther Considerations Concerning Our Simple Ideas of Sensation

Positive Ideas from Privative Causes.

1. Concerning the simple ideas of sensation, it is to be considered that whatsoever is constituted in nature as to be able by affecting our senses to cause any perception in the mind, doth thereby produce in the understanding a simple idea; which, whatever be the external cause of it, when it comes to be taken notice of by our discerning faculty, it is by the mind looked on and considered there to be a real positive idea in the understanding, as much as any other whatsoever; though perhaps the cause of it be but a privation of the subject.

Ideas in the Mind Distinguished from that in Things Which Gives Rise to Them.

2. Thus the ideas of heat and cold, light and darkness, white and black, motion and rest, are equally clear and positive ideas in the mind; though perhaps some of the causes which produce them are barely privations in those subjects from whence our senses derive those ideas. These the understanding, in its view of them, considers all as distinct positive ideas without taking notice of the causes that produce them; which is an inquiry not belonging to the idea as it is in the understanding, but to the nature of things existing without us. These are two very different things, and carefully to be distinguished; it being one thing to perceive and know the idea of white or black, and quite another to examine what kind of particles they must be, and how ranged in the superficies, to make any object appear white or black.

We May Have the Ideas When We Are Ignorant of Their Physical Causes.

3. A painter or dyer who never inquired into their causes hath the ideas of white and black and other colours as clearly, perfectly, and distinctly in his understanding, and perhaps more distinctly than the philosopher who hath busied himself in considering their natures, and thinks he knows how far either of them is in its cause positive or privative; and the idea of black is no less positive in his mind than that of white, however the cause of that colour in the external object may be only a privation.

Why a Privative Cause in Nature May Occasion a Positive Ideas.

4. If it were the design of my present undertaking to inquire into the natural causes and manner of perception, I should offer this as a reason why a privative cause might, in some cases at least, produce a positive idea; viz. that all sensation being produced in us only by different degrees and modes of motion in our animal spirits, variously agitated by external objects, the abatement of any former motion must as necessarily produce a new sensation as the variation or increase of it; and so introduce a new idea, which depends only on a different motion of the animal spirits in that organ.

Negative Names Need Not Be Meaningless.

5. But whether this be so or not I will not here determine, but appeal to everyone's own experience, whether the shadow of a man, though it consists of nothing but the absence of light (and the more the absence of light is, the more discernible is the shadow), does not, when a man looks on it, cause as clear and positive an idea in his mind as a man himself, though covered over with clear sunshine? And the picture of shadow is a positive thing. Indeed, we have negative names, [which stand not directly for positive ideas, but for their absence, such as *insipid*, *silence*, *nihil*, etc., which words denote positive ideas, v.g., *taste*, *sound*, *being*, with a signification of their absence].

Whether Any Ideas Are Due to Causes Really Privative.

6. And thus one may truly be said to see darkness. For, sup-posing a hole perfectly dark, from whence no light is reflected, it is certain one may see the figure of it, or it may be painted; or whether the ink I write with makes any other idea, is a question. The privative causes I have here assigned of positive ideas are according to the common opinion; but, in truth, it will be hard to determine whether there be really any ideas from a privative cause, till it be determined whether rest be any more a privation than motion.

Ideas in the Mind, Qualities in Bodies.

7. To discover the nature of our *ideas* the better, and to dis-course of them intelligibly, it will be convenient to distinguish them *as they are ideas or perceptions in our minds*, and *as they are modifications of matter in the bodies that cause such perceptions in us*: that so we may not think (as perhaps usually is done) that they are exactly the images and resemblances of something inherent in the subject; most of those of sensation being in the mind no more the likeness of something existing without us, than the names that stand for them are the likeness of our ideas, which yet upon hearing they are apt to excite in us.

Our Ideas and the Qualities of Bodies.

8. Whatsoever the mind perceives *in itself*, or is the immediate object of perception, thought, or understanding, that I call *idea*; and the power to produce any idea in our mind, I call *quality* of the subject wherein that power is. Thus a snowball having the power to produce in us the ideas of white, cold, and round,—the power to produce those ideas in us as they are in the snowball, I call qualities; and as they are sensations or perceptions in our understandings, I call them ideas; which *ideas*, if I speak of [them] sometimes as in the things themselves, would be understood to mean those qualities in the object which produce them in us.

Primary Qualities of Bodies.

9. [Qualities thus considered in bodies are: *First* such as are utterly inseparable from the body, in what estate soever it be;] and such as, in all the alterations and changes it suffers, all the force can

be used upon it, it constantly keeps; and such as sense constantly finds in every particle of matter which has bulk enough to be perceived, and the mind finds inseparable from every particle of matter, though less than to make itself singly be perceived by our senses: v.g., Take a grain of wheat, divide it into two parts, each part has still solidity, extension, figure, and mobility; divide it again, and it still retains the same qualities: and so divide it on, till the parts become insensible; they must retain still each of them all those qualities. For division (which is all that a mill or pestle or any other body does upon another, in reducing it to insensible parts) can never take away either solidity, extension, figure, or mobility from any body, but only makes two or more distinct separate masses of matter of that which was but one before; all which distinct masses, reckoned as so many distinct bodies, after division, make a certain number. [These I call *original* or *primary qualities* of body, which I think we may observe to produce simple ideas in us, viz., solidity, extension, figure, motion or rest, and number.

Secondary Qualities of Bodies.

10. *Secondly*, such qualities, which in truth are nothing in the objects themselves, but powers to produce various sensations in us by their primary qualities, i.e., by the bulk, figure, texture, and motion of their insensible parts, as colours, sounds, tastes, etc. These I call *secondary* qualities. To these might be added a third sort, which are allowed to be barely powers, though they are as much real qualities in the subject as those which I, to comply with the common way of speaking, call qualities, but, for distinction, secondary qualities. For, the power in fire to produce a new colour or consistency in *wax* or *clay*, by its primary qualities, is as much a quality in fire as the power it has to produce in *me* a new idea or sensation of warmth or burning, which I felt not before, by the same primary qualities, viz., the bulk, texture, and motion of its insensible parts.]

[How Bodies Produce Ideas in Us.

11. The next thing to be considered is, how bodies produce ideas in us; and that is manifestly by impulse, the only way we can conceive bodies to operate in.]

By Motions, External, and in Our Organism.

12. If, then, external objects be not united to our minds when they produce ideas therein, and yet we perceive these *original* qualities in such of them as singly fall under our senses, it is evident that some motion must be thence continued by our nerves, or animal spirits, by some parts of our bodies, to the brains or the seat of sensation, there to produce in our minds the particular ideas we have of them. And since the extension, figure, number, and motion of bodies of an observable bigness, may be perceived at a distance by the sight, it is evident some singly imperceptible bodies must come from them to the eyes, and thereby convey to the brain some motion which produces these ideas which we have of them in us.

How Secondary Qualities Produce Their Ideas.

13. After the same manner that the ideas of these original qualities are produced in us, we may conceive that the ideas of *secondary* qualities are also produced, viz., by the operation of insensible particles on our senses. For it being manifest that there are bodies, and good store of bodies, each whereof are so small that we cannot by any of our senses discover either their bulk, figure, or motion,—as is evident in the particles of the air and water, and others extremely smaller than those, perhaps as much smaller than the particles of air and water as the particles of air and water are smaller than peas or hailstones;—let us suppose at present that the different motions and figures, bulk and number, of such particles, affecting the several organs of our senses, produce in us these different sensations which we have from the colours and smells of bodies, v.g., that a violet, by the impulse of such insensible particles of matter of peculiar figures and bulks, and in different degrees and modifications of their motions, causes the ideas of the blue colour and sweet scent of that flower to be produced in our minds; it being no more impossible to conceive that God should annex such ideas to such motions, with which they have no similitude, than that He should annex the idea of pain to the motion of a piece of steel dividing our flesh, with which the idea hath no resemblance.

They Depend on the Primary Qualities.

14. What I have said concerning colours and smells may be understood also of tastes and sounds, and other the like sensible qualities; which, whatever reality we by mistake attribute to them, are in truth nothing in the objects themselves, but powers to produce various sensations in us, and depend on those primary qualities, viz., bulk, figure, texture, and motion of parts [as I have said].

Ideas of Primary Qualities Are Resemblances; of Secondary, Not.

15. From whence I think it easy to draw this observation, that the ideas of primary qualities of bodies are resemblances of them, and their patterns do really exist in the bodies themselves; but the ideas produced in us by these secondary qualities have no resemblance of them at all. There is nothing like our ideas existing in the bodies themselves. They are, in the bodies we denominate from them, only a power to produce those sensations in us; and what is sweet, blue, or warm in idea, is but the certain bulk, figure, and motion of the insensible parts in the bodies themselves, which we call so.

Examples.

16. Flame is denominated hot and light; snow, white and cold; and manna, white and sweet, from the ideas they produce in us, which qualities are commonly thought to be the same in those bodies that those ideas are in us, the one the perfect resemblance of the other, as they are in a mirror; and it would by most men be judged very extravagant, if one should say otherwise. And yet he that will consider that the same fire that at one distance produces in us the sensation of warmth, does at a nearer approach produce in us the far different sensation of pain, ought to bethink himself what reason he has to say, that this idea of warmth which was produced in him by the fire, *is actually in the fire*, and his idea of pain which the same fire produced in him the same way is *not* in the fire. Why are whiteness and coldness in snow and pain not, when it produces the one and the other idea in us, and can do neither but by the bulk, figure, number, and motion of its solid parts?

The Ideas of the Primary Alone Really Exist.

17. The particular bulk, number, figure, and motion of the parts of fire or snow are really in them, whether anyone's senses perceive them or no; and therefore they may be called *real* qualities, because they really exist in those bodies. But light, heat, whiteness, or coldness, are no more really in them than sickness or pain is in manna. Take away the sensation of them; let not the eyes see light or colours, nor the ears hear sounds; let the palate not taste, nor the nose smell; and all colours, tastes, odors, and sounds, *as they are such particular ideas*, vanish and cease, and are reduced to their causes, i.e. bulk, figure, and motion of parts.

The Secondary Exist in Things Only as Modes of the Primary.

18. A piece of manna of a sensible bulk is able to produce in us the idea of a round or square figure; and, by being removed from one place to another, the idea of motion. This idea of motion represents it as it really is in the manna moving; a circle or square are the same, whether in idea or existence, in the mind or in the manna; and this, both motion and figure, are really in the manna, whether we take notice of them or no: this everybody is ready to agree to. Besides, manna, by the bulk, figure, texture, and motion of its parts, has a power to produce the sensations of sickness, and sometimes of acute pains or gripings, in us. That these ideas of sickness and pain are *not* in the manna, but effects of its operations on us, and are nowhere when we feel them not; this also everyone readily agrees to. And yet men are hardly to be brought to think that sweetness and whiteness are not really in manna, which are but the effects of the operations of manna by the motion, size, and figure of its particles on the eye and palate; as the pain and sickness caused by manna, are confessedly nothing but the effects of its operations on the stomach and guts by the size, motion, and figure of its insensible parts (for by nothing else can a body operate, as has been proved): as if it could not operate on the eyes and palate, and thereby produce in the mind particular distinct ideas which in itself it has not, as well as we allow it can operate on guts and stomach, and thereby produce distinct ideas which in itself it has not. These ideas being all effects of the operations of manna on several parts of our bodies, by the size,

figure, number, and motion of its parts, why those produced by the eyes and palate should rather be thought to be really in the manna than those produced by the stomach and guts; or why the pain and sickness, ideas that are the effects of manna, should be thought to be nowhere when they are not felt; and yet the sweetness and whiteness, effects of the same manna on other parts of the body, by ways equally as unknown, should be thought to exist in the manna, when they are not seen or tasted would need some reason to explain.

Examples.

19. Let us consider the red and white colours in porphyry; hinder light from striking on it, and its colours vanish; it no longer produces any such ideas in us. Upon the return of light, it produces these appearances on us again. Can anyone think any real alterations are made in the porphyry by the presence or absence of light, and that those ideas of whiteness and redness are really in porphyry in the light, when it is plain *it has no colour in the dark*? It has indeed such a configuration of particles, both night and day, as are apt, by the rays of light rebounding from some parts of that hard stone, to produce in us the idea of redness, and from others the idea of whiteness. But whiteness or redness are not in it at any time, but such a texture that hath the power to produce such a sensation in us.

20. Pound an almond, and the clear white colour will be altered into a dirty one, and the sweet taste into an oily one. What real alteration can the beating of the pestle make in any body, but an alteration of the texture of it?

Explains How Water Felt as Cold by One Hand May Be Warm to the Other.

21. Ideas being thus distinguished and understood, we may be able to give an account how the same water, at the same time, may produce the idea of cold by one hand, and of heat by the other; whereas it is impossible that the same water, if those ideas were really in it, should at the same time be both hot and cold. For, if we imagine *warmth*, as it is in our hands, to be nothing but

a certain sort and degree of motion in the minute particles of our nerves or animal spirits, we may understand how it is possible that the same water may at the same time produce the sensations of heat in one hand, and cold in the other; which yet *figure* never does, that never producing the idea of a square by one hand which has produced the idea of a globe by another. But if the sensation of heat and cold be nothing but the increase or diminution of the motion of the minute parts of our bodies, caused by the corpuscles of any other body, it is easy to be understood that if that motion be greater in one hand than in the other, if a body be applied to the two hands, which has in its minute particles a greater motion than in those of one of the hands, and a less than in those of the other, it will increase the motion of the one hand, and lessen it in the other, and so cause the different sensations of heat and cold that depend thereon.

An Excursion into Natural Philosophy.

22. I have, in what just goes before, been engaged in physical inquiries a little further than perhaps I intended. But it being necessary to make the nature of sensation a little understood, and to make the difference between the *qualities* in bodies, and the *ideas* produced by them in the mind, to be distinctly conceived, without which it were impossible to discourse intelligibly of them, I hope I shall be pardoned this little excursion into natural philosophy, it being necessary in our present inquiry to distinguish the *primary* and *real* qualities of bodies, which are always in them (viz., solidity, extension, figure, number, and motion or rest, and are sometimes perceived by us, viz., when the bodies they are in are big enough singly as to be discerned), from those *secondary and imputed* qualities, which are but the powers of several combinations of those primary ones, when they operate without being distinctly discerned; whereby we may also come to know what ideas are, and what are not, resemblances of something really existing in the bodies we denominate from them.

Three Sorts of Qualities in Bodies.

23. The qualities then that are in bodies, rightly considered, are of three sorts:

First, the bulk, figure, number, situation, and motion or rest of their solid parts; those are in them, whether we perceive them or not; and when they are of that size that we can discover them, we have by these ideas of the thing as it is in itself, as is plain in artificial things. These I call *primary qualities*.

Secondly, the power that is in any body, by reason of its insensible primary qualities, to operate after a peculiar manner on any of our senses, and thereby produce in us the different ideas of several colours, sounds, smells, tastes, etc. These are usually called *sensible qualities*.

Thirdly, the power that is in any body, by reason of the particular constitution of its primary qualities, to make such a change in the bulk, figure, texture, and motion of *another body*, as to make it operate on our senses differently from what it did before. Thus the sun has a power to make wax white, and fire, to make lead fluid. [These are usually called *powers*.]

The first of these, as has been said, I think may be properly called real, original, or primary qualities, because they are in the things themselves, whether they are perceived or not; and upon their different modifications it is that the secondary qualities depend.

The other two are only powers to act differently upon other things, which powers result from the different modifications of those primary qualities.

The First Are Resemblances; the Second [Are] Thought To Be Resemblances, but Are Not; the Third Neither Are, Nor Are Thought so.

24. But though these two latter sorts of qualities are powers barely, and nothing but powers, relating to several other bodies, and resulting from the different modifications of the original qualities, yet they are generally otherwise thought of. For the *second* sort, viz., the powers to produce several ideas in us by our senses, are looked upon as real qualities in the things thus affecting us; but the *third* sort are called and esteemed barely powers. V.g., the idea of heat or light which we receive by our eyes or touch from the sun, are commonly thought real qualities existing in the sun, and something more than mere powers in it. But when

we consider the sun in reference to wax, which it melts or blanch-
es, we look on the whiteness and softness produced in the wax,
not as qualities in the sun, but effects produced by powers in it.
Whereas, if rightly considered, these qualities of light and
warmth, which are perceptions in me when I am warmed or
enlightened by the sun, are no otherwise in the sun than the
changes made in the wax, when it is blanched or melted, are in
the sun. They are all of them equally *powers in the sun, depending
on its primary qualities*, whereby it is able in the one case so to alter
the bulk, figure, texture, or motion of some of the insensible parts
of my eyes or hands as thereby to produce in me the idea of light
or heat, and in the other it is able so to alter the bulk, figure, texture, or motion of the insensible parts of the wax as to make them
fit to produce in me the distinct ideas of white and fluid.

Why the Secondary Are Ordinarily Taken for Real Qualities, and Not for Bare Powers.

25. The reason why the one are ordinarily taken for the real
qualities, and the other only for bare powers, seems to be because
the ideas we have of distinct colours, sounds, etc. containing
nothing at all in them of bulk, figure, or motion, we are not apt to
think them the effects of these primary qualities which appear not
to our senses to operate in their production, and with which they
have not any apparent congruity or conceivable connection.
Hence it is that we are so forward to imagine that those ideas are
the resemblances of something really existing in the objects themselves, since sensation discovers nothing of bulk, figure, or
motion of parts, in their production, nor can reason show how
bodies *by their bulk, figure, and motion* should produce in the mind
the ideas of blue or yellow, etc. But, in the other case, in the operations of bodies changing the qualities one of another, we plainly
discover that the quality produced hath commonly no resemblance with anything in the thing producing it; wherefore, we
look on it as a bare effect of power. For though, receiving the idea
of heat or light from the sun, we are apt to think *it* is a perception
and resemblance of such a quality in the sun, yet when we see
wax, or a fair face, receive change of colour from the sun, we cannot imagine *that* to be the reception or resemblance of anything in
the sun, because we find not those different colours in the sun

itself. For, our senses being able to observe a likeness or unlikeness of sensible qualities in two different external objects, we forwardly enough conclude the production of any sensible quality in any subject to be an effect of bare power, and not the communication of any quality which was really in the efficient, when we find no such sensible quality in the thing that produced it. But our senses not being able to discover any unlikeness between the idea produced in us and the quality of the object producing it, we are apt to imagine that our ideas are resemblances of something in the objects, and not the effects of certain powers, placed in the modification of their primary qualities, with which primary qualities the ideas produced in us have no resemblance.

Secondary Qualities Twofold: First, Immediately Perceivable; Secondly, Mediately Perceivable.

26. To conclude: besides those before mentioned primary qualities in bodies, viz., bulk, figure, extension, number, and motion of their solid parts, all the rest whereby we take notice of bodies and distinguish them one from another, are nothing else but several powers in them depending on those primary qualities, whereby they are fitted, either by immediately operating on our bodies, to produce several different ideas in us; or else by operating on other bodies, so to change their primary qualities as to render them capable of producing ideas in us different from what before they did. The former of these, I think, may be called secondary qualities *immediately perceivable*; the latter, secondary qualities *mediately perceivable*.

* * *

Book III: Of Words

CHAPTER III

OF GENERAL TERMS

The Greatest Part of Words General.

1. All things that exist being particulars, it may perhaps be thought reasonable that words, which ought to be conformed to things, should be so too. I mean in their signification: but yet we find the quite contrary. The far greatest part of words, that make all languages, are general terms: which has not been the effect of neglect, or chance, but of reason, and necessity.

* * *

How General Words Are Made.

6. The next thing to be considered is, how general words come to be made. For since all things that exist are only particulars, how come we by general terms, or where find we those general natures they are supposed to stand for? Words become general, by being made the signs of general ideas: and ideas become general, by separating from them the circumstances of time, and place, and any other ideas, that may determine them to this or that particular existence. By this way of abstraction they are made capable of representing more individuals than one; each of which, having in it a conformity to that abstract idea, is (as we call it) of that sort.

Shown by the Way We Enlarge Our Complex Ideas from Infancy.

7. But to deduce this a little more distinctly, it will not perhaps be amiss to trace our notions, and names, from their beginning, and observe by what degrees we proceed, and by what steps we enlarge our ideas from our first infancy. There is nothing more evident, than that the ideas of the persons children converse with (to instance in them alone), are like the persons themselves, only

particular. The ideas of the nurse, and the mother, are well framed in their minds; and, like pictures of them there, represent only those individuals. The names they first gave to them, are confined to these individuals; and the names of *nurse* and *mamma*, the child uses, determine themselves to those persons. Afterwards, when time and a large acquaintance have made them observe, that there are a great many other things in the world, that in some common agreements of shape, and several other qualities, resemble their father and mother, and those persons they have been used to, they frame an idea, which they find those many particulars do partake in; and to that they give, with others, the name *man* for example. And thus they come to have a general name, and a general idea. Wherein they make nothing new, but only leave out of the complex idea they had of Peter and James, Mary and Jane, that which is peculiar to each, and retain only what is common to them all.

*   *   *

General Natures Are Nothing but Abstract and Partial Ideas of More Complex Ones.

9. That this is the way, whereby men first formed general ideas, and general names to them, I think, is so evident, there needs no other proof of it, but the considering of a man's self, or others, and the ordinary proceedings of their minds in knowledge: and he that thinks *general natures* or *notions*, are anything else but such abstract and partial ideas of more complex ones, taken at first from particular existences, will, I fear, be at a loss where to find them. For let anyone reflect, and then tell me, wherein does his idea of *man* differ from that of *Peter* and *Paul*; or his idea of *horse* from that of *Bucephalus*, but in the leaving out something that is peculiar to each individual; and retaining so much of those particular complex ideas, of several particular existences, as they are found to agree in? Of the complex ideas, signified by the name *man*, and *horse*, leaving out but those particulars wherein they differ, and retaining only those wherein they agree, and of those making a new distinct complex idea, and giving the name *animal* to it, one has a more general term, that comprehends, with man, several other creatures. Leave out of the idea of

animal, sense and spontaneous motion, and the remaining complex idea, made up of the remaining simple ones of body, life, and nourishment, becomes a more general one, under the more comprehensive term, *vivens*. And not to dwell longer upon this particular, so evident in itself, by the same way the mind proceeds to *body, substance*, and at last to *being, thing*, and such universal terms, which stand for any of our *ideas* whatsoever. To conclude, this whole mystery of genera and species, which make a noise in the schools, and are, with justice, so little regarded out of them, is nothing else but *abstract ideas*, more or less comprehensive, with names annexed to them. In all which, this is constant and unvariable. That every more general term stands for such an idea, as is but a part of any of those contained under it.

* * *

General and Universal Are Creatures of the Understanding and Belong Not to the Real Existence of Things.

11. To return to general words, it is plain, by what has been said, that *general* and *universal*, belong not to the real existence of things; but are the inventions and creatures of the understanding, made by it for its own use, and concern only signs, whether words, or ideas. Words are general, as has been said, when used for signs of general ideas; and so are applicable indifferently to many particular things; and ideas, are general, when they are set up as the representatives of many particular things: but universality belongs not to things themselves, which are all of them particular in their existence, even those words, and ideas, which in their signification, are general. When therefore we quit particulars, the generals that rest, are only creatures of our own making, their general nature being nothing but the capacity they are put into by the understanding of signifying or representing many particulars. For the signification they have, is nothing but a relation, that by the mind of man is added to them.

* * *

They are the Workmanship of the Understanding, but Have Their Foundation in the Similitude of Things.

13. I would not here be thought to forget, much less than to deny, that nature in the production of things, makes several of them alike: there is nothing more obvious, especially in the races of animals, and all things propagated by seed. But yet, I think, we may say, *the sorting of them under names is the workmanship of the understanding, taking occasion from the similitude it observes amongst them, to make abstract general ideas*, and set them up in the mind, with names annexed to them, as patterns or forms (for in that sense the word *form* has a very proper signification), to which, as particular things existing are found to agree, so they come to be of that species, have that denomination, or are put into that *classis*. For when we say, this is a man, that a horse; this justice, that cruelty; this a watch, that a jack; what do we else but rank things under different specific names, as agreeing to those abstract ideas, of which we have made those names the signs? And what are the essences of those species, set out and marked by names, but those abstract ideas in the mind; which are, as it were, the bonds between particular things that exist, and the names they are to be ranked under? And when general names have any connexion with particular beings, these abstract ideas are the medium that unites them: so that the essences of species, as distinguished and denominated by us, neither are nor can be anything but those precise abstract ideas we have in our minds. And therefore the supposed real essences of substances, if different from our abstract ideas, cannot be the essences of the species *we* rank things into. For two species may be one, as rationally, as two different essences be the essence of one species: And I demand, what are the alterations [which] may, or may not be in a *horse* or *lead*, without making either of them to be another species? In determining the species of things by *our* abstract ideas, this is easy to resolve: but if anyone will regulate himself herein, by supposed *real* essences, he will, I suppose, be at a loss: and he will never be able to know when anything precisely ceases to be of the species of a *horse*, or *lead*.

* * *

Several Significations of the Word Essence: Real Essences and Nominal Essences.

15. But since the essences of things are thought by some (and not without reason), to be wholly unknown: it may not be amiss to consider the several significations of the word *essence*.

First, essence may be taken for the being of any thing, whereby it is, what it is. And thus the real internal, but generally in substances, unknown constitution of things, whereon their discoverable qualities depend, may be called their essence. This is the proper original signification of the word, as is evident from the formation of it; *essentia*, in its primary notation, signifying properly being. And in this sense it is still used, when we speak of the essence of *particular* things, without giving them any name.

Secondly, the learning and disputes of the schools, having been much busied about *genus* and *species*, the word *essence* has almost lost its primary signification; and instead of the real constitution of things, has almost wholly applied to the artificial constitution of *genus* and *species*. It is true, there is ordinarily supposed a real constitution of the sorts of things; and it is past doubt, there must be some real constitution, on which any collection of simple ideas co-existing, must depend. But it being evident, that things are ranked under names into sorts or species, only as they agree to certain abstract ideas, to which we have annexed those names, the essence of each *genus*, or sort, comes to nothing but that abstract idea, which the general, or sortal (if I may have leave so to call it from sort, as I do general from genus,) name stands for. And this we shall find to be that which the word essence imports in its most familiar use.

These two sorts of essences, I suppose, may not unfitly be termed, the one the *real*, the other the *nominal essence*.

Constant Connection Between the Name and Nominal Essence.

16. Between the *nominal essence*, and the *name*, there is so near a connection, that the name of any sort of things cannot be attributed to any particular being, but what has this essence, whereby it answers that abstract idea, whereof the name is the sign.

Supposition that Species are Distinguished by Their Real Essences, Useless.

17. Concerning the *real essences* of corporeal substances (to mention those only), there are, if I mistake not, two opinions. The one is of those, who using the word essence, for they know not what, suppose a certain number of those essences, according to which, all natural things are made, and wherein they do exactly every one of them partake, and so become of this or that species. The other, and more rational opinion, is of those, who look on all natural things to have a real, but unknown constitution of their insensible parts, from which flow those sensible qualities, which serve us to distinguish the one from another, according as we have occasion to rank them into sorts under common denominations. The former of these opinions, which supposes these essences, as a certain number of forms or moulds, wherein all natural things, that exist, are cast, and do equally partake, has, I imagine, very much perplexed the knowledge of natural things. The frequent productions of monsters, in all the species of animals, and of changelings, and other strange issues of human birth, carry with them difficulties, not possible to consist with this hypothesis; since it is as impossible, that two things, partaking exactly of the same real essence, should have different properties, as that two figures partaking in the same real essence of a circle, should have different properties. But were there no other reason against it, yet the supposition of essences, that cannot be known; and the making them nevertheless to be that which distinguishes the species of things, is so wholly useless, and unserviceable to any part of our knowledge, that that alone were sufficient to make us lay it by, and content ourselves with such essences of the sorts or species of things, as come within the reach of our knowledge; which, when seriously considered, will be found, as I have said, to be nothing else but those *abstract* complex ideas to which we have annexed distinct general names.

* * *

Recapitulation.

20. To conclude, this is that which in short I would say, (viz.) that all the great business of *genera* and *species*, and their *essences*, amount to no more than this, that men making abstract ideas, and settling them in their minds with names annexed to them, do thereby enable themselves to consider things, and discourse of them, as it were in bundles, for the easier and readier improvement and communication of their knowledge, which would advance but slowly were their words and thoughts confined only to particulars.

Book IV: Of Knowledge and Probability

CHAPTER IX

OF OUR THREEFOLD KNOWLEDGE
OF EXISTENCE

General Propositions That Are Certain Concern Not Existence.

1. Hitherto we have only considered the essences of things; which being only abstract ideas, and thereby removed in our thoughts from particular existence, (that being the proper operation of the mind, in abstraction, to consider an idea under no other existence but what it has in the understanding,) gives us no knowledge of real existence at all. Where, by the way, we may take notice, that universal propositions of whose truth or falsehood we can have certain knowledge concern not existence: and further, that all particular affirmations or negations that would not be certain if they were made general, are only concerning existence; they declaring only the accidental union or separation of ideas in things existing, which, in their abstract natures, have no known necessary union or repugnancy.

A Threefold Knowledge of Existence.

2. But, leaving the nature of proposition, and different ways of

predication to be considered more at large in another place, let us proceed now to inquire concerning our knowledge of the *existence of things*, and how we come by it. I say, then, that we have the knowledge of *our own* existence by intuition; of the existence of *God* by demonstration; and of *other things* by sensation.

* * *

CHAPTER XVIII

OF FAITH AND REASON,
AND THEIR DISTINCT PROVINCES

Necessary To Know Their Boundaries.

1. It has been above shown, 1. That we are of necessity ignorant, And want knowledge of all sorts, where we want ideas. 2. That we are ignorant, and want rational knowledge, where we want proofs. 3. That we ant certain knowledge and certainty, as far as we want clear and determined specific ideas. 4. That we want probability to direct our assent in matters where we have neither knowledge of our own nor testimony of other men to bottom our reason upon.

From these things just premised, I think we may come to lay down *the measures and boundaries between faith and reason*: the want whereof may possibly have been the cause, if not of great disorders, yet at least of great disputes, and perhaps mistakes in the world. For till it be resolved how far we are to be guided by reason, and how far by faith, we shall in vain dispute, and endeavour to convince one another in matters of religion.

Faith and Reason, What, as Contradistinguished.

2. I find every sect, as far as reason will help them, make use of it gladly: and where it fails them, they cry out, It is matter of faith, and above reason. And I do not see how they can argue with any one, or ever convince a gainsayer who makes use of the same plea, without setting down strict boundaries between faith and reason; which ought to be the first point established in all

questions where faith has anything to do.

Reason, therefore, here, as contradistinguished to *faith,* I take to be the discovery of the certainty or probability of such propositions or truths, which the mind arrives at by deduction made from such ideas, which it has got by the use of its natural faculties; viz. by sensation and reflection.

Faith, on the other side, is the assent to any proposition, not thus made out by the deductions of reason, but upon the credit of the proposer, as coming from God, in some extraordinary way of communication. This way of discovering truths to men, we call *revelation.*

First, No New Simple Idea.

3. *First,* then I say, that *no man inspired by God can by any revelation communicate to others any new simple ideas which they had not before from sensation or reflection.* For, whatsoever impressions he himself may have from the immediate hand of God, this revelation, if it be of new simple ideas, cannot be conveyed to another, either by words or any other signs. Because words, by their immediate operation on us, cause no other ideas but of their natural sounds: and it is by the custom of using them for signs, that they excite and revive in our minds latent ideas; but yet only such ideas as were there before. For words, seen or heard, recall to our thoughts those ideas only which to us they have been wont to be signs of, but cannot introduce any perfectly new, and formerly unknown simple ideas. The same holds in all other signs; which cannot signify to us things of which we have before never had any idea at all.

Thus whatever things were discovered to St. Paul, when he was rapt up to the third heaven; whatever new ideas his mind there received, all the description he can make to others of that place, is only this, that there are such things, "as eye hath not seen, nor ear heard, nor hath it entered into the heart of man to conceive." And supposing God should discover to any one, supernaturally, a species of creatures inhabiting, for example, Jupiter or Saturn, (for that it is possible there may be such, nobody can deny,) which had six senses; and imprint on his mind the ideas conveyed to theirs by that sixth sense: he could no more, by words, produce in the minds of other men those ideas imprinted by that sixth sense, than one of us could convey the idea of any colour, by the sound of words, into a man who, having the other four senses perfect, had always totally wanted the fifth, of seeing. For our simple ideas, then, which are the foundation, and sole matter of all our notions and knowledge, we must depend wholly on our reason, I mean our natural faculties; and can by no means receive them, or any of them, from traditional revelation. I say, *traditional revelation*, in distinction to *original revelation*. By the one, I mean that first impression which is made immediately by God on the mind of any man, to which we cannot set any bounds; and by the other, those impressions delivered over to others in words, and the ordinary ways of conveying our conceptions one to another.

Secondly, Traditional Revelation May Make Us Know Propositions Knowable also by Reason, but Not with the Same Certainty that Reason Doth.

4. *Secondly,* I say that *the same truths may be discovered, and conveyed down from revelation, which are discoverable to us by reason, and by those ideas we naturally may have.* So God might, by revelation, discover the truth of any proposition in Euclid; as well as men, by the natural use of their faculties, come to make the discovery themselves. In all things of this kind there is little need or use of revelation, God having furnished us with natural and surer means to arrive at the knowledge of them. For whatsoever truth we come to the clear discovery of, from the knowledge and contemplation of our own ideas, will always be certainer to us than those which are conveyed to us by *traditional revelation.* For the knowledge we have that this revelation came at first from God, can never be so sure as the knowledge we have from the clear and distinct perception of the agreement or disagreement of our own ideas: v.g. if it were revealed some ages since, that the three angles of a triangle were equal to two right ones, I might assent to the truth of that proposition, upon the credit of the tradition, that it was revealed: but that would never amount to so great a certainty as the knowledge of it, upon the comparing and measuring my own ideas of two right angles, and the three angles of a triangle. The like holds in matter of fact knowable by our senses; v.g. the history of the deluge is conveyed to us by writings which had

their original from revelation: and yet nobody, I think, will say he has certain and clear knowledge of the flood as Noah, that saw it; or that he himself would have had, had he been alive and seen it. For he has no greater an assurance than that of his senses, that it is writ in the book supposed writ by Moses inspired: but he has not so great an assurance that Moses wrote that book as if he had seen Moses write it. So that the assurance of its being revelation is less still than the assurance of his senses.

Even Original Revelation Cannot be Admitted Against the Clear Evidence of Reason.

5. In propositions, then, whose certainty is built upon the clear perception of the agreement or disagreement of our ideas, attained either by immediate intuition, as in self-evident propositions, or by evident deductions of reason in demonstrations we need not the assistance of revelation, as necessary to gain our assent, and introduce them into our minds. Because the natural ways of knowledge could settle them there, or had done it already; which is the greatest assurance we can possibly have of anything, unless where God immediately reveals it to us: and there too our assurance can be no greater than our knowledge is, that it *is* a revelation from God. But yet nothing, I think, can, under that title, shake or overrule plain knowledge; or rationally prevail with any man to admit it for true, in a direct contradiction to the clear evidence of his own understanding. For, since no evidence of our faculties, by which we receive such revelations, can exceed, if equal, the certainty of our intuitive knowledge, we can never receive for a truth anything that is directly contrary to our clear and distinct knowledge; v.g. the ideas of one body and one place do so clearly agree, and the mind has so evident a perception of their agreement, that we can never assent to a proposition that affirms the same body to be in two distant places at once, however it should pretend to the authority of a divine revelation: since the evidence, first, that we deceive not ourselves, in ascribing it to God; secondly, that we understand it right; can never be so great as the evidence of our own intuitive knowledge, whereby we discern it impossible for the same body to be in two places at once. And therefore *no proposition can be received for divine revelation, or obtain the assent due to all such, if it be contradictory to our*

clear intuitive knowledge. Because this would be to subvert the principles and foundations of all knowledge, evidence, and assent whatsoever: and there would be left no difference between truth and falsehood, no measures of credible and incredible in the world, if doubtful propositions shall take place before self-evident; and what we certainly know give way to what we may possibly be mistaken in. In propositions therefore contrary to the clear perception of the agreement or disagreement of any of our ideas, it will be in vain to urge them as matters of faith. They cannot move our assent under that or any other title whatsoever. For faith can never convince us of anything that contradicts our knowledge. Because, though faith be founded on the testimony of God (who cannot lie) revealing any proposition to us; yet we cannot have an assurance of the truth of its being a divine revelation greater than our own knowledge. Since the whole strength of the certainty depends upon our knowledge that God revealed it; which, in this case, where the proposition supposed revealed contradicts our knowledge or reason, will always have this objection hanging to it, viz. that we cannot tell how to conceive that to come from God, the bountiful Author of our being, which, if received for true, must overturn all the principles and foundations of knowledge he has given us; render all our faculties useless; wholly destroy the most excellent part of his workmanship, our understandings; and put a man in a condition wherein he will have less light, less conduct than the beast that perisheth. For if the mind of man can never have a clearer (and perhaps not so clear) evidence of anything to be a divine revelation, as it has of the principles of its own reason, it can never have a ground to quit the clear evidence of its reason, to give a place to a proposition, whose revelation has not a greater evidence than those principles have.

Traditional Revelation Much Less.

6. Thus far a man has use of reason, and ought to hearken to it, even in immediate and original revelation, where it is supposed to be made to himself. But to all those who pretend not to immediate revelation, but are required to pay obedience, and to receive the truths revealed to others, which, by the tradition of writings, or word of mouth, are conveyed down to them, reason

has a great deal more to do, and is that only which can induce us to receive them. For matter of faith being only divine revelation, and nothing else, faith, as we use the word, (called commonly *divine faith*), has to do with no propositions, but those which are supposed to be divinely revealed. So that I do not see how those who make revelation alone the sole object of faith can say, that it is a matter of faith, and not of reason, to believe that such or such a proposition to be found in such or such a book, is of divine inspiration; unless it be revealed that that proposition, or all in that book, was communicated by divine inspiration. Without such a revelation, the believing, or not believing, that proposition, or book, to be of divine authority, can never be matter of faith, but matter of reason; and such as I must come to an assent to only by use of my reason, which can never require or enable me to believe that which is contrary to itself: it being impossible for reason ever to procure any assent to that which to itself appears unreasonable.

In all things, therefore, where we have clear evidence from our ideas, and those principles of knowledge I have above mentioned, reason is the proper judge; and revelation, though it may, in consenting with it, confirm its dictates, yet cannot in such cases invalidate its decrees: nor can we be obliged, where we have the clear and evident sentence of reason, to quit it for the contrary opinion, under a pretence that it is a matter of faith: [which can have no authority against the plain and clear dictates of reason].

Thirdly, Things Above Reason Are, When Revealed, the Proper Matter of Faith.

7. But, *thirdly*, there being many things wherein we have very imperfect notions, or none at all; and other things, of whose past, present, or future existence, by the natural use of our faculties, we can have no knowledge at all; these, as being beyond the discovery of our natural faculties, and *above reason*, are, when revealed, the *proper matter of faith*. Thus, that part of the angels rebelled against God, and thereby lost their first happy state: and that [the dead shall rise, and live again]: these and the like, being beyond the discovery of reason, are purely matters of faith, with which reason has directly nothing to do.

Or Not Contrary To Reason, if Revealed, Are Matter of Faith; and Must Carry It Against Probable Conjectures of Reason.

8. But since God, in giving us the light of reason, has not thereby tied up his own hands from affording us, when he thinks fit, the light of revelation in any of those matters wherein our natural faculties are able to give a probable determination; *revelation*, where God has been pleased to give it, *must carry against the probable conjectures of reason*. Because the mind not being certain of the truth of that it does not evidently know, but only yielding to the probability that appears in it, is bound to give up its assent to such testimony which, it is satisfied, comes from one who cannot err, and will not deceive. But yet, it still belongs to reason to judge the truth of its being a revelation, and of the signification of the words wherein it is delivered. Indeed, if anything shall be thought revelation which is contrary to the plain principles of reason, and the evident knowledge the mind has of its own clear and distinct ideas; there reason must be hearkened to, as to a matter within its province. Since a man can never have so certain a knowledge, that a proposition which contradicts the clear principles and evidence of his own knowledge was divinely revealed, or that he understands the words rightly wherein it is delivered, as he has that the contrary is true, and so is bound to consider and judge of it as a matter of reason, and not swallow it, without examination, as a matter of faith.

Revelation in Matters Where Reason Cannot Judge, or but Probably, Ought To Be Hearkened to.

9. First, whatever proposition is revealed, of whose truth our mind, by its natural faculties and notions, cannot judge, that is purely matter of faith, and above reason.

Secondly, all propositions whereof the mind, by the use of its natural faculties, can come to determine and judge, from naturally acquired ideas, are matters of reason; with this difference still, that, in those concerning which it has but an uncertain evidence, and so is persuaded of their truth only upon probable grounds, which still admit a possibility of the contrary to be true, without doing violence to the certain evidence of its own knowledge, and overturning the principles of all reason; in such probable propositions, I say, an evident revelation ought to determine our assent, even against probability. For where the principles of reason have not evidenced a proposition to be certainly true or false, there clear revelation, as another principle of truth and ground of assent, may determine; and so it may be matter of faith, and be also above reason. Because reason, in that particular matter, being able to reach no higher than probability, faith gave the determination where reason came short; and revelation discovered on which side the truth lay.

In Matters Where Reason Can Afford Certain Knowledge, that is to be Hearkened to.

10. Thus far the dominion of faith reaches, and that without any violence or hindrance to reason; which is not injured or disturbed, but assisted and improved by new discoveries of truth, coming from the eternal fountain of all knowledge. Whatever God hath revealed is certainly true: no doubt can be made of it. This is the proper object of faith: but whether it be a *divine* revelation or no, reason must judge; which can never permit the mind to reject a greater evidence to embrace what is less evident, nor allow it to entertain probability in opposition to knowledge and certainty. There can be no evidence that any traditional revelation is of divine original, in the words we receive it, and in the sense we understand it, so clear and so certain as that of the principles of reason: and therefore *nothing that is contrary to, and inconsistent with, the clear and self-evident dictates of reason, has a right to be urged or assented to as a matter of faith, wherein reason hath nothing to do.* Whatsoever is divine revelation, ought to overrule all our opinions, prejudices, and interest, and hath a right to be received with full assent. Such a submission as this, of our reason to faith, takes not away the landmarks of knowledge: this shakes not the foundations of reason, but leaves us that use of our faculties for which they were given us.

*   *   *

Chapter XIX

(Of Enthusiasm)

Love of Truth Necessary.

1. He that would seriously set upon the search of truth, ought in the first place to prepare his mind with a love of it. For he that loves it not, will not take much pains to get it; nor be much concerned when he misses it. There is nobody in the commonwealth of learning who does not profess himself a lover of truth: and there is not a rational creature that would not take it amiss to be thought otherwise of. And yet, for all this, one may truly say that there are very few lovers of truth, for truth's sake, even amongst those who persuade themselves that they are so. How a man may know whether he be so in earnest, is worth inquiry: and I think there is one unerring mark of it, viz. The not entertaining any proposition with greater assurance than the proofs it is built upon will warrant. Whoever goes beyond this measure of assent, it is plain receives not the truth in the love of it; loves not truth for truth's sake, but for some other bye-end. For the evidence that any proposition is true (except such as are self-evident) lying only in the proofs a man has of it, whatsoever degrees of assent he affords it beyond the degrees of that evidence, it is plain that all the surplusage of assurance is owing to some other affection, and not to the love of truth: it being as impossible that the love of truth should carry my assent above the evidence there is to me, that it is true, as that the love of truth should make me assent to any proposition for the sake of that evidence which it has not, that it is true: which is in effect to love it as a truth, because it is possible or probable that it may not be true. In any truth that gets not possession of our minds by the irresistible light of self-evidence, or by the force of demonstration, the arguments that gain it assent are the vouchers and gage of its probability to us; and we can receive it for no other than such as they deliver it to our understandings. Whatsoever credit or authority we give to any proposition more than it receives from the principles and proofs it supports itself upon, is owing to our inclinations that way, and is so far a derogation from the love of truth as such: which, as it can

receive no evidence from our passions or interests, so it should receive no tincture from them.

A Forwardness To Dictate Another's Beliefs, from Whence.

2. The assuming an authority of dictating to others, and forwardness to prescribe to their opinions, is a constant concomitant of this bias and corruption of our judgments. For how almost can it be otherwise, but that he should be ready to impose on another's belief, who has already imposed on his own? Who can reasonably expect arguments and conviction from him in dealing with others, whose understanding is not accustomed to them in his dealing with himself? Who does violence to his own faculties, tyrannizes over his own mind, and usurps the prerogative that belongs to truth alone, which is to command assent by only its own authority, i.e. by and in proportion to that evidence which it carries with it.

Force of Enthusiasm, in Which Reason Is Taken Away.

3. Upon this occasion I shall take the liberty to consider *a third ground of assent*, which with some men has the same authority, and is as confidently relied on as either faith or reason; I mean *enthusiasm*: which, laying by reason, would set up revelation without it. Whereby in effect it takes away both reason and revelation, and substitutes in the room of them the ungrounded fancies of a man's own brain, and assumes them for a foundation both of opinion and conduct.

Reason and Revelation.

4. *Reason* is *natural revelation*, whereby the eternal Father of light and fountain of all knowledge, communicates to mankind that portion of truth which he has laid within the reach of their natural faculties: *revelation* is *natural reason enlarged* by a new set of discoveries communicated by God immediately; which reason vouches the truth of, by the testimony and proofs it gives that they come from God. So that he that takes away reason to make way for revelation, puts out the light of both, and does muchwhat the same as if he would persuade a man to put out his eyes, the better to receive the remote light of an invisible star by telescope.

Rise of Enthusiasm.

5. Immediate revelation being a much easier way for men to establish their opinions and regulate their conduct, than the tedious and not always successful labour of strict reasoning, it is no wonder that some have been very apt to pretend to revelation, and to persuade themselves that they are under the peculiar guidance of heaven in their actions and opinion, especially in those of them which they cannot account for by the ordinary methods of knowledge and principles of reason. Hence we see, that, in all ages, men in whom melancholy has mixed with devotion, or whose conceit of themselves has raised them into an opinion of a greater familiarity with God, and a nearer admittance to his favour than is afforded to others, have often flattered themselves with a persuasion of an immediate intercourse with the Deity, and frequent communications from the Divine Spirit. God, I own, cannot be denied to be able to enlighten the understanding by a ray darted into the mind immediately from the fountain of light: this they understand he has promised to do, and who then has so good a title to expect it as those who are his peculiar people, chosen by him, and depending in him?

Enthusiastic Impulse.

6. Their minds being thus prepared, whatever groundless opinion comes to settle itself strongly upon their fancies, is an illumination from the Spirit of God, and presently of divine authority: and whatsoever odd action they find in themselves a strong inclination to do, that impulse is concluded to be a call or direction from heaven, and must be obeyed: it is a commission from above, and they cannot err in executing it.

What Is Meant by Enthusiasm.

7. This I take to be properly *enthusiasm*, which, though founded neither on reason nor divine revelation, but rising from the conceits of a warmed or overweening brain, works yet, where it once gets footing, more powerfully on the persuasions and actions of men than either of those two, or both together: men being most forwardly obedient to the impulses they receive from themselves; and the whole man is sure to act more vigorously

where the whole man is carried by a natural motion. For strong conceit, like a new principle, carries all easily with it, when got above common sense, and freed from all restraint of reason and check of reflection, it is heightened into a divine authority, in concurrence with our own temper and inclination.

Enthusiasm Accepts Its Supposed Illumination Without Search and Proof.

8. Though the odd opinions and extravagant actions enthusiasm has run men into were enough to warn them against this wrong principle, so apt to misguide them both in their belief and conduct: yet the love of something extraordinary, the ease and glory it is to be inspired, and be above the common and natural ways of knowledge, so flatters many men's laziness, ignorance, and vanity, that, when once they are got into this way of immediate revelation, of illumination without search, and of certainty without proof and without examination, it is a hard matter to get them out of it. Reason is lost upon them, they are above it: they see the light infused into their understandings, and cannot be mistaken; it is clear and visible there, like the light of bright sunshine; shows itself, and needs no other proof but its own evidence: they feel the hand of God moving them within, and the impulses of the Spirit, and cannot be mistaken in what they feel. Thus they support themselves, and are sure reasoning hath nothing to do with what they see and feel in themselves: what they have a sensible experience of admits no doubt, needs no probation. Would he not be ridiculous, who should require to have it proved to him that the light shines, and that he sees it? It is its own proof and can have no other. When the Spirit brings light into our minds, it dispels darkness. We see it as we do that of the sun at noon, and need not the twilight of reason to show it us. This light from heaven is strong, clear, and pure; carries its own demonstration with it: and we may as naturally take a glow-worm to assist us to discover the sun, as to examine the celestial ray by our dim candle, reason.

Enthusiasm How To Be Discovered.

9. This is the way of talking of these men: they are sure, because they are sure: and their persuasions are right, because

they are strong in them. For, when what they say is stripped of the metaphor of seeing and feeling, this is all it amounts to: and yet these similes so impose on them, that they serve them for certainty in themselves, and demonstration to others.

The Supposed Internal Light Examined.

10. But to examine a little soberly this internal light, and this feeling on which they build so much. These men have, they say, clear light, and they see; they have awakened sense, and they feel: this cannot, they are sure, be disputed them. For when a man says he sees or feels, nobody can deny him that he does so. But here let me ask: This seeing, is it the perception of the truth of the proposition or of this that it is a revelation from God? This feeling, is it a perception of an inclination or fancy to do something, or of the Spirit of God moving that inclination? These are two very different perceptions, and must be carefully distinguished, if we would not impose upon ourselves. I may perceive the truth of a proposition, and yet not perceive that it is an immediate revelation from God. I may perceive the truth of a proposition in Euclid, without its being, or my perceiving it to be, a revelation: nay, I may perceive I came not by this knowledge in a natural way, and so may conclude it revealed, without perceiving that it is a revelation of God. Because there be spirits which, without being divinely commissioned, may excite those ideas in me, and lay them in such order before my mind, that I may perceive their connexion. So that the knowledge of any proposition coming into my mind, I know not how, is not a perception that it is from God. Much less is a strong persuasion that it is true, a perception that it is from God, or so much as true. But however it be called light and seeing, I suppose it is at most but belief and assurance: and the proposition taken for a revelation, is not such as they *know* to be true, but *take* to be true. For where a proposition is known to be true, revelation is needless: and it is hard to conceive how there can be a revelation to any one of what he knows already. If therefore it be a proposition which they are persuaded, but do not know, to be true, whatever they may call it, it is not seeing, but believing. For these are two ways whereby truth comes into the mind, wholly distinct, so that one is not the other. What I see, I know to be so, by the evidence of the thing itself: what I believe, I

take to be so upon the testimony of another. But this testimony I must know to be given, or else what ground have I of believing? I must see that it is God that reveals this to me, or else I see nothing. The question then here is: How do I know that God is the revealer of this to me; that this impression is made upon my mind by his Holy Spirit; and that therefore I ought to obey it? If I know not this, how great soever the assurance is that I am possessed with, it is groundless; whatever light I pretend to, it is but *enthusiasm*. For, whether the proposition supposed to be revealed be in itself evidently true, or visibly probable, or, by the natural ways of knowledge, uncertain, the proposition that must be well grounded and manifested to be true, is this, That God is the revealer of it, and that what I take to be a revelation is certainly put into my mind by Him, and is not an illusion dropped in by some other spirit, or raised by my own fancy. For, if I mistake not, these men receive it for true, because they presume God revealed it. Does it not, then, stand them upon to examine upon what grounds they presume it to be a revelation from God? or else all their confidence is mere presumption: and this light they are so dazzled with is nothing but an *ignis fatuus*, that leads them constantly round in this circle; *It is a revelation, because they firmly believe it*; and *they believe it, because it is a revelation*.

Enthusiasm Fails of Evidence, that the Proposition Is from God.

11. In all that is of divine revelation, there is need of no other proof but that it is an inspiration from God: for he can neither deceive nor be deceived. But how shall it be known that any proposition in our minds is a truth infused by God; a truth that is revealed to us by him, which he declares to us, and therefore we ought to believe? Here it is that enthusiasm fails of the evidence it pretends to. For men thus possessed, boast of a light whereby they say they are enlightened, and brought into the knowledge of this or that truth. But if they know it to be truth, they must know it to be so, either by its own self-evidence to natural reason, or by the rational proofs that make it out to be so. If they see and know it to be a truth, either of these two ways, they in vain suppose it to be a revelation. For they know it to be true the same way that any other man naturally may know that it is so, without the help of revelation. For thus, all the truths, of what kind soever, that men

uninspired are enlightened with, came into their minds, and are established there. If they say they know it to be true, because it is a revelation from God, the reason is good: but then it will be demanded how they know it to be a revelation from God. If they say, by the light it brings with it, which shines bright in their minds, and they cannot resist: I beseech them to consider whether this be any more than what we have taken notice of already, viz. that it is a revelation, because they strongly believe it to be true. For all the light they speak of is but a strong, though ungrounded persuasion of their own minds, that it is a truth. For rational grounds from proofs that it is a truth, they must acknowledge to have none; for then it is not received as a revelation, but upon the ordinary grounds that other truths are received: and if they believe it to be true because it is a revelation, and have no other reason for its being a revelation, but because they are fully persuaded, without any other reason, that it is true, then they believe it to be a revelation only because they strongly believe it to be a revelation; which is a very unsafe ground to proceed on, either in our tenets or actions. And what readier way can there be to run ourselves into the most extravagant errors and miscarriages, than thus to set up fancy for our supreme and sole guide, and to believe any proposition to be true, any action to be right, only because we believe it to be so? The strength of our persuasions is no evidence at all of their own rectitude: crooked things may be as stiff and inflexible as straight: and men may be as positive and peremptory in error as in truth. How come else the untractable zealots in different and opposite parties? For if the light, which every one thinks he has in his mind, which in this case is nothing but the strength of his own persuasion, be an evidence that it is from God, contrary opinions have the same title to be inspirations; and God will be not only the Father of lights, but of opposite and contradictory lights, leading men contrary ways; and contradictory propositions will be divine truths, if an ungrounded strength of assurance be an evidence that any proposition is a Divine Revelation.

Firmness of Persuasion No Proof that Any Proposition Is from God.

12. This cannot be otherwise, whilst firmness of persuasion is made the cause of believing, and confidence of being in the right

is made an argument of truth. St. Paul himself believed he did well, and that he had a call to it, when he persecuted the Christians, whom he confidently thought in the wrong: but yet it was he, and not they, who were mistaken. Good men are men still liable to mistakes, and are sometimes warmly engaged in errors, which they take for divine truths, shining in their minds with the clearest light.

Light in the Mind, What.

13. Light, true light, in the mind is, or can be, nothing else but the evidence of the truth of any proposition; and if it be not a self-evident proposition, all the light it has, or can have, is from the clearness and validity of those proofs upon which it is received. To talk of any other light in the understanding is to put ourselves in the dark, or in the power of the Prince of Darkness, and, by our own consent, to give ourselves up to delusion to believe a lie. For, if strength of persuasion be the light which must guide us; I ask how shall any one distinguish between the delusions of Satan, and the inspirations of the Holy Ghost? He can transform himself into an angel of light. And they who are led by this Son of the Morning are as fully satisfied of the illumination, i.e. are as strongly persuaded that they are enlightened by the Spirit of God as any one who is so: they acquiesce and rejoice in it, are actuated by it: and nobody can be more sure, nor more in the right (if their own strong belief may be judge) than they.

Revelation Must Be Judged of by Reason.

14. He, therefore, that will not give himself up to all the extravagances of delusion and error must bring this guide of his *light within* to the trial. God when he makes the prophet does not unmake the man. He leaves all his faculties in the natural state, to enable him to judge of his inspirations, whether they be of *divine* original or no. When he illuminates the mind with supernatural light, he does not extinguish that which is natural. If he would have us assent to the truth of any proposition, he either evidences that truth by the usual methods of natural reason, or else makes it known to be a truth which he would have us assent to by his authority, and convinces us that it is from him, by some marks

which reason cannot be mistaken in. *Reason must be our last judge and guide in everything*. I do not mean that we must consult reason, and examine whether a proposition revealed from God can be made out by natural principles, and if it cannot, that then we may reject it: but consult it we must, and by it examine whether it be a revelation from God or no: and if reason finds it to be revealed from God, reason then declares for it as much as for any other truth, and makes it one of her dictates. Every conceit that thoroughly warms our fancies must pass for an inspiration, if there be nothing but the strength of our persuasions, whereby to judge of our persuasions: if reason must not examine their truth by something extrinsical to the persuasions themselves, inspirations and delusions, truth and falsehood, will have the same measure, and will not be possible to be distinguished.

Belief No Proof of Revelation.

15. If this internal light, or any proposition which under that title we take for inspired, be conformable to the principles of reason, or to the word of God, which is attested revelation, reason warrants it, and we may safely receive it for true, and be guided by it in our belief and actions: if it receive no testimony nor evidence from either of these rules, we cannot take it for a revelation, or so much as for true, till we have some other mark that it is a revelation, besides our believing that it is so. Thus we see the holy men of old, who had revelations from God, had something else besides that internal light of assurance in their own minds, to testify to them that it was from God. They were not left to their own persuasions alone, that those persuasions were from God, but had *outward signs* to convince them of the Author of those revelations. And when they were to convince others, they had a power given them to justify the truth of their commission from heaven, and by visible signs to assert the divine authority of a message they were sent with. Moses saw the bush burn without being consumed, and heard a voice out of it: this was something besides finding an impulse upon his mind to go to Pharaoh, that he might bring his brethren out of Egypt: and yet he thought not this enough to authorize him to go with that message till God, by another miracle of his rod turned into a serpent, had assured him of a power to testify his mission, by the same miracle repeated

before them whom he was sent to. Gideon was sent by an angel to deliver Israel from the Midianites, and yet he desired a sign to convince him that this commission was from God. These, and several the like instances to be found among the prophets of old, are enough to show that they thought not an inward seeing or persuasion of their own minds, without any other proof, a sufficient evidence that it was from God; though the Scripture does not everywhere mention their demanding or having such proofs.

Criteria of a Divine Revelation.

16. In what I have said I am far from denying, that God can, or doth sometimes enlighten men's minds in the apprehending of certain truths or excite them to good actions, by the immediate influence and assistance of the Holy Spirit, *without any extraordinary signs accompanying it.* But in such cases too we have reason and Scripture; unerring rules to know whether it be from God or no. Where the truth embraced is consonant to the revelation in the written word of God, or the action conformable to the dictates of right reason or holy writ, we may be assured that we run no risk in entertaining it as such: because, though perhaps it be not an immediate revelation from God, extraordinarily operating on our minds, yet we are sure it is warranted by that revelation which has given us truth. But it is not the strength of our private persuasion within ourselves, that can warrant it to be a light or motion from heaven: nothing can do that but the written Word of God without us, or that standard of reason which is common to us with all men. Where reason or Scripture is express for any opinion or action, we may receive it as of divine authority: but it is not the strength of our own persuasions which can by itself give it that stamp. The bent of our own minds may favour it as much as we please: that may show it or be a fondling of our own, but will by no means prove it to be an offspring of heaven, and of divine original.

CHAPTER XXI

OF THE DIVISION OF THE SCIENCES

Science May Be Divided into Three Sorts.

1. All that can fall within the compass of human understanding, being either, *First*, the nature of things, as they are in themselves, their relations, and their manner of operation: or, *Secondly*, that which man himself ought to do, as a rational and voluntary agent, for the attainment of any end, especially happiness: or, *Thirdly*, the ways and means whereby the knowledge of both the one and the other of these is attained and communicated; I think science may be divided properly into these three sorts:—

First, Physica.

2. *First*, The knowledge of things, as they are in their own proper beings, then constitution, properties, and operation; whereby I mean not only matter and body, but spirits also, which have their proper natures, constitutions, and operations, as well as bodies. This, in a little more enlarged sense of the word, I call Φυσικὴ, or *natural philosophy*. The end of this is bare speculative truth: and whatsoever can afford the mind of man any such, falls under this branch, whether is be God himself, angels, spirits, bodies; or any of their affections, as number, and figure, &c.

Secondly, Practica.

3. *Secondly*, Πρακτικὴ, The skill of right applying our own powers and actions, for the attainment of things good and useful. The most considerable under this head is *ethics*, which is the seeking out those rules and measures of human actions, which lead to happiness, and the means to practice them. The end of this is not bare speculation and the knowledge of truth; but right, and a conduct suitable to it.

Thirdly, Λογικὴ

4. *Thirdly*, the third branch may be called Σημειωτικὴ, or *the doctrine of signs*; the most usual whereof being words, it is aptly enough termed also, Λογικὴ, *logic:* the business whereof is to consider the nature of signs, the mind makes use of for the understanding of things, or conveying its knowledge to others. For, since the things the mind contemplates are none of them, besides itself, present to the understanding, it is necessary that something else, as a sign or representation of the thing it considers, should be present to it: and these are *ideas*. And because the scene of ideas that makes one man's thoughts cannot be laid open to the immediate view of another, nor laid up anywhere but in the memory, a no very sure repository: therefore to communicate our thoughts to one another, as well as record them for our own use, signs of our ideas are also necessary: those which men have found most convenient, and therefore generally make use of, are *articulate sounds*. The consideration, then, of *ideas* and *words* as the great instruments of knowledge, makes no despicable part of their contemplation who would take a view of human knowledge in the whole extent of it. And perhaps if they were distinctly weighed, and duly considered, they would afford us another sort of logic and critic, that what we have been hitherto acquainted with.

This is the First and Most General Division of the Objects of Our Understanding.

5. This seems to me the first and most general, as well as natural division of the objects of our understanding. For a man can employ his thoughts about nothing, but either, the contemplation of *things* themselves, for the discovery of truth; or about the things in his own power, which are his own *actions*, for the attainment of his own ends; or the *signs* the mind makes use of both in the one and the other, and the right ordering of them for its clearer information. All which three, viz. *things*, as they are in themselves knowable; *actions* as they depend on us, in order to happiness; and the right use of *signs* in order to knowledge, being *toto coelo* different, they seemed to me to be the three great provinces of the intellectual world, wholly separate and distinct one from another.

STUDY QUESTIONS

Book II, Chapter I

1. What does Locke mean by "idea"?

2. What is Locke's model of mind and against what philosophical position is it directed?

3. What does Locke understand by "experience"?

4. What does Locke understand by "sensation"?

5. What does Locke understand by "reflection"?

6. What does Locke understand by "operations of our minds"?

7. What, according to Locke, is the origin of all ideas, original as well as compound, imprinted on the mind?

8. To what empirical evidence does Locke appeal to support his view concerning the origin of ideas?

9. What is Locke's opinion concerning when the soul begins to perceive? Whom does he have in mind?

10. In Locke's opinion is man always thinking?

Book II, Chapter II

1. What does Locke mean by a "simple idea"?

2. What does Locke mean by a "complex idea"?

3. According to Locke, can man invent or destroy simple ideas? Explain.

4. Does Locke admit the possibility of a creature with more than our five senses?

5. Does Locke admit that there can be in bodies other qualities besides sounds, tastes, smells, and visible and tangible qualities by which they can be known by us?

Book II, Chapter VIII

1. According to Locke, what is it in perception that is "taken notice of by our discerning faculty"?

2. What does Locke mean by positive and privative cause? (You may not be able to answer this question until you have read this entire section.)

3. Give Locke's distinction between knowing an idea and knowing its cause.

4. What is Locke's tentative explanation of how a privation can cause a positive idea?

5. Why does Locke think it important to distinguish ideas as they

are perceptions in our minds and as they are modifications of matter?

6. What does Locke mean by "quality"?

7. What does Locke mean by "primary quality"?

8. What, according to Locke, are the primary qualities?

9. What does Locke mean by "secondary quality"?

10. What, according to Locke, are the secondary qualities?

11. What does Locke mean by a "third sort" of quality?

12. What, according to Locke, are some examples of the third sort of quality?

13. How does Locke explain the production of ideas by the primary qualities?

14. How does Locke explain the production of ideas by the secondary qualities?

15. How, according to Locke, are the ideas of primary qualities related to the primary qualities themselves?

16. How, according to Locke, are the ideas of secondary qualities related to the secondary qualities themselves?

17. What evidence does Locke adduce to support his claim that our ideas of secondary qualities do not resemble anything in the things themselves?

18. What does Locke mean by saying that the primary qualities are "real" while the secondary qualities are not?

19. Give one of Locke's three analyses of secondary qualities (manna, porphyry, water).

20. How does Locke summarize his position on qualities?

Book III, Chapter III

1. For Locke, how do words become general?

2. For Locke, how do ideas become general?

3. Give Locke's account of how "we enlarge our *ideas* from our first infancy."

4. What does Locke understand by abstraction?

5. For Locke, to what do "general" and "universal" properly belong?

6. According to Locke, what are the "essences of species"?

7. According to Locke, on what are our abstract ideas founded?

8. What, according to Locke, are the several meanings of "essence"?

9. What, according to Locke, are the two opinions concerning the real essences of corporeal substances?

10. What arguments does Locke adduce against the supposition of essences that cannot be known?

Book IV, Chapter IX

1. What does Locke understand by "the essence of things"?
2. How do we know our existence? the existence of God? the existence of "other things" such as tables and chairs, horses and cats?

Book IV, Chapter XVIII

1. Why might it be important to draw clearly the boundary between faith and reason?
2. What does Locke understand by "reason"? by "faith"?
3. In what specific ways does Locke try to demarcate reason and faith?

Book IV, Chapter XIX

1. What role, if any, ought the love of truth to play in the search for truth?
2. If Locke were writing today, what word would he most probably use instead of "enthusiasm"?
3. What does Locke mean by "enthusiasm"?
4. What is the relationship between "enthusiasm" and "the supposed internal Light"?
5. What is Locke's evaluation of this supposed internal Light?
6. What criteria does Locke propose for judging the validity and authenticity of a divine revelation?

Book IV, Chapter XXI

1. What division of the sciences does Locke propose in this concluding chapter?

5

George Berkeley
(1685–1753)

ALTHOUGH GEORGE BERKELEY was born in Ireland (in 1685 in Kilkenny), his family was of English descent. He studied at Trinity College, Dublin, from 1700 to 1707 when, having earned his Bachelor's, Master's, and Doctor's degrees, he was appointed fellow. From 1707 to 1713 he served as philosophy tutor and lecturer. It was during this period that his own basic philosophical positions were formed, in particular, his immaterialist hypothesis. He was convinced that the Hobbesian and freethinking opinions of his day could not be definitively refuted so long as one accepted the reality of matter.

It was during this period that he published *An Essay Towards a New Theory of Vision* (1709), *A Treatise Concerning the Principles of Human Knowledge* (1710), and *Three Dialogues Between Hylas and Philonous* (1713). These are three of his best-known and most important philosophical pieces. Hence, before he was thirty, Berkeley had worked out his entire philosophical position.

In 1710 he was ordained a priest in the Church of Ireland, and in 1713 he went to London where he met with many of the chief literary figures of his day: Swift, Addison, Steele, and Pope, among others. He published in Steele's *Guardian* a series of anonymous articles attacking the freethinking of the day. Between 1713 and 1724 he held various minor academic posts including a second fellowship at Trinity. Finally, in 1724 he was appointed Dean of Derry, an ecclesiastical post which required his resignation from his Trinity fellowship. He planned to found a college (St. Paul's) in Bermuda for which he obtained a royal charter and for which he raised considerable money. In 1729 he and his new wife visited America. He left his estate at Newport, Rhode Island, and a considerable portion of his library to Yale University.

In 1734 Berkeley, in recognition of his service to the Church of Ireland, was made Bishop of Cloyne, in which post he labored diligently for nearly twenty years. He died in January 1753.

In *Principles*, Berkeley pushes Locke's phenomenalism to its logical conclusion. Whereas Locke holds that "ideas" are the objects of our thoughts about a world which includes material objects, Berkeley held that "ideas" are the *sole* objects of our knowledge and hence "sensible things" *are* ideas." There are no material *substances*.

SUGGESTED READING

Collins, J. *A History of Modern European Philosophy*. Milwaukee: Bruce, 1956.

Copleston, F., S.J. *A History of Philosophy*. V. *Hobbes to Hume*. Westminster, Md.: Newman, 1964.

Grayling, A. C. *Berkeley: The Central Arguments*. La Salle, Ill.: Open Court, 1986.

Locke and Berkeley. Edd. C. B. Martin and D. M. Armstrong. Garden City, N.Y.: Doubleday Anchor, 1968.

Luce, A. A. *Berkeley's Immaterialism: A Commentary on his* A TREATISE CONCERNING THE PRINCIPLES OF HUMAN KNOWLEDGE. London: Nelson, 1945.

From

A Treatise
Concerning
the Principles of Human Knowledge

Part I

1. It is evident to anyone who takes a survey of the *objects of human knowledge*, that they are either *ideas* actually imprinted on the senses; or else such as are perceived by attending to the passions and operations of the mind; or lastly, *ideas* formed by the help of memory and imagination—either compounding, dividing, or barely representing those originally perceived in the aforesaid ways. By sight I have the ideas of light and colours, with their several degrees and variations. By touch I perceive hard and soft, heat and cold, motion and resistance, and of all these more or less either as to quantity or degree. Smelling furnishes me with odors; the palate with tastes; and hearing conveys sounds to the mind in all their variety of tone and composition.

And as several of these are observed to accompany each other, they come to be marked by one name, and so to be reputed as one thing. Thus, for example, a certain colour, taste, smell, figure and consistence having been observed to go together, are accounted as one distinct thing, signified by the name *apple*; other collections of ideas constitute a stone, a tree, a book, and the like sensible things—which as they are pleasing or disagreeable excite the passions of love, hatred, joy, grief, and so forth.

2. But, besides all that endless variety of ideas or objects of knowledge, there is likewise something which knows or perceives them, and exercises diverse operations, as willing, imagining, remembering, about them. This perceiving, active being is what I call *mind, spirit, soul* or *myself*. By which words I do not denote any one of my ideas, but a thing entirely distinct from them, wherein they exist, or, which is the same thing, whereby they are perceived; for the existence of an idea consists in being perceived.

3. That neither our thoughts, nor passions, nor ideas formed by the imagination, exist without the mind, is what everybody will allow. And to me it seems no less evident that the various sensations or ideas imprinted on the Sense, however blended or combined together (that is, whatever objects they compose), cannot exist otherwise than in a mind perceiving them. I think an intuitive knowledge may be obtained of this, by any one that shall attend to what is meant by the term *exist*, when applied to sensible things. The table I write on I say exists, that is, I see and feel it; and if I were out of my study I should say it existed—meaning thereby that if I was in my study I might perceive it, or that some other spirit actually does perceive it. There was an odour, that is, it was smelt; there was a sound, that is, it was heard; a colour or figure, and it was perceived by sight or touch. This is all that I can understand by these and the like expressions. For as to what is said of the absolute existence of unthinking things without any relation to their being perceived, that is to me perfectly unintelligible. Their *esse* is *percipi*, nor is it possible they should have any existence out of the minds of thinking things which perceive them.

4. It is indeed an opinion strangely prevailing amongst men, that houses, mountains, rivers, and in a word all sensible objects, have an existence, natural or real, distinct from their being perceived by the understanding. But, with how great an assurance and acquiescence soever this principle may be entertained in the world, yet whoever shall find in his heart to call it in question may, if I mistake not, perceive it to involve a manifest contradiction. For, what are the aforementioned objects but the things we perceive by sense? And what do we perceive besides our own ideas or sensations? And is it not plainly repugnant that any one of these, or any combination of them, should exist unperceived?

5. If we thoroughly examine this tenet it will, perhaps, be found at bottom to depend on the doctrine of *abstract ideas*. For can there be a nicer strain of abstraction than to distinguish the existence of sensible objects from their being perceived, so as to conceive them existing unperceived? Light and colours, heat and cold, extension and figures—in a word the things we see and feel—what are they but so many sensations, notions, ideas, or impressions [of] sense? and is it possible to separate, even in

thought, any of these from perception? For my part, I might as easily divide a thing from itself. I may, indeed, divide in my thoughts, or conceive apart from each other, those things which, perhaps, I never perceived by sense so divided. Thus, I imagine the trunk of a human body without the limbs, or conceive the smell of a rose without thinking on the rose itself. So far, I will not deny, I can abstract—if that may properly be called *abstraction* which extends only to the conceiving separately such objects as it is possible may really exist or be actually perceived asunder. But my conceiving or imagining power does not extend beyond the possibility of real existence or perception. Hence, as it is impossible for me to see or feel anything without an actual sensation of that thing, so is it impossible for me to conceive in my thoughts any sensible thing or object distinct from the sensation or perception of it. [In truth, the object and the sensation are the same thing, and cannot therefore be abstracted from each other.]

6. Some truths there are so near and obvious to the mind that a man need only open his eyes to see them. Such I take this important one to be, viz., that all the choir of heaven and furniture of the earth, in a word all those bodies which compose the mighty frame of the world, have not any subsistence without a mind; that their *being* is to be perceived or known; that consequently so long as they are not actually perceived by me, or do not exist in my mind, or that of any other created spirit, they must either have no existence at all, or else subsist in the mind of some Eternal Spirit—it being perfectly unintelligible, and involving all the absurdity of abstraction, to attribute to any single part of them an existence independent of a spirit. [To be convinced of which, the reader need only reflect, and try to separate in his own thoughts the *being* of a sensible thing from its *being perceived*.]

7. From what has been said it is evident there is not any other Substance than *Spirit*, or that which perceives. But, for the fuller proof of this point, let it be considered the sensible qualities are colour, figure, motion, smell, taste, etc. and such like, that is, the ideas perceived by sense. Now, for an idea to exist in an unperceiving thing is a manifest contradiction, for to have an idea is all one as to perceive; that therefore wherein colour, figure, and the like qualities exist must perceive them; hence it is clear there can be no unthinking substance or *substratum* of those ideas.

8. But, say you, though the ideas themselves do not exist without the mind, yet there may be things like them, whereof they are copies or resemblances, which things exist without the mind in an unthinking substance. I answer, an idea can be like nothing but an idea; a colour or figure can be like nothing but another colour or figure. If we look but never so little into our thoughts, we shall find it impossible for us to conceive a likeness except only between our ideas. Again, I ask whether those supposed *originals* or external things, of which our ideas are the pictures or representations, be themselves perceivable or no? If they are, then they are ideas and we have gained our point; but if you say they are not, I appeal to anyone whether it be sense to assert a colour is like something which is invisible; hard or soft, like something which is intangible; and so of the rest.

9. Some there are who make a distinction betwixt *primary* and *secondary* qualities. By the former they mean extension, figure, motion, rest, solidity or impenetrability, and number; by the latter they denote all other sensible qualities, as colours, sounds, tastes, and so forth. The ideas we have of these they acknowledge not to be the resemblances of anything existing without the mind, or unperceived, but they will have our ideas of primary qualities to be patterns or images of things which exist without the mind, in an unthinking substance which they call Matter. By Matter, therefore, we are to understand an inert, senseless substance, in which extension, figure, and motion do actually subsist. But it is evident from what we have already shown, that extension, figure, and motion are only ideas existing in the mind, and that an idea can be like nothing but another idea, and that consequently neither they nor their archetypes can exist in an unperceiving substance. Hence, it is plain that the very notion of what is called *Matter* or *corporeal substance*, involves a contradiction in it. . . .

10. They who assert that figure, motion, and the rest of the primary or original qualities do exist without the mind in unthinking substances, do at the same time acknowledge that colours, sounds, heat, cold, and such-like secondary qualities, do not—which they tell us are sensations existing in the mind alone, that depend on and are occasioned by the different size, texture, and motion of the minute particles of matter. This they take for an undoubted truth, which they can demonstrate beyond all excep-

tion. Now, if it be certain that those *original* qualities are inseparably united with the other sensible qualities, and not, even in
thought, capable of being abstracted from them, it plainly follows
that *they* exist only in the mind. But I desire any one to reflect and
try whether he can, by any abstraction of thought, conceive the
extension and motion of a body without all other sensible qualities. For my own part, I see evidently that it is not in my power to
frame an idea of a body extended and moving, but I must withal
give it some colour or other sensible quality which is acknowledged to exist only in the mind. In short, extension, figure, and
motion, abstracted from all other qualities, are inconceivable.
Where therefore the other sensible qualities are, there must these
be also, to wit, in the mind and nowhere else.

11. Again, *great* and *small, swift* and *slow,* are allowed to exist
nowhere without the mind, being entirely relative, and changing
as the frame or position of the organs of sense varies. The extension therefore which exists without the mind is neither great nor
small, the motion neither swift nor slow, that is, they are nothing
at all. But, say you, they are extension in general, and motion in
general: thus we see how much the tenet of extended movable
substances existing without the mind depends on that strange
doctrine of *abstract ideas.* And here I cannot but remark how nearly the vague and indeterminate description of Matter or corporeal
substance, which the modern philosophers are run into by their
own principles, resembles that antiquated and so much ridiculed
notion of *materia prima,* to be met with in Aristotle and his followers. Without extension solidity cannot be conceived; since therefore it has been shown that extension exists not in an unthinking
substance, the same must also be true of solidity.

* * *

16. But let us examine a little the received opinion. It is said
extension is a *mode* or *accident* of Matter, and that Matter is the
substratum that supports it. Now I desire that you would explain
to me what is meant by Matter's *supporting* extension. Say you, I
have no idea of Matter and therefore cannot explain it. I answer,
though you have no positive, yet, if you have any meaning at all,
you must at least have a relative idea of Matter; though you know

not what it is, yet you must be supposed to know what relation it bears to accidents, and what is meant by its supporting them. It is evident "support" cannot here be taken in its usual or literal sense—as when we say that pillars support a building; in what sense therefore must it be taken? . . .

17. If we inquire into what the most accurate philosophers declare themselves to mean by *material substance*, we shall find they acknowledge they have no other meaning annexed to those sounds but the idea of Being in general, together with the relative notion of its supporting accidents. The general idea of Being appeareth to me the most abstract and incomprehensible of all other; and as for its supporting accidents, this, as we have just now observed, cannot be understood in the common sense of those words; it must therefore be taken in some other sense, but what that is they do not explain. So that when I consider the two parts or branches which make the signification of the words *material substance*, I am convinced there is no distinct meaning annexed to them. But why should we trouble ourselves any farther, in discussing this material *substratum* or support of figure and motion, and other sensible qualities? Does it not suppose they have an existence without the mind? And is not this a direct repugnancy, and altogether inconceivable?

18. But, though it were possible that solid, figured, movable substances may exist without the mind, corresponding to the ideas we have of bodies, yet how is it possible for us to know this? Either we must know it by sense or by reason. As for our senses, by them we have the knowledge only of our sensations, ideas, or those things that are immediately perceived by sense, call them what you will: but they do not inform us that things exist without the mind, or unperceived, like to those which are perceived. This the materialists themselves acknowledge. It remains therefore that if we have any knowledge at all of external things, it must be by reason, inferring their existence from what is immediately perceived by sense. But (I do not see) what reason can induce us to believe the existence of bodies without the mind, from what we perceive, since the very patrons of Matter themselves do not pretend there is any necessary connection betwixt them and our ideas? I say it is granted on all hands (and what happens in dreams, frenzies, and the like, puts it beyond dispute)

that it is possible we might be affected with all the ideas we have now, though no bodies existed without resembling them. Hence, it is evident the supposition of external bodies is not necessary for the producing our ideas; since it is granted they are produced sometimes, and might possibly be produced always in the same order, we see them in at present, without their concurrence.

19. But, though we might possibly have all our sensations without them, yet perhaps it may be thought easier to conceive and explain the manner of their production, by supposing external bodies in their likeness rather than otherwise; and so it might be at least probable there are such things as bodies that excite their ideas in our minds. But neither can this be said; for, though we give the materialists their external bodies, they by their own confession are never the nearer knowing how our ideas are produced; since they own themselves unable to comprehend in what manner body can act upon spirit, or how it is possible it should imprint any idea in the mind. Hence it is evident the production of ideas or sensations in our minds can be no reason why we should suppose Matter or corporeal substances, since that is acknowledged to remain equally inexplicable with or without this supposition. If therefore it were possible for bodies to exist without the mind, yet to hold they do so, must needs be a very precarious opinion; since it is to suppose, without any reason at all, that God has created innumerable beings that are entirely useless, and serve to no manner of purpose.

20. In short, if there were external bodies, it is impossible we should ever come to know it; and if there were not, we might have the very same reasons to think there were that we have now. Suppose—what no one can deny possible—an intelligence without the help of external bodies, to be affected with the same train of sensations or ideas that you are, imprinted in the same order and with like vividness in his mind. I ask whether that intelligence hath not all the reason to believe the existence of corporeal substances, represented by his ideas, and exciting them in his mind, that you can possibly have for believing the same thing? Of this there can be no question—which one consideration were enough to make any reasonable person suspect the strength of whatever arguments he may think himself to have, for the existence of bodies without the mind.

21. Were it necessary to add any further proof against the existence of Matter after what has been said, I could instance several of those errors and difficulties (not to mention impieties) which have sprung from that tenet. It has occasioned numberless controversies and disputes in philosophy, and not a few of far greater moment in religion. But I shall not enter into the detail of them in this place, as well because I think arguments *a posteriori* are unnecessary for confirming what has been, if I mistake not, sufficiently demonstrated *a priori*, as because I shall hereafter find occasion to speak somewhat of them.

* * *

25. All our ideas, sensations, notions, or the things which we perceive, by whatsoever names they may be distinguished, are visibly inactive—there is nothing of power or agency included in them. So that one idea or object of thought cannot produce or make any alteration in another. To be satisfied of the truth of this, there is nothing else requisite but a bare observation of our ideas. For, since they and every part of them exist only in the mind, it follows that there is nothing in them but what is perceived: but whoever shall attend to his ideas, whether of sense or reflection, will not perceive in them any power or activity; there is, therefore, no such thing contained in them. A little attention will discover to us that the very being of an idea implies passiveness and inertness in it, insomuch that it is impossible for an idea to do anything, or, strictly speaking, to be the cause of anything; neither can it be the resemblance or pattern of any active being, as is evident from sect. 8. Whence it plainly follows that extension, figure, and motion cannot be the cause of our sensations. To say, therefore, that these are the effects of powers resulting from the configuration, number, motion, and size of corpuscles, must certainly be false.

26. We perceive a continual succession of ideas, some are anew excited, others are changed or totally disappear. There is therefore *some* cause of these ideas, whereon they depend, and which produces and changes them. That this cause cannot be any quality or idea or combination of *ideas*, is clear from the preceding section. It must therefore be a *substance*; but it has been shown

that there is no corporeal or material substance: it remains therefore that the cause of ideas is an incorporeal active substance or
Spirit.

27. A spirit is one simple, undivided, active being—as it perceives ideas it is called the *understanding*, and as it produces or
otherwise operates about them it is called the *will*. Hence there
can be no *idea* formed of a soul or spirit; for all ideas whatever,
being passive and inert (Vide sect. 25), they cannot represent unto
us, by way of image or likeness, that which acts. A little attention
will make it plain to any one, that to have an idea which shall be
like that active principle of motion and change of ideas is
absolutely impossible. Such is the nature of Spirit, or that which
acts, that it cannot be of itself perceived, but only by the effects
which it produceth. If any man shall doubt of the truth of what is
here delivered, let him but reflect and try if he can frame the idea
of any power or active being, and whether he has ideas of two
principal powers, marked by their names *will* and *understanding*,
distinct from each other as well as from a third idea of Substance
or Being in general, with a relative notion of its supporting or
being the subject of the aforesaid powers—which is signified by
the name *soul* or *spirit*. This is what some hold; but, so far as I can
see, the words *will, soul, spirit*, do not stand for different ideas, or,
in truth, for any idea at all, but for something which is very different from ideas, and which, being an agent, cannot be like unto, or
represented by, any idea whatsoever. [Though it must be owned
at the same time that we have some *notion* of soul, spirit, and the
operations of mind: such as willing, loving, hating—inasmuch as
we know or understand the meaning of these words.]

28. I find I can excite ideas in my mind at pleasure, and vary
and shift the scene as oft as I think fit. It is no more than willing,
and straightway this or that idea arises in my fancy; and by the
same power it is obliterated and makes way for another. This
making and unmaking of ideas doth very properly denominate
the mind active. Thus much is certain and grounded on experience; but when we talk of unthinking agents or of exciting ideas
exclusive of volition, we only amuse ourselves with words.

29. But, whatever power I may have over my own thoughts, I
find the ideas actually perceived by Sense have not a like dependence on *my* will. When in broad daylight I open my eyes, it is

not in my power to choose whether I shall see or no, or to determine what particular objects shall present themselves to my view; and so likewise as to the hearing and other senses; the ideas imprinted on them are not creatures of *my* will. There is therefore some *other* Will or Spirit that produces them.

30. The ideas of Sense are more strong, lively and distinct than those of imagination; they have likewise a steadiness, order, and coherence, and are not excited at random, as those which are the effects of human wills often are, but in a regular train or series, the admirable connection whereof sufficiently testifies the wisdom and benevolence of its Author. Now the set rules or established methods wherein the Mind we depend on excites in us the ideas of Sense, are called the *laws of nature*; and these we learn by experience, which teaches us that such and such ideas are attended with such and such other ideas, in the ordinary course of things.

31. This gives us a sort of foresight which enables us to regulate our actions for the benefit of life. And without this we should be eternally at a loss; we could not know how to act anything that might procure us the least pleasure, or remove the least pain of sense. That food nourishes, sleep refreshes, and fire warms us; that to sow in the seed-time is the way to reap in the harvest; and in general that to obtain such or such ends, such or such means are conducive—all this we know, not by discovering any *necessary connection* between our ideas, but only by the observation of the *settled laws* of nature, without which we should be all in uncertainty and confusion, and a grown man no more know how to manage himself in the affairs of life than an infant just born.

32. And yet this consistent uniform working, which so evidently displays the goodness and wisdom of that Governing Spirit whose Will constitutes the laws of nature, is so far from leading our thoughts to Him, that it rather sends them wandering after second causes. For, when we perceive certain ideas of Sense constantly followed by other ideas and we know this is not of our own doing, we forthwith attribute power and agency to the ideas themselves, and make one the cause of another, than which nothing can be more absurd and unintelligible. Thus, for example, having observed that when we perceive by sight a certain round luminous figure we at the same time perceive by touch the idea

or sensation called heat, we do from thence conclude the sun to be the cause of heat. And in like manner perceiving the motion and collision of bodies to be attended with sound, we are inclined to think the latter the effect of the former.

33. The ideas imprinted on the Senses by the Author of nature are called *real things*; and those excited in the imagination being less regular, vivid, and constant, are more properly termed *ideas*, or *images of things*, which they copy and represent. But then our *sensations*, be they never so vivid and distinct, are nevertheless ideas, that is, they exist in the mind, or are perceived by it, as truly as the ideas of its own framing. The ideas of Sense are allowed to have more reality in them, that is, to be more strong, orderly, and coherent than the creatures of the mind; but this is no argument that they exist without the mind. They are also less dependent on the spirit, or thinking substance which perceives them, in that they are excited by the will of another and more powerful spirit; yet still they are *ideas*, and certainly no idea, whether faint or strong, can exist otherwise than in a mind perceiving it.

34. Before we proceed any farther it is necessary we spend some time in answering objections which may probably be made against the principles we have hitherto laid down. In doing of which, if I seem too prolix to those of quick apprehensions; I desire to be excused, since all men do not equally apprehend things of this nature, and I am willing to be understood by every one.

First, then, it will be objected that by the foregoing principles all that is real and substantial in nature is banished out of the world, and instead thereof a chimerical scheme of *ideas* takes place. All things that exist, exist only in the mind, that is, they are purely notional. What therefore becomes of the sun, moon, and stars? What must we think of houses, rivers, mountains, trees, stones; nay even of our own bodies? Are all these but so many chimeras and illusions on the fancy? To all which, and whatever else of the same sort may be objected, I answer, that by the principles premised we are not deprived of any one thing in nature. Whatever we see, feel, hear, or anywise conceive or understand remains as secure as ever, and is as real as ever. There is a *rerum natura*, and the distinction between realities and chimeras retains its full force. This is evident from sect. 29, 30, and 33, where we have shown what is meant by *real things* in opposition to *chimeras* or *ideas of our own framing*; but then they both equally exist in the mind, and in that sense they are alike *ideas*.

35. I do not argue against the existence of any one thing that we can apprehend either by sense or reflexion. That the things I see with my eyes and touch with my hands do exist, really exist, I make not the least question. The only thing whose existence we deny is that which *philosophers* call Matter or corporeal substance. And in doing of this there is no damage done to the rest of mankind, who, I dare say, will never miss it. The Atheist indeed will want the colour of an empty name to support his impiety; and the Philosophers may possibly find they have lost a great handle for trifling and disputation. [But that is all the harm that I can see done.]

36. If any man thinks this detracts from the existence or reality of things, he is very far from understanding what hath been premised in the plainest terms I could think of. Take here an abstract of what has been said:—There are spiritual substances, minds, or human souls, which will or excite ideas in themselves at pleasure; but these are faint, weak, and unsteady in respect of others they perceive by sense—which, being impressed upon them according to certain rules or laws of nature, speak themselves the effects of a mind more powerful and wise than human spirits. These latter are said to have *more reality* in them than the former:—by which is meant that they are more affecting, orderly, and distinct, and that they are not fictions of the mind perceiving them. And in this sense the sun that I see by day is the real sun, and that which I imagine by night is the idea of the former. In the sense here given of *reality* it is evident that every vegetable, star, mineral, and in general each part of the mundane system, is as much a *real being* by our principles as by any other. Whether others mean anything by the term *reality* different from what I do, I entreat them to look into their own thoughts and see.

37. It will be urged that thus much at least is true, to wit, that we take away all *corporeal substances*. To this my answer is, that if the word *substance* be taken in the vulgar sense—for a combination of sensible qualities, such as extension, solidity, weight, and the like—this we cannot be accused of taking away: but if it be

taken in a philosophic sense—for the support of accidents or qualities without the mind—then indeed I acknowledge that we take it away, if one may be said to take away that which never had any existence, not even in the imagination.

38. But after all, say you, it sounds very harsh to say we eat and drink ideas, and are clothed with ideas. I acknowledge it does so—the word *idea* not being used in common discourse to signify the several combinations of sensible qualities which are called *things*; and it is certain that any expression which varies from the familiar use of language will seem harsh and ridiculous. But this doth not concern the truth of the proposition, which in other words is no more than to say, we are fed and clothed with those things which we perceive immediately by our senses. The hardness or softness, the colour, taste, warmth, figure, or suchlike qualities, which combined together constitute the several sorts of victuals and apparel, have been shown to exist only in the mind that perceives them; and this is all that is meant by calling them *ideas*; which word if it was as ordinarily used as *thing*, would sound no harsher nor more ridiculous than it. I am not for disputing about the propriety, but the truth of the expression. If therefore you agree with me that we eat and drink and are clad with the immediate objects of sense, which cannot exist unperceived or without mind, I shall readily grant it is more proper or comformable to custom that they should be called *things* rather than *ideas*.

39. If it be demanded why I make use of the word *idea*, and do not rather in compliance with custom call them *things*; I answer, I do it for two reasons:—first, because the term *thing* in contradistinction to *idea*, is generally supposed to denote somewhat existing without the mind; secondly, because *thing* hath a more comprehensive signification than *idea*, including spirit or thinking things as well as ideas. Since therefore the objects of sense exist only in the mind, and are withal thoughtless and inactive, I chose to mark them by the word *idea*, which implies those properties.

40. But, say what we can, some one perhaps may be apt to reply, he will still believe his senses, and never suffer any arguments, how plausible soever, to prevail over the certainty of them. Be it so; assert the evidence of sense as high as you please, we are willing to do the same. That what I see, hear, and feel doth exist,

that is to say, is perceived by me, I no more doubt than I do of my own being. But I do not see how the testimony of sense can be alleged as a proof for the existence of anything which is *not* perceived by Sense. We are not for having any man turn sceptic and disbelieve his Senses; on the contrary, we give them all the stress and assurance imaginable; nor are there any principles more opposite to Skepticism than those we have laid down, as shall be hereafter clearly shown.

41. *Secondly,* it will be objected that there is a great difference betwixt real fire for instance, and the idea of fire, betwixt dreaming or imagining oneself burnt, and actually being so. [If you suspect it to be only the idea of fire which you see, do but put your hand into it and you will be convinced with a witness.] This and the like may be urged in opposition to our tenets. To all which the answer is evident from what hath been already said; and I shall only add in this place, that if real fire be very different from the idea of fire, so also is the real pain that it occasions very different from the idea of the same pain, and yet nobody will pretend that real pain either is, or can possibly be, in an unperceiving thing, or without mind, any more than its idea.

*   *   *

45. *Fourthly,* it will be objected that from the foregoing principles it follows that things are every moment annihilated and created anew. The objects of Sense exist only when they are perceived; the trees therefore are in the garden, or the chairs are in the parlour, no longer than while there is somebody by to perceive them. Upon shutting my eyes all the furniture in this room is reduced to nothing, and barely upon opening them is it again created. In answer to all which, I refer the reader to what has been said in sect. 3, 4, &c., and desire he will consider whether he means anything by the actual existence of an idea distinct from its being perceived. For my part, after the nicest inquiry I could make, I am not able to discover that anything else is meant by those words; and I once more entreat the reader to sound his own thoughts, and not suffer himself to be imposed on by words. If he can conceive it possible either for his ideas or their archetypes to exist without being perceived, then I give up the cause; but if he

cannot, he will acknowledge it is unreasonable for him to stand up in defence of he knows not what, and pretend to charge on me as an absurdity the not assenting to those propositions which at bottom have no meaning in them.

46. It will not be amiss to observe how far the received principles of philosophy are themselves chargeable with those pretended absurdities. It is thought strangely absurd that upon closing my eyelids all the visible objects around me should be reduced to nothing; and yet is not this what philosophers commonly acknowledge, when they agree on all hands that light and colours, which alone are the proper and immediate objects of sight, are mere sensations that exist no longer than they are perceived? Again, it may to some perhaps seem very incredible that things should be every moment creating, yet this very notion is commonly taught in the schools. For the Schoolmen, though they acknowledge the existence of Matter, and that whole mundane fabric is framed out of it, are nevertheless of opinion that it cannot subsist without the divine conservation, which by them is expounded to be a continual creation.

47. Farther, a little thought will discover to us that though we allow the existence of Matter or corporeal substance, yet it will unavoidably follow, from the principles which are now generally admitted, that the particular bodies, of what kind soever, do none of them exist whilst they are not perceived. For, it is evident from sect. 11 and the following sections, that the Matter philosophers contend for is an incomprehensible somewhat, which hath none of those particular qualities whereby the bodies falling under our senses are distinguished one from another. But, to make this more plain, it must be remarked that the infinite divisibility of Matter is now universally allowed, at least, by the most approved and considerable philosophers, who on the received principles demonstrate it beyond all exception. Hence, it follows there is an infinite number of parts in each particle of Matter which are not perceived by sense. The reason therefore that any particular body seems to be of a finite magnitude, or exhibits only a finite number of parts to sense, is, not because it contains no more, since in itself it contains an infinite number of parts, but because the sense is not acute enough to discern them. In proportion therefore as the sense is rendered more acute, it perceives a greater number of

parts in the object, that is, the object appears greater, and its figure varies, those parts in its extremities which were before unperceivable appearing now to bound it in very different lines and angles from those perceived by an obtuser sense. And at length, after various changes of size and shape, when the sense becomes infinitely acute the body shall seem infinite. During all which there is no alteration in the body, but only in the sense. Each body therefore, considered in itself, is infinitely extended, and consequently void of all shape and figure. From which it follows that, though we should grant the existence of Matter to be never so certain, yet it is withal as certain, the materialists themselves are by their own principles forced to acknowledge, that neither the particular bodies perceived by sense, nor anything like them, exists without the mind. Matter, I say, and each particle thereof, is according to them infinite and shapeless, and it is mind that frames all that the variety of bodies which compose the visible world, any one whereof does not exist longer than it is perceived.

48. But, after all, we consider it, the objection proposed in sect. 45 will not be found reasonably charged on the principles we have premised, so as in truth to make any objection at all against our notions. For, though we hold indeed the objects of Sense to be nothing else but ideas which cannot exist unperceived; yet we may not hence conclude they have no existence except only while they are perceived by *us*, since there may be some other spirit that perceives them though we do not. Wherever bodies are said to have no existence without the mind, I would not be understood to mean this or that particular mind, but all minds whatsoever. It does not therefore follow from the foregoing principles that bodies are annihilated and created every moment, or exist not at all during the intervals between our perception of them.

STUDY QUESTIONS

Part I

1. According to Berkeley, what are the objects of human knowledge?

2. According to Berkeley, how do we come to the idea of a thing like an "apple" or a "stone" or a "tree"?

3. For Berkeley, what is "mind," "spirit," "soul," "myself"?

4. What does Berkeley mean by "exist" when applied to sensible things?

5. According to Berkeley, what leads men mistakenly to think that sensible objects exist unperceived?

6. What does Berkeley mean by "abstraction"?

7. Give the list of minds, on some or all of which, according to Berkeley, sensible things depend for their existence?

8. For Berkeley, what is the only true substance and why?

9. How does Berkeley handle Locke's copy or resemblance theory?

10. How does Berkeley handle Locke's distinction of primary and secondary qualities?

11. Why does Berkeley think that the notion of corporeal substance (matter) is self-contradictory?

12. How does Berkeley show that primary qualities cannot be conceived without secondary qualities and what conclusion does he draw?

13. How does Berkeley attack the notion of matter as a substratum?

14. How does Berkeley argue that even if material substance could exist without mind, we could never know it?

15. How does Berkeley argue that even if material substance could exist without mind, it could not explain how our ideas are produced?

16. What conclusion does Berkeley draw from the fact that ideas are inactive?

17. According to Berkeley, what causes our ideas?

18. What, according to Berkeley, is Spirit and why can we have no idea of it?

19. How, according to Berkeley, is Spirit known?

20. What conclusion does Berkeley draw from the fact that ideas of sense are not dependent on his will?

21. According to Berkeley, how do ideas of sense differ from ideas of imagination?

22. How does Berkeley account for the "laws of nature"?

23. What is a "second cause," and how does Berkeley think we come to that idea?

24. According to Berkeley, how are "real things" distinguished from "images of things"?

25. What objections does Berkeley raise against his position, and how does he answer them?

6

David Hume
(1711–1776)

DAVID HUME WAS BORN in Edinburgh, Scotland, in 1711, the younger son of the laird of Ninewells. His father died when he was a baby. He was educated at Edinburgh College and although his family wanted him to become a lawyer, his own preference was for literature and philosophy. He tried studying law and then pursued commerce in Bristol. When neither of these was successful, he decided to retire to France in 1734 where he studied privately until 1737. During this time he wrote his famous work *A Treatise of Human Nature*, which upon his return to London in 1738 was published in three volumes. Hume says of this work that it "fell dead-born from the press," although it did get the attention of Francis Hutcheson through whom Hume was offered the chair of moral philosophy at Glasgow.

In 1741-1742 he published *Essays Moral and Political* which was well received. In 1745 he tried for a post at the University of Edinburgh, but was turned down because he had a reputation of being a skeptic and atheist.

In 1745 he accompanied General St. Clair on a diplomatic mission as secretary. During this time he prepared a revision of the first part of the *Treatise*, now known as *An Enquiry Concerning Human Understanding* (1748). Hume returned to Edinburgh in 1749 where he continued his writing on moral, religious, and political topics. In 1752 he was appointed Keeper of the Advocate's Library in Edinburgh and undertook to write a history of England. It appeared in four volumes between 1754 and 1761. This history is what really made Hume's reputation among his contemporaries.

In 1763 he served as acting secretary to the British embassy in Paris. Hume returned to London with Rousseau in 1766, intending to obtain for the latter a safe place to live. They later broke up their friendship in a public quarrel. Hume retired to Edinburgh in 1769 where he died in 1776.

Hume's philosophy is the outcome of Locke's phenomenalism as developed by Berkeley, i.e., skepticism. Since ideas alone are what we know, how we actually do think and how we *must think* the world is one thing, while how the world *is* is quite another. Thus although we must *think* the world as ordered causally, we have no grounds whatsoever for assuming that the world *is* causally ordered. Again, although Berkeley denied material substances, while admitting spiritual ones, Hume denies any objective ground for our asserting the existence of any substance, material or spiritual. Hence the self is, for all we know, a mere bundle of habits since this is how we encounter it in experience. It was this radical skepticism which so disturbed Kant and roused him from his dogmatic slumber.

SUGGESTED READING

Collins, J. *A History of Modern European Philosophy.* Milwaukee: Bruce, 1956.

Copleston, F., s.J. *A History of Philosophy. V. Hobbes to Hume.* Westminster, Md.: Newman, 1964.

Hume: A Collection of Critical Essays. Ed. V. C. Chappell. Garden City, N.Y.: Doubleday Anchor, 1966.

Hume: A Re-evaluation. Edd. Donald W. Livingston and James T. King. New York: Fordham University Press, 1976.

From

An Enquiry Concerning Human Understanding

Section II

Of the Origin of Ideas

Everyone will readily allow, that there is a considerable difference between the perceptions of the mind, when a man feels the pain of excessive heat, or the pleasure of moderate warmth, and when he afterwards recalls to his memory this sensation, or anticipates it by his imagination. These faculties may mimic or copy the perceptions of the senses; but they never can entirely reach the force and vivacity of the original sentiment. The utmost we say of them, even when they operate with greatest vigour, is, that they represent their object in so lively a manner, that we could *almost* say we feel or see it: But, except the mind be disordered by disease or madness, they never can arrive at such pitch of vivacity, as to render these perceptions altogether undistinguishable. All the colours of poetry, however splendid, can never paint natural objects in such a manner as to make the description be taken for a real landscape. The most lively thought is still inferior to the dullest sensation.

We may observe a like distinction to run through all the other perceptions of the mind. A man in a fit of anger, is actuated in a very different manner from one who only thinks of that emotion. If you tell me, that any person is in love, I easily understand your meaning, and form a just conception of his situation; but never can mistake that conception for the real disorders and agitations of the passion. When we reflect on our past sentiments and affections, our thought is a faithful mirror, and copies its objects truly; but the colours which it employs are faint and dull, in comparison of those in which our original perceptions were clothed. It requires no nice discernment or metaphysical head to mark the distinction between them.

Here therefore we may divide all the perceptions of the mind into two classes or species, which are distinguished by their different degrees of force and vivacity. The less forcible and lively are commonly denominated *Thoughts* or *Ideas*. The other species want a name in our language, and in most others; I suppose, because it was not requisite for any, but philosophical purposes, to rank them under a general term or appellation. Let us, therefore, use a little freedom, and call them *Impressions*; employing that word in a sense somewhat different from the usual. By the term *impression*, then, I mean all our more lively perceptions, when we hear, or see, or feel, or love, or hate, or desire, or will. And impressions are distinguished from ideas, which are the less lively perceptions, of which we are conscious, when we reflect on any of those sensations or movements above mentioned.

Nothing, at first view, may seem more unbounded than the thought of man, which not only escapes all human power and authority, but is not even restrained within the limits of nature and reality. To form monsters, and join incongruous shapes and appearances, costs the imagination no more trouble than to conceive the most natural and familiar objects. And while the body is confined to one planet, along which it creeps with pain and difficulty; the thought can in an instant transport us to the most distant regions of the universe; or even beyond the universe, into the unbounded chaos, where nature is supposed to lie in total confusion. What never was seen, or heard of, may yet be conceived; nor is anything beyond the power of thought, except what implies an absolute contradiction.

But though our thought seems to possess this unbounded liberty, we shall find, upon a nearer examination, that it is really confined within very narrow limits, and that all this creative power of the mind amounts to no more than the faculty of compounding, transposing, augmenting, or diminishing the materials afforded us by the senses and experience. When we think of a golden mountain, we only join two consistent ideas, *gold* and *mountain*, with which we were formerly acquainted. A virtuous horse we can conceive; because, from our own feeling, we can conceive virtue; and this we may unite to the figure and shape of a horse, which is an animal familiar to us. In short, all the materials of thinking are derived either from our outward or inward sentiment: the mixture and composition of these belongs alone to the mind and will. Or, to express myself in philosophical language, all our ideas or more feeble perceptions are copies of our impressions or more lively ones.

To prove this, the two following arguments will, I hope, be sufficient. First, when we analyze our thoughts or ideas, however compounded or sublime, we always find that they resolve themselves into such simple ideas as were copied from a precedent feeling or sentiment. Even those ideas, which, at first view, seem the most wide of this origin, are found, upon a nearer scrutiny, to be derived from it. The idea of God, as meaning an infinitely intelligent, wise, and good Being, arises from reflecting on the operations of our mind, and augmenting, without limit, those qualities of goodness and wisdom. We may prosecute this inquiry to what length we please; where we shall always find, that every idea which we examine is copied from a similar impression. Those who would assert that this position is not universally true nor without exception, have only one, and that an easy method of refuting it; by producing that idea, which, in their opinion, is not derived from this source. It will then be incumbent on us, if we would maintain our doctrine, to produce the impression, or lively perception, which corresponds to it.

Secondly, if it happen, from a defect of the organ, that a man is not susceptible of any species of sensation, we always find that he is as little susceptible of the correspondent ideas. A blind man can form no notion of colours; a deaf man of sounds. Restore either of them that sense in which he is deficient; by opening this new inlet for his sensations, you also open an inlet for the ideas; and he finds no difficulty in conceiving these objects. The case is the same, if the object, proper for exciting any sensation, has never been applied to the organ. A Laplander or Negro has no notion of the relish of wine. And though there are few or no instances of a like deficiency in the mind, where a person has never felt or is wholly incapable of a sentiment or passion that belongs to his species; yet we find the same observation to take place in a less degree. A man of mild manners can form no idea of inveterate revenge or cruelty; nor can a selfish heart easily conceive the heights of friendship and generosity. It is readily allowed, that other beings may possess many senses of which we can have no conception; because the ideas of them have never been introduced to us in the only manner by which an idea can have access to the mind, to wit, by the actual feeling and sensation.

There is, however, one contradictory phenomenon, which may prove that it is not absolutely impossible for ideas to arise, independent of their correspondent impressions. I believe it will readily be allowed, that the several distinct ideas of colour, which enter by the eye, or those of sound, which are conveyed by the ear, are really different from each other; though, at the same time, resembling. Now if this be true of different colours, it must be no less so of the different shades of the same colour; and each shade produces a distinct idea, independent of the rest. For if this should be denied, it is possible, by the continual gradation of shades, to run a colour insensibly into what is most remote from it; and if you will not allow any of the means to be different, you cannot, without absurdity, deny the extremes to be the same. Suppose, therefore, a person to have enjoyed his sight for thirty years, and to have become perfectly acquainted with colours of all kinds except one particular shade of blue, for instance, which it has never been his fortune to meet with. Let all the different shades of that colour, except that single one, be placed before him, descending gradually from the deepest to the lightest; it is plain that he will perceive a blank, where that shade is wanting, and will be sensible that there is a greater distance in that place between the contiguous colours than in any other. Now I ask, whether it be possible for him, from his own imagination, to supply this deficiency, and raise up to himself the idea of that particular shade, though it had never been conveyed to him by his senses? I believe there are few but will be of opinion that he can; and this may serve as a proof that the simple ideas are not always, in every instance, derived from the correspondent impressions; though this instance is so singular, that it is scarcely worth our observing, and does not merit that for it alone we should alter our general maxim.

Here, therefore, is a proposition, which not only seems, in itself, simple and intelligible; but, if a proper use were made of it, might render every dispute equally intelligible, and banish all that jargon, which has so long taken possession of metaphysical reasonings, and drawn disgrace upon them. All ideas, especially abstract ones, are naturally faint and obscure: the mind has but a slender hold of them: they are apt to be confounded with other resembling ideas; and when we have often employed any term, though without a distinct meaning, we are apt to imagine it has a determinate idea annexed to it. On the contrary, all impressions, that is, all sensations, either outward or inward, are strong and vivid: the limits between them are more exactly determined: nor is it easy to fall into any mistake or error with regard to them. When we entertain, therefore, any suspicion that a philosophical term is employed without any meaning or idea (as is but too frequent), we need but inquire, *from what impression is that supposed idea derived*? And if it be impossible to assign any, this will serve to confirm our suspicion. By bringing ideas into so clear a light we may reasonably hope to remove all dispute, which may arise, concerning their nature and reality.

Section III

Of the Association of Ideas

It is evident that there is a principle of connexion between the different thoughts or ideas of the mind, and that, in their appearance to the memory or imagination, they introduce each other with a certain degree of method and regularity. In our more serious thinking or discourse this is so observable that any particular thought, which breaks in upon the regular tract or chain of ideas, is immediately remarked and rejected. And even in our wildest and most wandering reveries, nay in our very dreams, we shall find, if we reflect, that the imagination ran not altogether at adventures, but that there was still a connexion upheld among the different ideas, which succeeded each other. Were the loosest and freest conversation to be transcribed, there would immediately be observed something which connected it in all its transitions. Or where this is wanting, the person who broke the thread of discourse might still inform you, that there had secretly revolved in his mind a succession of thought, which had gradually led him from the subject of conversation. Among different languages, even where we cannot suspect the least connexion or communication, it is found, that the words, expressive of ideas, the most compounded, do yet nearly correspond to each other: a certain proof that the simple ideas, comprehended in the compound ones, were bound together by some universal principle, which had an equal influence on all mankind.

Though it be too obvious to escape observation, that different ideas are connected together; I do not find that any philosopher has attempted to enumerate or class all the principles of association; a subject, however, that seems worthy of curiosity. To me, there appear to be only three principles of connexion among ideas, namely, *Resemblance, Contiguity* in time or place, and *Cause* or *Effect*.

That these principles serve to connect ideas will not, I believe, be much doubted. A picture naturally leads our thoughts to the original: the mention of one apartment in a building naturally introduces an enquiry or discourse concerning the others: and if we think of a wound, we can scarcely forbear reflecting on the pain which follows it. But that this enumeration is complete, and that there are no other principles of association except these, may be difficult to prove to the satisfaction of the reader, or even to a man's own satisfaction. All we can do, in such cases, is to run over several instances, and examine carefully the principle which binds the different thoughts to each other, never stopping till we render the principle as general as possible. The more instances we examine, and the more care we employ, the more assurance shall we acquire, that the enumeration, which we form from the whole, is complete and entire.

Section IV

Sceptical Doubts Concerning
the Operations of the Understanding

PART I

All the objects of human reason or inquiry may naturally be divided into two kinds, to wit, *Relations of Ideas*, and *Matters of Fact*. Of the first kind are the sciences of Geometry, Algebra, and Arithmetic; and in short, every affirmation which is either intuitively or demonstratively certain. *That the square of the hypothenuse is equal to the square of the two sides*, is a proposition which expresses a relation between these figures. *That three times five is equal to the half of thirty*, expresses a relation between these numbers. Propositions of this kind are discoverable by the mere operation of thought, without dependence on what is anywhere existent in the universe. Though there never were a circle or triangle in nature, the truths demonstrated by Euclid would for ever retain their certainty and evidence.

Matters of fact, which are the second objects of human reason, are not ascertained in the same manner; nor is our evidence of their truth, however great, of a like nature with the foregoing. The contrary of every matter of fact is still possible; because it can never imply a contradiction, and is conceived by the mind with the same facility and distinctness, as if ever so conformable to reality. *That the sun will not rise tomorrow* is no less intelligible a proposition, and implies no more contradiction than the affirmation, *that it will rise*. We should in vain, therefore, attempt to demonstrate its falsehood. Were it demonstratively false, it would imply a contradiction, and could never be distinctly conceived by the mind.

It may, therefore, be a subject worthy of curiosity, to enquire what is the nature of that evidence which assures us of any real existence and matter of fact, beyond the present testimony of our senses, or the records of our memory. This part of philosophy, it is observable, has been little cultivated, either by the ancients or the moderns; and therefore our doubts and errors, in the prosecution of so important an enquiry, may be the more excusable; while we march through such difficult paths without any guide or direction. They may even prove useful, by exciting curiosity, and destroying that implicit faith and security, which is the bane of all reasoning and free enquiry. The discovery of defects in the common philosophy, if any such there be, will not, I presume, be a discouragement, but rather an incitement, as is usual, to attempt something more full and satisfactory than has yet been proposed to the public.

All reasonings concerning matter of fact seem to be founded on the relation of Cause and Effect. By means of that relation alone we can go beyond the evidence of our memory and senses. If you were to ask a man, why he believes any matter of fact, which is absent; for instance, that his friend is in the country, or in France; he would give you a reason; and this reason would be some other fact; as a letter received from him, or the knowledge of his former resolutions and promises. A man finding a watch or any other machine in a desert island, would conclude that there had once been men in that island. All our reasonings concerning fact are of the same nature. And here it is constantly supposed that there is a connexion between the present fact and that which is inferred from it. Were there nothing to bind them together, the inference would be entirely precarious. The hearing of an articulate voice and rational discourse in the dark assures us of the presence of some person: Why? because these are the effects of the human make and fabric, and closely connected with it. If we anatomize all the other reasonings of this nature, we shall find that they are founded on the relation of cause and effect, and that this relation is either near or remote, direct or collateral. Heat and light are collateral effects of fire, and the one effect may justly be inferred from the other.

If we would satisfy ourselves, therefore, concerning the nature of that evidence, which assures us of matters of fact, we must inquire how we arrive at the knowledge of cause and effect.

I shall venture to affirm, as a general proposition, which admits of no exception, that the knowledge of this relation is not, in any instance, attained by reasonings *a priori*; but arises entirely from experience, when we find that any particular objects are constantly conjoined with each other. Let an object be presented to a man of ever so strong natural reason and abilities; if that object be entirely new to him, he will not be able, by the most accurate examination of its sensible qualities, to discover any of its causes or effects. Adam, though his rational faculties be supposed, at the very first, entirely perfect, could not have inferred from the fluidity and transparency of water that it would suffocate him, or from the light and warmth of fire that it would consume him. No object ever discovers, by the qualities which appear to the senses, either the causes which produced it, or the effects which will arise from it; nor can our reason, unassisted by experience, ever draw any inference concerning real existence and matter of fact.

This proposition, *that causes and effects are discoverable, not by reason but by experience*, will readily be admitted with regard to such objects, as we remember to have once been altogether unknown to us; since we must be conscious of the utter inability, which we then lay under, of foretelling what would arise from them. Present two smooth pieces of marble to a man who has no tincture of natural philosophy; he will never discover that they will adhere together in such a manner as to require great force to separate them in a direct line, while they make so small a resistance to a lateral pressure. Such events, as bear little analogy to the common course of nature, are also readily confessed to be known only by experience; nor does any man imagine that the explosion of gunpowder, or the attraction of a loadstone, could ever be discovered by arguments *a priori*. In like manner, when an effect is supposed to depend upon an intricate machinery or secret structure of parts, we make no difficulty in attributing all our knowledge of it to experience. Who will assert that he can give the ultimate reason, why milk or bread is proper nourishment for a man, not for a lion or a tiger?

But the same truth may not appear, at first sight, to have the same evidence with regard to events, which have become familiar to us from our first appearance in the world, which bear a close analogy to the whole course of nature, and which are supposed to depend on the simple qualities of objects, without any secret structure of parts. We are apt to imagine that we could discover these effects by the mere operation of our reason, without experience. We fancy, that were we brought on a sudden into this world, we could at first have inferred that one Billiard-ball would communicate motion to another upon impulse; and that we needed not to have waited for the event, in order to pronounce with certainty concerning it. Such is the influence of custom, that, where it is strongest, it not only covers our natural ignorance, but even conceals itself, and seems not to take place, merely because it is found in the highest degree.

But to convince us that all the laws of nature, and all the operations of bodies without exception, are known only by experience, the following reflections may, perhaps, suffice. Were any object presented to us, and were we required to pronounce concerning the effect, which would result from it, without consulting past observation: after what manner, I beseech you, must the mind proceed in this operation? It must invent or imagine some event, which it ascribes to the object as its effect; and it is plain that this invention must be entirely arbitrary. The mind can never possibly find the effect in the supposed cause, by the most accurate scrutiny and examination. For the effect is totally different from the cause, and consequently can never be discovered in it. Motion in the second Billiard-ball is a quite distinct event from motion in the first: nor is there anything in the one to suggest the smallest hint of the other. A stone or piece of metal raised into the air, and left without any support, immediately falls: but to consider the matter *a priori*, is there anything we discover in this situation which can beget the idea of a downward, rather than an upward, or any other motion, in the stone or metal?

And as the first imagination or invention of a particular effect, in all natural operations, is arbitrary, where we consult not experience; so must we also esteem the supposed tie or connexion between the cause and effect, which binds them together, and renders it impossible that any other effect could result from the operation of that cause. When I see, for instance, a Billiard-ball moving in a straight line towards another; even suppose motion in the second ball should by accident be suggested to me, as the result of their contact or impulse; may I not conceive, that a hundred different events might as well follow from that cause? May not both these balls remain at absolute rest? May not the first ball return in a straight line, or leap off from the second in any line or direction? All these suppositions are consistent and conceivable. Why then should we give the preference to one, which is no more consistent or conceivable than the rest? All our reasonings *a priori* will never be able to show us any foundation for this preference.

In a word, then, every effect is a distinct event from its cause. It could not, therefore, be discovered in the cause, and the first invention or conception of it, *a priori*, must be entirely arbitrary. And even after it is suggested, the conjunction of it with the cause must appear equally arbitrary; since there are always many other effects, which, to reason, must seem fully as consistent and natural. In vain, therefore, should we pretend to determine any single event, or infer any cause or effect, without the assistance of observation and experience.

Hence we may discover the reason why no philosopher, who is rational and modest, has ever pretended to assign the ultimate cause of any natural operation, or to show distinctly the action of that power, which produces any single effect in the universe. It is confessed, that the utmost effort of human reason is to reduce the principles, productive of natural phenomena, to a greater simplicity, and to resolve the many particular effects into a few general causes, by means of reasonings from analogy, experience, and observation. But as to the causes of these general causes, we should in vain attempt their discovery; nor shall we ever be able to satisfy ourselves, by any particular explication of them. These ultimate springs and principles are totally shut up from human curiosity and enquiry. Elasticity, gravity, cohesion of parts, communication of motion by impulse; these are probably the ultimate causes and principles which we shall ever discover in nature; and we may esteem ourselves sufficiently happy, if, by accurate enquiry and reasoning, we can trace up the particular phenomena to, or near to, these general principles. The most perfect philosophy of the natural kind only staves off our ignorance a little longer; as perhaps the most perfect philosophy of the moral or metaphysical kind serves only to discover larger portions of it. Thus the observation of human blindness and weakness is the result of all philosophy, and meets us at every turn, in spite of our endeavours to elude or avoid it.

Nor is geometry, when taken into the assistance of natural philosophy, ever able to remedy this defect, or lead us into the knowledge of ultimate causes, by all that accuracy of reasoning for which it is so justly celebrated. Every part of mixed mathematics proceeds upon the supposition that certain laws are established by nature in her operations; and abstract reasonings are employed, either to assist experience in the discovery of these laws, or to determine their influence in particular instances, where it depends upon any precise degree of distance and quantity. Thus, it is a law of motion, discovered by experience, that the moment or force of any body in motion is in the compound ratio or proportion of its solid contents and its velocity; and consequently, that a small force may remove the greatest obstacle or raise the greatest weight, if, by any contrivance or machinery, we can increase the velocity of that force, so as to make it an overmatch for its antagonist. Geometry assists us in the application of this law, by giving us the just dimensions of all the parts and figures which can enter into any species of machine; but still the discovery of the law itself is owing merely to experience, and all the abstract reasonings in the world could never lead us one step towards the knowledge of it. When we reason *a priori*, and consider merely any object or cause, as it appears to the mind, independent of all observation, it never could suggest to us the notion of any distinct object, such as its effect; much less, show us the inseparable and inviolable connexion between them. A man must be very sagacious who could discover by reasoning that crystal is the effect of heat, and ice of cold, without being previously acquainted with the operation of these qualities.

PART II

But we have not yet attained any tolerable satisfaction with regard to the question first proposed. Each solution still gives rise to a new question as difficult as the foregoing, and leads us on to farther enquiries. When it is asked, *What is the nature of all our reasonings concerning matter of fact?* the proper answer seems to be, that they are founded on the relation of cause and effect. When again it is asked, *What is the foundation of all our reasonings and conclusions concerning that relation?* it may be replied in one word, Experience. But if we still carry on our sifting humour, and ask,

What is the foundation of all conclusions from experience? this implies a new question, which may be of more difficult solution and explication. Philosophers, that give themselves airs of superior wisdom and sufficiency, have a hard task when they encounter persons of inquisitive dispositions, who push them from every corner to which they retreat, and who are sure at last to bring them to some dangerous dilemma. The best expedient to prevent this confusion, is to be modest in our pretensions; and even to discover the difficulty ourselves before it is objected to us. By this means, we may make a kind of merit of our very ignorance.

I shall content myself, in this section, with an easy task, and shall pretend only to give a negative answer to the question here proposed. I say then, that, even after we have experience of the operations of cause and effect, our conclusions from that experience are *not* founded on reasoning, or any process of the understanding. This answer we must endeavour both to explain and to defend.

It must certainly be allowed, that nature has kept us at a great distance from all her secrets, and has afforded us only the knowledge of a few superficial qualities of objects; while she conceals from us those powers and principles on which the influence of those objects entirely depends. Our senses inform us of the colour, weight, and consistence of bread; but neither sense nor reason can ever inform us of those qualities which fit it for the nourishment and support of a human body. Sight or feeling conveys an idea of the actual motion of bodies; but as to that wonderful force or power, which would carry on a moving body for ever in a continued change of place, and which bodies never lose but by communicating it to others; of this we cannot form the most distant conception. But notwithstanding this ignorance of natural powers and principles, we always presume, when we see like sensible qualities, that they have like secret powers, and expect that effects, similar to those which we have experienced, will follow from them. If a body of like colour and consistence with that bread, which we have formerly eat [sic], be presented to us, we make no scruple of repeating the experiment, and foresee, with certainty, like nourishment and support. Now this is a process of the mind or thought, of which I would willingly know the foundation. It is allowed on all hands that there is no known connexion between the sensible qualities and the secret powers; and consequently, that the mind is not led to form such a conclusion concerning their constant and regular conjunction, by anything which it knows of their nature. As to past *Experience*, it can be allowed to give *direct* and *certain* information of those precise objects only, and that precise period of time, which fell under its cognizance: but why this experience should be extended to future times, and to other objects, which, for aught we know, may be only in appearance similar; this is the main question on which I would insist. The bread, which I formerly eat [sic], nourished me; that is, a body of such sensible qualities was, at that time, endued with such secret powers: but does it follow, that other bread must also nourish me at another time, and that like sensible qualities must always be attended with like secret powers? The consequence seems nowise necessary. At least, it must be acknowledged that there is here a consequence drawn by the mind; that there is a certain step to be taken; a process of thought, and an inference, which wants to be explained. These two propositions are far from being the same, *I have found that such an object has always been attended with such an effect*, and *I foresee, that other objects, which are, in appearance, similar, will be attended with similar effects*. I shall allow, if you please, that the one proposition may justly be inferred from the other; I know, in fact, that it always is inferred. But if you insist that the inference is made by a chain of reasoning, I desire you to produce that reasoning. The connexion between these propositions is not intuitive. There is required a medium, which may enable the mind to draw such an inference, if indeed it be drawn by reasoning and argument. What that medium is, I must confess, passes my comprehension; and it is incumbent on those to produce it, who assert that it really exists, and is the origin of all our conclusions concerning matter of fact.

This negative argument must certainly, in process of time, become altogether convincing, if many penetrating and able philosophers shall turn their inquiries this way and no one be ever able to discover any connecting proposition or intermediate step, which supports the understanding in this conclusion. But as the question is yet new, every reader may not trust so far to his own penetration, as to conclude, because an argument escapes his enquiry, that therefore it does not really exist. For this reason it may be requisite to venture upon a more difficult task; and enumerating all the branches of human knowledge, endeavour to show that none of them can afford such an argument.

All reasonings may be divided into two kinds, namely, demonstrative reasoning, or that concerning relations of ideas, and moral reasoning, or that concerning matter of fact and existence. That there are no demonstrative arguments in the case seems evident; since it implies no contradiction that the course of nature may change, and that an object, seemingly like those which we have experienced, may be attended with different or contrary effects. May I not clearly and distinctly conceive that a body, falling from the clouds, and which, in all other respects, resembles snow, has yet the taste of salt or feeling of fire? Is there any more intelligible proposition than to affirm, that all the trees will flourish in December and January, and decay in May and June? Now whatever is intelligible, and can be distinctly conceived, implies no contradiction, and can never be proved false by any demonstrative argument or abstract reasoning *a priori*.

If we be, therefore, engaged by arguments to put trust in past experience, and make it the standard of our future judgment, these arguments must be probable only, or such as regard matter of fact and real existence, according to the division above mentioned. But that there is no argument of this kind, must appear, if our explication of that species of reasoning be admitted as solid and satisfactory. We have said that all arguments concerning existence are founded on the relation of cause and effect; that our knowledge of that relation is derived entirely from experience; and that all our experimental conclusions proceed upon the supposition that the future will be conformable to the past. To endeavour, therefore, the proof of this last supposition by probable arguments, or arguments regarding existence, must be evidently going in a circle, and taking that for granted, which is the very point in question.

In reality, all arguments from experience are founded on the similarity which we discover among natural objects, and by which we are induced to expect effects similar to those which we have found to follow from such objects. And though none but a fool or a madman will ever pretend to dispute the authority of experience, or to reject that great guide of human life, it may surely be allowed a philosopher to have so much curiosity at least as to examine the principle of human nature, which gives this mighty authority to experience, and makes us draw advantage from that similarity which nature has placed among different objects. From causes which appear *similar* we expect similar effects. This is the sum of all our experimental conclusions. Now it seems evident that, if this conclusion were formed by reason, it would be as perfect at first, and upon one instance, as after ever so long a course of experience. But the case is far otherwise. Nothing so like as eggs; yet no one, on account of this appearing similarity, expects the same taste and relish in all of them. It is only after a long course of uniform experiments in any kind, that we attain a firm reliance and security with regard to a particular event. Now where is that process of reasoning which, from one instance, draws a conclusion, so different from that which it infers from a hundred instances that are nowise different from that single one? This question I propose as much for the sake of information, as with an intention of raising difficulties. I cannot find, I cannot imagine any such reasoning. But I keep my mind still open to instruction, if any one will vouchsafe to bestow it on me.

Should it be said that, from a number of uniform experiments, we *infer* a connexion between the sensible qualities and the secret powers; this, I must confess, seems the same difficulty, couched in different terms. The question still recurs, on what process of argument this *inference* is founded? Where is the medium, the interposing ideas, which join propositions so very wide of each other? It is confessed that the colour, consistence, and other sensible qualities of bread appear not, of themselves, to have any connexion with the secret powers of nourishment and support. For otherwise we could infer these secret powers from the first appearance of these sensible qualities, without the aid of experience; contrary to the sentiment of all philosophers, and contrary to plain matter of fact. Here, then, is our natural state of ignorance with regard to the powers and influence of all objects. How is this remedied by experience? It only shows us a number of uniform effects, resulting from certain objects, and teaches us that those particular objects, at that particular time, were endowed with such powers and forces. When a new object, endowed with similar sensible qualities, is produced, we expect similar powers and forces, and look for a like effect. From a body of like colour and consistence with bread we expect like nourishment and support. But this surely is a step or progress of the mind, which wants to be explained. When a man says, *I have found, in all past instances, such sensible qualities conjoined with such secret powers*: And when he says, *Similar sensible qualities will always be conjoined with similar secret powers*, he is not guilty of a tautology, nor are these propositions in any respect the same. You say that the one proposition is an inference from the other. But you must confess that the inference is not intuitive; neither is it demonstrative: Of what nature is it, then? To say it is experimental, is begging the question. For all inferences from experience suppose, as their foundation, that the future will resemble the past, and that similar powers will be conjoined with similar sensible qualities. If there be any suspicion that the course of nature may change, and that the past may be no rule for the future, all experience becomes useless, and can give rise to no inference or conclusion. It is impossible, therefore, that any arguments from experience can prove this resemblance of the past to the future; since all these arguments are founded on the supposition of that resemblance. Let the course of things be allowed hitherto ever so regular; that alone, without some new argument or inference, proves not that, for the future, it will continue so. In vain do you pretend to have learned the nature of bodies from your past experience. Their secret nature, and consequently all their effects and influence, may change, without any change in their sensible qualities. This happens sometimes, and with regard to some objects: Why may it not happen always, and with regard to all objects? What logic, what process of argument secures you against this supposition? My practice, you say, refutes my doubts. But you mistake the purport of my question. As an agent, I am quite satisfied in the point; but as a philosopher, who has some share of curiosity, I will not say skepticism, I want to learn the foundation of this inference. No reading, no enquiry has yet been able to remove my difficulty, or give me satisfaction in a matter of such importance. Can I do better than propose the difficulty to the public, even though, perhaps, I have small hopes of obtaining a solution? We shall, at least, by this means, be sensible of our ignorance, if we do not augment our knowledge.

I must confess that a man is guilty of unpardonable arrogance who concludes, because an argument has escaped his own investigation, that therefore it does not really exist. I must also confess that, though all the learned, for several ages, should have employed themselves in fruitless search upon any subject, it may still, perhaps, be rash to conclude positively that the subject must, therefore, pass human comprehension. Even though we examine all the sources of our knowledge, and conclude them unfit for such a subject, there may still remain a suspicion, that the enumeration is not complete, or the examination not accurate. But with regard to the present subject, there are some considerations which seem to remove all this accusation of arrogance or suspicion of mistake.

It is certain that the most ignorant and stupid peasants—nay infants, nay even brute beasts—improve by experience, and learn the qualities of natural objects, by observing the effects which result from them. When a child has felt the sensation of pain from touching the flame of a candle, he will be careful not to put his hand near any candle; but will expect a similar effect from a cause which is similar in its sensible qualities and appearance. If you assert, therefore, that the understanding of the child is led into this conclusion by any process of argument or ratiocination, I may justly require you to produce that argument; nor have you any pretence to refuse so equitable a demand. You cannot say that the argument is abstruse, and may possibly escape your inquiry; since you confess that it is obvious to the capacity of a mere infant. If you hesitate, therefore, a moment, or if, after reflection, you produce any intricate or profound argument, you, in a manner, give up the question, and confess that it is not reasoning which engages us to suppose the past resembling the future, and to expect similar effects from causes which are, to appearance, similar. This is the proposition I intended to enforce in the present section. If I be right, I pretend not to have made any mighty discovery. And if I be wrong, I must acknowledge myself to be indeed a very backward scholar; since I cannot now discover an argument which, it seems, was perfectly familiar to me long before I was out of my cradle.

Section XII

On the Academical or Sceptical Philosophy

PART III

There is, indeed, a more *mitigated* scepticism or *academical* philosophy which may be both durable and useful, and which may, in part, be the result of this Pyrrhonism or *excessive* scepticism when its undistinguished doubts are, in some measure, corrected by common sense and reflection. The greater part of mankind are naturally apt to be affirmative and dogmatical in their opinions, and while they see objects only on one side and have no idea of any counterpoising argument, they throw themselves precipitately into the principles to which they are inclined, nor have they any indulgence for those who entertain opposite sentiments. To hesitate or balance perplexes their understanding, checks their passion, and suspends their action. They are, therefore, impatient till they escape from a state which to them is so uneasy, and they think that they can never remove themselves far enough from it by the violence of their affirmations and obstinacy of their belief. But could such dogmatical reasoners become sensible of the strange infirmities of human understanding, even in its most perfect state and when most accurate and cautious in it determinations—such a reflection would naturally inspire them with more modesty and reserve, and diminish their fond opinion of themselves and their prejudice against antagonists. The illiterate may reflect on the disposition of the learned, who, amidst all the advantages of study and reflection, are commonly still diffident in their determinations. And if any of the learned be inclined, from their natural temper, to haughtiness and obstinacy, a small tincture of Pyrrhonism might abate their pride by showing them that the few advantages which they may have attained over their fellows are but inconsiderable if compared with the universal perplexity and confusion which is inherent in human nature. In general, there is a degree of doubt and caution and modesty which, in all kinds of scrutiny and decision, ought forever to accompany a just reasoner.

Another species of *mitigated* scepticism which may be of advantage to mankind, and which may be the natural result of the Pyrrhonian doubts and scruples, is the limitation of our inquiries to such subjects as are best adapted to the narrow capacity of human understanding. The *imagination* of man is naturally sublime, delighted with whatever is remote and extraordinary, and running, without control, into the most distant parts of space and time in order to avoid the objects which custom has rendered too familiar to it. A correct *judgment* observes a contrary method and, avoiding all distant and high inquiries, confines itself to common life and to such subjects as fall under daily practice and experience, leaving the more sublime topics to the embellishment of poets and orators or to the arts of priests and politicians. To bring us to so salutary a determination, nothing can be more serviceable than to be once thoroughly convinced of the force of the Pyrrhonian doubt and of the impossibility that anything but the strong power of natural instinct could free us from it. Those who have a propensity to philosophy will still continue their researches, because they reflect that, besides the immediate pleasure attending such an occupation, philosophical decisions are nothing but the reflections of common life, methodized and corrected. But they will never be tempted to go beyond common life so long as they consider the imperfection of those faculties which they employ, their narrow reach, and their inaccurate operations. While we cannot give a satisfactory reason why we believe, after a thousand experiments, that a stone will fall or fire burn, can we ever satisfy ourselves concerning any determination which we may form with regard to the origin of worlds and the situation of nature from and to eternity?

This narrow limitation, indeed, of our enquiries is in every respect so reasonable that it suffices to make the slightest examination into the natural powers of the human mind, and to compare them with their objects, in order to recommend it to us. We shall then find what are the proper subjects of science and enquiry.

It seems to me that the only objects of the abstract science, or of demonstration, are quantity and number, and that all attempts to extend this more perfect species of knowledge beyond these bounds are mere sophistry and illusion. As the component parts of quantity and number are entirely similar, their relations become intricate and involved, and nothing can be more curious, as well as useful, than to trace, by a variety of mediums, their equality or inequality through their different appearances. But as all other ideas are clearly distinct and different from each other, we can never advance farther, by our utmost scrutiny, than to observe this diversity and, by an obvious reflection, pronounce one thing not to be another. Or if there be any difficulty in these decisions, it proceeds entirely from the undeterminate meaning of words, which is corrected by juster definitions. That *the square of the hypotenuse is equal to the squares of the other two sides* cannot be known. let the terms be ever so exactly defined, without a train of reasoning and inquiry. But to convince us of this proposition, *that where there is no property there can be no injustice*, it is only necessary to define the terms and explain injustice to be a violation of property. This proposition is, indeed, nothing but a more imperfect definition. It is the same case with all those pretended syllogistical reasonings which may be found in every other branch of learning except the sciences of quantity and number; and these may safely, I think, be pronounced the only proper objects of knowledge and demonstration.

All other inquiries of men regard only matter of fact and existence, and these are evidently incapable of demonstration. Whatever *is* may *not be*. No negation of a fact can involve a contradiction. The non-existence of any being, without exception, is as clear and distinct an idea as its existence. The proposition which affirms it not to be, however false, is no less conceivable and intelligible than that which affirms it to be. The case is different with the sciences, properly so called. Every proposition which is not true is there confused and unintelligible. That the cube root of 64 is equal to the half of 10 is a false proposition and can never be distinctly conceived. But that Caesar, or the angel Gabriel, or any being never existed may be a false proposition, but still is perfectly conceivable and implies no contradiction.

The existence, therefore, of any being can only be proved by arguments from its cause or its effect, and these arguments are founded entirely on experience. If we reason *a priori*, anything may appear able to produce anything. The falling of a pebble may, for aught we know, extinguish the sun, or the wish of a man control the planets in their orbits. It is only experience which teaches us the nature and bounds of cause and effect and enables us to infer the existence of one object from that of another. Such is the foundation of moral reasoning, which forms the greater part of human knowledge and is the source of all human action and behavior.

Moral reasonings are either concerning particular or general facts. All deliberations in life regard the former; as also all disquisitions in history, chronology, geography, and astronomy.

The sciences which treat of general facts are politics, natural philosophy, physics, chemistry, etc., where the qualities, causes, and effects of a whole species of objects are inquired into.

Divinity or theology, as it proves the existence of a deity and the immortality of souls, is composed partly of reasonings concerning particular, partly concerning general facts. It has a foundation in *reason* so far as it is supported by experience. But its best and most solid foundation is *faith* and divine revelation.

Morals and criticism are not so properly objects of the understanding as of taste and sentiment. Beauty, whether moral or natural, is felt more properly than perceived. Or if we reason concerning it and endeavour to fix its standard, we regard a new fact, to wit, the general tastes of mankind, or some such fact which may be the object of reasoning and inquiry.

When we run over libraries, persuaded of these principles, what havoc must we make? If we take in our hand any volume—of divinity or school metaphysics, for instance—let us ask, *Does it contain any abstract reasoning concerning quantity or number*? No. *Does it contain any experimental reasoning concerning matter of fact and existence*? No. Commit then to the flames, for it can contain nothing but sophistry and illusion.

STUDY QUESTIONS

Section II

1. According to Hume, what is the difference between memory and imagination, on the one hand, and perception, on the other?
2. How does Hume divide all perceptions?
3. What does Hume mean by the term "impression"?
4. Within what limits, according to Hume, are the "unbounded limits of thought" confined?
5. How does Hume "prove" that ideas are copies of impressions?
6. What is Hume's criterion for determining whether an idea has any meaning?

Section III

1. According to Hume, what is the function of the association of ideas?
2. According to Hume, what are the principles of association?
3. For Hume, how are these principles of association related to habit?

Section IV
Part I

1. How does Hume divide the objects of human reason? Are there examples?
2. What does Hume mean by saying that claims concerning matters of fact cannot be *demonstrated* to be false?
3. According to Hume, upon what evidence, beyond that of sense and memory, might one claim assurance of any matter of fact?
4. What general proposition does Hume assert relative to our knowledge of cause and effect?
5. How does Hume explain our conviction that one billiard ball causes the motion in another?
6. What reason does Hume give why we cannot possibly find the effect in the supposed cause (that is, by mere analysis without the aid of experience)?

Section IV
Part II

1. How does Hume answer the question, "What is the foundation of all conclusions from experience of cause and effect"?

2. According to Hume, what grounds our inference from past experience of regularities to future regularities?

3. How does Hume divide all reasoning? Explain.

4. How does Hume tell whether something is self-contradictory or not?

5. Why does Hume claim that there is no "moral reasoning" (i.e., reasoning concerning matters of fact) to support our trust in past experience?

6. According to Hume, what principle of human nature gives such great authority to experience?

Section XII
Part III

1. What does Hume understand by "mitigated" or "academical" skepticism? In what ways does Hume think it may be of advantage to mankind?

2. According to Hume, what are the only objects of the "abstract sciences" or of demonstration?

3. According to Hume, why are matters of fact and existence incapable of demonstration?

4. What are the only arguments for the existence of something which Hume will allow as legitimate?

5. What does Hume understand by "moral reasoning"?

6. What is Hume's final judgment about theology and metaphysics? Why does he hold this?

7

Immanuel Kant
(1724–1804)

IMMANUEL KANT, the son of a saddler, was born in Koenigsberg, East Prussia, in 1724. Aside from his intellectual achievements, the most remarkable thing about his life is how extraordinarily unremarkable it was. He is said never to have traveled beyond his native East Prussia. As a professor, his habits were so regular that you could set your clock by his daily walk. For all that, Kant liked to entertain his friends at a luncheon or dinner party at which good wine and good conversation were mixed in equal parts.

Kant came from a religious family and was brought up at home and in school in the Pietist tradition of Protestantism. He attended the University of Koenigsberg (1740) and came under the influence of a certain professor Martin Knutzen who introduced him both to philosophy (of the Wolffian sort) and to Newtonian physics. Kant never lost his interest in science, and many of his early works dealt with the philosophical implications of Newton's principles. This combination of religious, philosophical, and scientific elements in his education makes more understandable the sorts of issues Kant took up as a mature thinker and to some extent explains the way in which he handled them.

From the time he left the university until 1755 Kant took various posts as a private tutor in various East Prussian families. Finally in that year he received what today would be called a doctorate awarded for a scientific treatise on fire and was admitted as lecturer (*Privatdozent*) at the University of Koenigsberg after having presented an essay entitled *A New Exposition of the First Principles of Metaphysical Knowledge*. This essay contains some criticism of the rationalism of Leibniz and Wolff. Kant soon became convinced that philosophy must pattern itself more after the model of physics (not mathematics), and this empirical thrust led him to be more and more skeptical concerning metaphysics as understood by the rationalists.

Although Kant did not travel abroad, his intellectual interests were far from provincial. He kept track of developments among the British moralists (Shaftesbury, Hutcheson, and Hume) and the philosophers of the French Enlightenment (Rousseau). In 1770 these influences came together with the rationalism of Leibniz in Kant's inaugural dissertation

(*Dissertation on the Form and Principles of the Sensible and Intelligible World*). The presentation of this work marked his promotion to professor of logic and metaphysics at Koenigsberg.

In about 1772 it dawned on Kant that Hume's criticism of causality was correct, and this aroused him from his "dogmatic slumber." As a result he entered into what is now known as his "critical" period, that is, the period in which he wrote the three *Critiques* (*of Pure Reason, of Practical Reason,* and *of Judgment*). The first edition of the *Critique of Pure Reason* appeared in 1781, and in 1783 Kant wrote the *Prolegomena to Any Future Metaphysics* as an introduction to the *Critique* which apparently had fallen on uncomprehending ears. He wished to offer his reader a map or guide to the *Critique*. In 1785 he published *Foundations of the Metaphysics of Morals* and in 1788 the *Critique of Practical Reason*. Finally, in 1790, the *Critique of Judgment* appeared.

A brief word about the three *Critiques* is in order. *The Critique of Pure Reason* attempts to give the *a priori* conditions of possibility of human knowing, where "knowing" is understood in the sense of scientific knowledge. Kant, then, has in mind empirical knowledge of the world as presented by Newton. This knowledge was certain; it dealt with causes; and the world it revealed was completely deterministic. Scientific knowledge, however, is confined to the world as it appears to us through the senses (phenomenal world). There can be no "knowledge" of things-in-themselves, that is, as pure, intelligible essences.

Still, Kant understood that scientific knowledge and discovery did not exhaust man's experience of the world. Man also experienced the realm of value, responsibility, and freedom precisely because he is a *moral* agent. But then there must be another, inner, world which is not subject to the iron necessity of Newtonian physics. He sets out to give the *a priori* conditions of possibility of this moral experience in the *Critique of Practical Reason*. Here Kant brings back as "postulates" what in the first critique he had thrown out as objects of "knowledge" (that is, empirical, scientific knowledge), namely, the ideas of God, freedom, and immortality. The ideas are required that there be any moral experience and so they are necessary postulates for the *practical* use of reason (but not for its speculative or scientific use).

Finally, Kant would not settle for two worlds, one outer and determined, the other inner and free. He had somehow to try to bridge them. He set out to give the *a priori* conditions of possibility of the transition from physical nature to moral freedom. While the two realms could not be reconciled objectively (that is, on the part of the realms themselves), they could, in some way, be united in our consciousness. Kant thought he had discovered the key to this reconciliation in the power of judgment and feeling. Hence the third *Critique* examines the notions of beauty and purposiveness. Through our aesthetic and teleological judgments the outer world becomes a symbolic representation of the inner; or perhaps, better, the inner world of value and moral freedom is given symbolic expression and interpretation in the outer world of physical nature.

In 1793 Kant published *Religion Within the Limits of Reason Alone* (which got him into hot water with the civil authorities). In 1795 he wrote an interesting political essay on *Perpetual Peace*. Kant retired from teaching in 1796 and died in 1804 still working on his philosophy.

SUGGESTED READING

Collins, J. *A History of Modern European Philosophy*. Milwaukee: Bruce, 1956.

Copleston, F., S.J. *A History of Philosophy*. VI. *Wolff to Kant*. Westminster, Md.: Newman, 1960.

Kant: A Collection of Critical Essays. Ed. Robert Paul Wolff. Garden City, N.Y.: Doubleday Anchor, 1967.

Kemp Smith, N. *A Commentary to Kant's `Critique of Pure Reason.'* 2nd ed. rev. London: Macmillan, 1930.

Paton, H. J. *The Categorical Imperative: A Study of Kant's Moral Philosophy*. Chicago: The University of Chicago Press, 1948.

———. *Kant's Metaphysic of Experience: A Commentary on the First Half of the* KRITIK DER REINEN *Vernunft*. 2 vols. New York: Macmillan, 1936.

From

Prolegomena to Any Future Metaphysics

Introduction

My object is to persuade all those who think Metaphysics worth studying, that it is absolutely necessary to pause a moment, and, neglecting all that has been done, to propose first the preliminary question, "Whether such a thing as metaphysics be at all possible?"

If it be a science, how comes it that it cannot, like other sciences, obtain universal and permanent recognition? If not, how can it maintain its pretensions, and keep the human mind in suspense with hopes, never ceasing, yet never fulfilled? Whether then we demonstrate our knowledge or our ignorance in this field, we must come once for all to a definite conclusion respecting the nature of this so-called science, which cannot possibly remain on its present footing. It seems almost ridiculous, while every other science is continually advancing, that in this, which pretends to be Wisdom incarnate, for whose oracle every one inquires, we should constantly move round the same spot, without gaining a single step. And so its followers having melted away, we do not find men confident of their ability to shine in other sciences venturing their reputation here, where everybody, however ignorant in other matters, may deliver a final verdict, as in this domain there is as yet no standard weight and measure to distinguish sound knowledge from shallow talk.

After all it is nothing extraordinary in the elaboration of a science, when men begin to wonder how far it has advanced, that the question should at last occur, whether and how such a science is possible? Human reason so delights in constructions, that it has several times built up a tower, and then razed it to examine the nature of the foundation. It is never too late to become wise; but if the change comes late, there is always more difficulty in stating a reform.

The question whether a science be possible, presupposes a doubt as to its actuality. But such a doubt offends the man whose whole possessions consist of this supposed jewel; hence he who raises the doubt must expect opposition from all sides. Some, in the proud consciousness of their possessions, which are ancient, and therefore considered legitimate, will take their metaphysical compendia in their hands, and look down on him with contempt; others, who never see anything except it be identical with what they have seen before, will not understand him, and everything will remain for a time, as if nothing had happened to excite the concern, or the hope, for an impending change.

Nevertheless, I venture to predict that the independent reader of these Prolegomena will not only doubt his previous science, but ultimately be fully persuaded, that it cannot exist unless the demands here stated on which its possibility depends, be satisfied; and, as this has never been done, that there is, as yet, no such thing as Metaphysics. But as it can never cease to be in demand—since the interests of common sense are intimately interwoven with it, he must confess that a radical reform, or rather a new birth of the science after an original plan, are unavoidable, however men may struggle against it for a while.

Since the Essays of Locke and Leibnitz, or rather since the origin of metaphysics so far as we know its history, nothing has ever happened which was more decisive to its fate than the attack made upon it by David Hume. He threw no light on this species of knowledge, but he certainly struck a spark from which light might have been obtained, had it caught some inflammable substance and had its smouldering fire been carefully nursed and developed.

Hume started from a single but important concept in Metaphysics, viz., that of cause and effect (including its derivatives force and action, etc). He challenges reason, which pretends to have given birth to this idea from herself, to answer him by what right she thinks anything to be so constituted, that if that thing be posited, something else also must necessarily be posited; for this is the meaning of the concept of cause. He demonstrated irrefutably that it was perfectly possible for reason to think *a priori* and by means of concepts a combination involving necessity. We cannot at all see why, in the consequence of the existence of one thing, another must necessarily exist, or how the concept of such a combination can arise *a priori*. Hence he inferred, that reason was altogether deluded with reference to this concept, which she erroneously considered as one of her children, whereas in reality it was nothing but a bastard of imagination, impregnated by experience, which subsumed certain representations under the Law of Association, and mistook the subjective necessity of habit for an objective necessity arising from insight. Hence he inferred that reason had no power to think such combinations, even generally, because her concepts would then be purely fictitious, and all her pretended *a priori* cognitions nothing but common experiences marked with a false stamp. In plain language there is not, and cannot be, any such thing as metaphysics at all.

However hasty and mistaken Hume's conclusion may appear, it was at least founded upon investigation, and this investigation deserved the concentrated attention of the brighter spirits of his day as well as determined efforts on their part to discover, if possible, a happier solution of the problem in the sense proposed by him, all of which would have speedily resulted in a complete reform of the science.

But Hume suffered the usual misfortune of metaphysicians, of not being understood. It is positively painful to see how utterly his opponents, Reid, Oswald, Beattie, and lastly Priestley, missed the point of the problem; for while they were forever taking for granted that which he doubted, and demonstrating with zeal and often with impudence that which he never thought of doubting, they so misconstrued his valuable suggestion that everything remained in its old condition, as if nothing had happened.

The question was not whether the concept of cause was right, useful, and even indispensable for our knowledge of nature, for this Hume had never doubted; but whether that concept could be thought by reason *a priori*, and consequently whether it possessed an inner truth, independent of all experience, implying a wider application than merely to the objects of experience. This was Hume's problem. It was a question concerning the *origin*, not concerning the *indispensable need* of the concept. Were the former decided, the conditions of the use and the sphere of its valid application would have been determined as a matter of course.

But to satisfy the conditions of the problem, the opponents of the great thinker should have penetrated very deeply into the nature of reason, so far as it is concerned with pure thinking—a task which did not suit them. They found a more convenient method of being defiant without any insight, viz., the appeal to common sense. It is indeed a great gift of God, to possess right, or (as they now call it) plain common sense. But this common sense must be shown practically, by well-considered and reasonable thoughts and words, not by appealing to it as an oracle, when no rational justification can be advanced. To appeal to common sense, when insight and science fail, and no sooner—this is one of the subtle discoveries of modern times, by means of which the most superficial ranter can safely enter the lists with the most thorough thinker, and hold his own. But as long as a particle of insight remains, no one would think of having recourse to this subterfuge. For what is it but an appeal to the opinion of the multitude, of whose applause the philosopher is ashamed, while the popular charlatan glories and confides in it? I should think that Hume might fairly have laid as much claim to common sense as Beattie, and in addition to a critical reason (such as the latter did not possess), which keeps common sense in check and prevents it from speculating, or, if speculations are under discussion, restrains the desire to decide because it cannot satisfy itself concerning its own arguments. By this means alone can common sense remain sound. Chisels and hammers may suffice to work a piece of wood, but for steel-engraving we require an engraver's needle. Thus common sense and speculative understanding are each serviceable in their own way, the former in judgments which apply immediately to experience, the latter when we judge universally from mere concepts, as in metaphysics, where sound common sense, so called in spite of all inapplicability of the word, has no right to judge at all.

I openly confess, the suggestion of David Hume was the very thing, which many years ago first interrupted my dogmatic slumber, and gave my investigations in the field of speculative philosophy quite a new direction. I was far from following him in the conclusions at which he arrived by regarding, not the whole of his problem, but a part, which by itself can give us no information. If we start from a well-founded, but undeveloped, thought, which another has bequeathed to us, we may well hope by continued reflection to advance farther than the acute man, to whom we owe the first spark of light.

I therefore first tried whether Hume's objections could not be put into general form, and soon found that the concept of the connexion of cause and effect was by no means the only idea by which the understanding thinks the connexion of things *a priori*, but rather that metaphysics consists altogether of such connexions. I sought to ascertain their number, and when I had satisfactorily succeeded in this by starting from a single principle, I proceeded to the deduction of these concepts, which I was now certain were not deduced from experience, as Hume had apprehended, but sprang from the pure understanding. This deduction (which seemed impossible to my acute predecessor, which had never even occurred to anyone else, though no one had hesitated to use the concepts without investigating the basis of their objective validity) was the most difficult task ever undertaken in the service of metaphysics; and the worst was that metaphysics, such as it then existed could not assist me in the least, because this deduction alone can render metaphysics possible. But as soon as I had succeeded in solving Hume's problem not merely in a particular case, but with respect to the whole faculty of pure reason, I could proceed safely, to determine the whole sphere of pure reason completely and from general principles, in its circumference as well as in its contents. This was required for metaphysics in order to construct its system according to a reliable method.

* * *

Preamble on the Peculiarities of All Metaphysical Cognition

1. OF THE SOURCE OF METAPHYSICS.

If it becomes desirable to formulate any cognition as science, it will be necessary first to determine accurately those peculiar features which no other science has in common with it, constituting its characteristics; otherwise the boundaries of all sciences become confused, and none of them can be treated thoroughly according to its nature.

The characteristics of a science may consist of a simple difference of object, or of the sources of cognition, or of the kind of cognition, or perhaps of all three conjointly. On this, therefore, depends the idea of a possible science and its territory.

First, as concerns the sources of metaphysical cognition, its very concept implies that they cannot be empirical. Its principles (including not only its maxims but its basic notions) must never be derived from experience. It must not be physical but metaphysical knowledge, viz., knowledge lying beyond experience. It can therefore have for its basis neither external experience, which is the source of physics proper, nor internal, which is the basis of empirical psychology. It is therefore *a priori* knowledge, coming from pure Understanding and pure Reason.

But so far Metaphysics would not be distinguishable from pure Mathematics; it must therefore be called pure philosophical cognition; and for the meaning of this term I refer to the Critique of Pure Reason (II. "Method of Transcendentalism," Chap. 1, Sec. 1), where the distinction between these two employments of the reason is sufficiently explained. So far concerning the sources of metaphysical cognition.

2. CONCERNING THE KIND OF COGNITION WHICH CAN ALONE BE CALLED METAPHYSICAL.

a. Of the Distinction between Analytical and Synthetical Judgments in General.

The peculiarity of its sources demands that metaphysical cognition must consist of nothing but *a priori* judgments. But whatever be their origin, or their logical form, there is a distinction in judgments, as to their content, according to which they are merely explicative, adding nothing to the content of the cognition, or expansive, increasing the given cognition: the former may be called analytical, the latter synthetical, judgments. ·

Analytical judgments express nothing in the predicate but what has been already actually thought in the concept of the subject, though not so distinctly or with the same (full) consciousness. When I say: All bodies are extended, I have not amplified in the least my concept of body, but have only analysed it, as extension was really thought to belong to that concept before the judgment was made, though it was not expressed; this judgment is therefore analytical. On the contrary, this judgment, All bodies have weight, contains in its predicate something not actually thought in the general concept of the body; it amplifies my knowledge by adding something to my concept, and must therefore be called synthetical.

b. The Common Principle of All Analytical Judgments Is the Law of Contradiction.

All analytical judgments depend wholly on the law of Contradiction, and are in their nature *a priori* cognitions, whether the concepts that supply them with matter be empirical or not. For the predicate of an affirmative analytical judgment is already contained in the concept of the subject, of which it cannot be denied without contradiction. In the same way its opposite is necessarily denied of the subject in an analytical, but negative, judgment, by the same law of contradiction. Such is the nature of the judgments: all bodies are extended, and no bodies are unextended (i.e., simple).

For this very reason all analytical judgments are *a priori* even when the concepts are empirical, as, for example, Gold is a yellow metal; for to know this I require no experience beyond my concept of gold as a yellow metal: it is, in fact, the very concept, and I need only analyse it, without looking beyond it elsewhere.

c. Synthetical Judgments Require a Different Principle from the Law of Contradiction.

There are synthetical *a posteriori* judgments of empirical origin; but there are also others which are proved to be certain *a priori*, and which spring from pure Understanding and Reason. Yet they both agree in this, that they cannot possibly spring from the principle of analysis, viz,, the law of contradiction, alone; they require a quite different principle, though, from whatever they may be deduced, they must be subject to the law of contradiction, which must never be violated, even though everything cannot be deduced from it. I shall first classify synthetical judgments.

1. Empirical Judgments are always synthetical. For it would be absurd to base an analytical judgment on experience, as our

concept suffices for the purpose without requiring any testimony from experience. That a body is extended, is a judgment established *a priori*, and not an empirical judgment. For before appealing to experience, we already have all the conditions of the judgment in the concept, from which we have but to elicit the predicate according to the law of contradiction, and thereby to become conscious of the necessity of the judgment, which experience could not even teach us.

2. Mathematical Judgments are all synthetical. This fact seems hitherto to have altogether escaped the observation of those who have analysed human reason; it even seems directly opposed to all their conjectures, though incontestably certain, and most important in its consequences. For as it was found that the conclusions of mathematicians all proceed according to the law of contradiction (as is demanded by all apodeictic certainty), men persuaded themselves that the fundamental principles were known from the same law. This was a great mistake, for a synthetical proposition can indeed be comprehended according to the law of contradiction, but only by presupposing another synthetical proposition from which it follows, but never in itself.

First of all, we must observe that all proper mathematical judgments are *a priori*, and not empirical, because they carry with them necessity, which cannot be obtained from experience. But if this be not conceded to me, very good; I shall confine my assertion to *pure Mathematics*, the very notion of which implies that it contains pure *a priori* and not empirical cognitions.

It might at first be thought that the proposition 7 + 5 = 12 is a mere analytical judgment, following from the concept of the sum of seven and five, according to the law of contradiction. But on closer examination it appears that the concept of the sum of 7 + 5 contains merely their union in a single number, without its being at all thought what the particular number is that unites them. The concept of twelve is by no means thought by merely thinking of the combination of seven and five; and analyse this possible sum as we may, we shall not discover twelve in the concept. We must go beyond these concepts, by calling to our aid some concrete image (*Anschauung*), i.e., either our five fingers, or five points (as Segner has it in his *Arithmetic*), and we must add successively the units of the five, given in some concrete image (*Anschauung*), to the concept of seven. Hence our concept is really amplified by the proposition 7 + 5 = 12, and we add to the first a second, not thought in it. Arithmetical judgments are therefore synthetical, and the more plainly according as we take larger numbers; for in such cases it is clear that, however closely we analyse our concepts without calling visual images (*Anschauungen*) to our aid, we can never find the sum by such mere dissection.

Nor is any principle of geometry analytical. That a straight line is the shortest path between two points, is a synthetical proposition. For my concept of straight contains nothing of quantity, but only a quality. The attribute of shortness is therefore altogether additional, and cannot be obtained by any analysis of the concept. Here, too, visualisation (*Anschauung*) must come to aid us. It alone makes the synthesis possible.

Some other principles, assumed by geometers, are indeed actually analytical, and dependent on the law of contradiction; but they only serve, as identical propositions, as a method of concatenation, and not as principles, e.g., a = a, the whole is equal to itself, or a + b > a, the whole is greater than its parts. And yet even these, though they are recognized as valid from mere concepts, are only admitted in mathematics, because they can be represented in some visual form (*Anschauung*). What usually makes us believe that the predicate of such apodeictic judgments is already contained in our concept, and that the judgment is therefore analytical, is the duplicity of the expression, requesting us to think a certain predicate as of necessity implied in the thought of a given concept, which necessity attaches to the concept. But the question is not what we are requested to join in thought *to* the given concept, but what we actually think together with and in it, though obscurely; and so it appears that the predicate belongs to these concepts necessarily indeed, yet not directly but indirectly by an added visualisation (*Anschauung*).

The essential and distinguishing feature of pure mathematical cognition among all other *a priori* cognitions is, that it cannot at all proceed from concepts, but only by means of the construction of concepts (see Critique II., "Method of Transcendentalism," Chap. 1, Sec. 1). As therefore in its judgments it must proceed beyond the concept to that which its corresponding visualisation (*Anschauung*) contains, these judgments neither can, nor ought to,

arise analytically, by dissecting the concept, but are all synthetical.
I cannot refrain from pointing out the disadvantage resulting to philosophy from the neglect of this easy and apparently insignificant observation. Hume being prompted (a task worthy of a philosopher) to cast his eye over the whole field of *a priori* cognitions in which human understanding claims such mighty possessions, heedlessly severed from it a whole, and indeed its most valuable province, viz., pure mathematics: for he thought its nature, or, so to speak, the state-constitution of this empire, depended on totally different principles, namely, on the law of contradiction alone; and although he did not divide judgments in this manner formally and universally as I have done here, what he said was equivalent to this: that mathematics contains only analytical, but metaphysics synthetical, *a priori* judgments. In this, however, he was greatly mistaken, and the mistake had a decidedly injurious effect upon his whole conception. But for this, he would have extended his question concerning the origin of our synthetical judgments far beyond the metaphysical concept of Causality, and included in it the possibility of mathematics *a priori* also, for this latter he must have assumed to be equally synthetical. And then he could not have based his metaphysical judgments on mere experience without subjecting the axioms of mathematics equally to experience, a thing which he was far too acute to do. The good company into which metaphysics would thus have been brought, would have saved it from the danger of a contemptuous ill-treatment, for the thrust intended for it must have reached mathematics, which was not and could not have been Hume's intention. Thus that acute man would have been led into considerations which must needs be similar to those that now occupy us, but which would have gained inestimably by his inimitably elegant style.

Metaphysical judgments, properly so called, are all synthetical. We must distinguish judgments pertaining to metaphysics from metaphysical judgments properly so called. Many of the former are analytical, but they only afford the means for metaphysical judgments, which are the whole end of the science, and which are always synthetical. For if there be concepts pertaining to metaphysics (as, for example, that of substance), the judgments springing from simple analysis of them also pertain to metaphysics, as, for example, substance is that which only exists as subject; and by means of several such analytical judgments, we seek to approach the definition of the concept. But as the analysis of a pure concept of the understanding pertaining to metaphysics, does not proceed in any different way from the dissection of any other, even empirical, concepts, not pertaining to metaphysics (such as: air is an elastic fluid, the elasticity of which is not destroyed by any known degree of cold), it follows that the concept indeed, but not the analytical judgment, is properly metaphysical. This science has something peculiar in the production of its *a priori* cognitions, which must therefore be distinguished from the features it has in common with other rational knowledge. Thus the judgment, that all the substance in things is permanent, is a synthetical and properly metaphysical judgment.

If the *a priori* principles, which constitute the materials of metaphysics, have first been collected according to fixed principles, then their analysis will be of great value; it might be taught as a particular part (as a *philosophia definitiva*), containing nothing but analytical judgments pertaining to metaphysics, and could be treated separately from the synthetical which constitute metaphysics proper. For indeed these analyses are not elsewhere of much value, except in metaphysics, i.e., as regards the synthetical judgments, which are to be generated by these previously analysed concepts.

The conclusion drawn in this section then is, that metaphysics is properly concerned with synthetical propositions *a priori*, and these alone constitute its end, for which it indeed requires various dissections of its concepts, viz,, of its analytical judgments, but wherein the procedure is not different from that in every other kind of knowledge, in which we merely seek to render our concepts distinct by analysis. But the generation of *a priori* cognition by concrete images as well as by concepts, in fine of synthetical propositions *a priori* in philosophical cognition, constitutes the essential subject of Metaphysics.

*   *   *

4. THE GENERAL QUESTION OF THE PROLEGOMENA: IS METAPHYSICS AT ALL POSSIBLE?

Were a metaphysics, which could maintain its place as a science, really in existence; could we say, here is metaphysics, learn it, and it will convince you irresistibly and irrevocably of its truth: this question would be useless, and there would only remain that other question (which would rather be a test of our acuteness, than a proof of the existence of the thing itself), "How is the science possible, and how does reason come to attain it?" But human reason has not been so fortunate in this case. There is no single book to which you can point as you do to Euclid and say: This is Metaphysics; here you may find the noblest objects of this science, the knowledge of a highest Being, and of a future existence, proved from principles of pure reason. We can indeed be shown many judgments, demonstrably certain, and never questioned; but these are all analytical, and rather concern the materials and the scaffolding for Metaphysics, than the extension of knowledge, which is our object in studying it (#2). Even supposing you produce synthetical judgments (such as the law of Sufficient Reason, which you have never proved, as you ought to, from pure reason *a priori* though we gladly concede its truth), you lapse when they come to be employed for your principal object, into such doubtful assertions, that in all ages one Metaphysics has contradicted another, either in its assertions, or their proofs, and thus has itself destroyed its own claim to lasting assent. Nay, the very attempts to set up such a science are the main cause of the early appearance of scepticism, a mental attitude in which reason treats itself with such violence that it could never have arisen save from complete despair of ever satisfying our most important aspirations. For long before men began to inquire into nature methodically, they consulted abstract reason, which had to some extent been exercised by means of ordinary experience; for reason is ever present, while laws of nature must usually be discovered with labor. So Metaphysics floated to the surface, like foam, which dissolved the moment it was scooped off. But immediately there appeared a new supply on the surface, to be ever eagerly gathered up by some, while others, instead of seeking in the depths the cause of the phenomenon, thought they showed their wisdom by ridiculing the idle labor of their neighbors.

Weary therefore as well of dogmatism, which teaches us nothing, as of scepticism, which does not even promise us anything, not even the quiet state of a contented ignorance; disquieted by the importance of knowledge so much needed; and lastly, rendered suspicious by long experience of all knowledge which we believe we possess, or which offers itself, under the title of pure reason: there remains but one critical question on the answer to which our future procedure depends, viz., *Is Metaphysics at all possible?* But this question must be answered not by sceptical objections to the asseverations of some actual system of metaphysics (for we do not as yet admit such a thing to exist), but from the conception, as yet only problematical, of a science of this sort.

In the *Critique of Pure Reason* I have treated this question synthetically, by making inquiries into pure reason itself, and endeavoring in this source to determine the elements as well as the laws of its pure use according to principles. The task is difficult, and requires a resolute reader to penetrate by degrees into a system, based on no data but reason itself, which therefore seeks, without resting upon any fact, to unfold knowledge from its original germs. *Prolegomena*, however, are designed for preparatory exercises; they are intended rather to point out what we have to do in order if possible to actualise a science, than to propound it. They must therefore rest upon something already known as trustworthy, from which we can set out with confidence, and ascend to sources as yet unknown, the discovery of which will not only explain to us what we knew, but exhibit a sphere of many cognitions which all spring from the same source. The method of *Prolegomena*, especially of those designed as a preparation for future metaphysics, is consequently analytical.

But it happens fortunately, that though we cannot assume metaphysics to be an actual science, we can say with confidence that certain pure *a priori* synthetical cognitions, pure Mathematics and pure Physics are actual and given; for both contain propositions, which are thoroughly recognised as apodeictically certain, partly by mere reason, partly by general consent arising from experience, and yet as independent of experience. We have therefore some at least uncontested synthetical knowledge *a priori*, and need not ask *whether* it be possible, for it is actual, but *how* it is possible, in order that we may deduce from the principle which makes the given cognitions possible the possibility of all the rest.

5. THE GENERAL PROBLEM: HOW IS COGNITION FROM PURE REASON POSSIBLE?

We have above learned the significant distinction between analytical and synthetical judgments. The possibility of analytical propositions was easily comprehended, being entirely founded on the law of Contradiction. The possibility of synthetical *a posteriori* judgments, of those which are gathered from experience, also requires no particular explanation; for experience is nothing but a continual synthesis of perceptions. There remains therefore only synthetical propositions *a priori*, of which the possibility must be sought or investigated, because they must depend upon other principles than the law of contradiction.

But here we need not first establish the possibility of such propositions so as to ask whether they are possible. For there are enough of them which indeed are of undoubted certainty, and as our present method is analytical, we shall start from the fact, that such synthetical but purely rational cognition actually exists; but we must now inquire into the reason of this possibility, and ask, *how* such cognition is possible, in order that we may from the principles of its possibility be enabled to determine the conditions of its use, its sphere and its limits. The proper problem upon which all depends, when expressed with scholastic precision, is therefore: *How are Synthetic Propositions a priori possible?*

For the sake of popularity I have above expressed this problem somewhat differently, as an inquiry into purely rational cognition, which I could do for once without detriment to the desired comprehension, because, as we have only to do here with metaphysics and its sources, the reader will, I hope, after the foregoing remarks, keep in mind that when we speak of purely rational cognition, we do not mean analytical, but synthetical cognition.

Metaphysics stands or falls with the solution of this problem: its very existence depends on it. Let any one make metaphysical assertions with ever so much plausibility, let him overwhelm us with conclusions, if he has not previously proved able to answer this question satisfactorily, I have a right to say: this is all vain baseless philosophy and false wisdom. You speak through pure reason, and claim, as it were to create cognitions *a priori* by not only dissecting given concepts, but also by asserting connexions which do not rest upon the law of contradiction, and which you believe you conceive quite independently of all experience; how do you arrive at this, and how will you satisfy your pretensions? An appeal to the consent of the common sense of mankind cannot be allowed; for it is a witness whose authority depends merely upon rumor. Says Horace: "*Quodcunque ostendis mihi sic, incredulus odi.*" "To all that which thou provest me thus, I refuse to give credence."

The answer to this question, though indispensable, is difficult; and though the principal reason that it was not made long ago is, that the possibility of the question never occurred to anybody, there is yet another reason, which is this that a satisfactory answer to this one question requires a much more persistent, profound, and painstaking reflexion, than the most diffuse work on Metaphysics, which on its first appearance promised immortality to its author. And every intelligent reader, when he carefully reflects what this problem requires, must at first be struck with its difficulty, and would regard it as insoluble and even impossible, did there not actually exist pure synthetical cognitions *a priori*. This actually happened to David Hume, though he did not conceive the question in its entire universality as is done here, and as must be done, should the answer be decisive for all Metaphysics. For how is it possible, says that acute man, that when a concept is given me, I can go beyond it and connect with it another, which is not contained in it, in such a manner as if the latter necessarily belonged to the former? Nothing but experience can furnish us with such connexions (thus he concluded from the difficulty which he took to be an impossibility), and all that vaunted necessity, or, what is the same thing, all cognition assumed to be *a priori*, is nothing but a long habit of mistaking subjective necessity for objective.

Should my reader complain of the difficulty and the trouble which I occasion him in the solution of this problem, he is at liberty to solve it himself in an easier way. Perhaps he will then feel under obligation to the person who has undertaken for him a labor of so profound research, and will rather be surprised at the facility with which, considering the nature of the subject, the solution has been attained. Yet it has cost years of work to solve the problem in its whole universality (using the term in the mathematical sense, viz., for that which is sufficient for all cases), and finally to exhibit it in the analytical form, as the reader finds it here.

All metaphysicians are therefore solemnly and legally suspended from their occupations till they shall have answered in a satisfactory manner the question, "How are synthetic cognitions *a priori* possible?" For the answer contains the only credentials which they must show when they have anything to offer in the name of pure reason. But if they do not possess these credentials, they can expect nothing else of reasonable people, who have been deceived so often, than to be dismissed without further ado.

If they on the other hand desire to carry on their business, not as a science, but as an art of wholesome oratory suited to the common sense of man, they cannot in justice be prevented. They will then speak the modest language of a rational belief. They will grant that they are not allowed even to conjecture, far less to know, anything which lies beyond the bounds of all possible experience, but only to assume (not for speculative use, which they must abandon, but for practical purposes only) the existence of something that is possible and even indispensable for the guidance of the understanding and of the will in life. In this manner alone can they be called useful and wise men, and the more so as they renounce the title of metaphysicians; for the latter profess to be speculative philosophers, and since, when judgments *a priori* are under discussion, poor probabilities cannot be admitted (for what is declared to be known *a priori* is thereby announced as necessary), such men cannot be permitted to play with conjectures, but their assertions must be either science, or are worth nothing at all.

It may be said, that the entire transcendental philosophy, which necessarily precedes all metaphysics, is nothing but the complete solution of the problem here propounded, in systematical order and completeness, and hitherto we have never had any transcendental philosophy; for what goes by its name is properly a part of metaphysics, whereas the former science is intended first to constitute the possibility of the latter, and must therefore precede all metaphysics. And it is not surprising that when a whole science, deprived of all help from other sciences, and consequently in itself quite new, is required to answer a single question satisfactorily, we should find the answer troublesome and difficult, nay even shrouded in obscurity.

As we now proceed to this solution according to the analytical method, in which we assume that such cognitions from pure reason actually exist, we can only appeal to two sciences of theoretical cognition (which alone is under consideration here), pure mathematics and pure natural science (physics). For these alone can exhibit to us objects in a definite and actualisable form (*in der Anschauung*), and consequently (if there should occur in them a cognition *a priori*) can show the truth or conformity of the cognition to the object *in concreto*, that is, its actuality, from which we could proceed to the reason of its possibility by the analytic method. This facilitates our work greatly for here universal considerations are not only applied to facts, but even start from them, while in a synthetic procedure they must strictly be derived *in abstracto* from concepts.

But, in order to rise from these actual and at the same time well-grounded pure cognitions *a priori* to such a possible cognition of the same as we are seeking, viz., to metaphysics as a science, we must comprehend that which occasions it, I mean the mere natural, though in spite of its truth not unsuspected, cognition *a priori* which lies at the bottom of that science, the elaboration of which without any critical investigation of its possibility is commonly called metaphysics. In a word, we must comprehend the natural conditions of such a science as a part of our inquiry, and thus the transcendental problem will be gradually answered by a division into four questions:

1. How is pure mathematics possible?
2. How is pure natural science possible?
3. How is metaphysics in general possible?
4. How is metaphysics as a science possible?

It may be seen that the solution of these problems, though chiefly designed to exhibit the essential matter of the Critique, has yet something peculiar, which for itself alone deserves attention.

This is the search for the sources of given sciences in reason itself, so that its faculty of knowing something *a priori* may by its own deeds be investigated and measured. By this procedure these sciences gain, if not with regards to their contents, yet as to their proper use, and while they throw light on the higher question concerning their common origin, they give, at the same time, an occasion better to explain their own nature.

* * *

How Is Pure Science of Nature Possible?

* * *

We shall here be concerned with experience only, and the universal conditions of its possibility which are given *a priori*. Thence we shall determine nature as the whole object of all possible experience. I think it will be understood that I here do not mean the rules of the observation of a nature that is already given, for these already presuppose experience. I do not mean how (through experience) we can study the laws of nature; for these would not then be laws *a priori*, and would yield us no pure science of nature; but [I mean to ask] how the conditions *a priori* of the possibility of experience are at the same time the sources from which all the universal laws of nature must be derived.

18. In the first place we must state that, while all judgments of experience (*Erfahrungsurtheile*) are empirical (i.e., have their ground in immediate sense-perception), *vice versa*, all empirical judgments (*empirische Urtheile*) are not judgments of experience, but, besides the empirical, and in general besides what is given to the sensuous intuition, particular concepts must yet be superadded—concepts which have their origin quite *a priori* in the pure understanding, and under which every perception must be first of all subsumed and then by their means changed into experience.

Empirical judgments, so far as they have objective validity, are *judgments of experience*; but those which are only subjectively valid, I name mere *judgments of perception*. The latter require no pure concept of the understanding, but only the logical connexion of perception in a thinking subject. But the former always require, besides the representation of the sensuous intuition, particular *concepts originally begotten in the understanding*, which produce the objective validity of the judgment of experience.

All our judgments are at first merely judgments of perception; they hold good only for us (i.e., for our subject), and we do not till afterwards give them a new reference (to an object), and desire that they shall always hold good for us and in the same way for everybody else; for when a judgment agrees with an object, all judgments concerning the same object must likewise agree among themselves, and thus the objective validity of the judgment of experience signifies nothing else than its necessary universality of application. And conversely when we have reason to consider a judgment necessarily universal (which never depends upon perception, but upon the pure concept of the understanding, under which the perception is subsumed), we must consider it objective also, that is, that it expresses not merely a reference to our perception to a subject, but a quality of the object. For there would be no reason for the judgments of other men necessarily agreeing with mine, if it were not the unity of the object to which they all refer, and with which they accord; hence they must all agree with one another.

19. Therefore objective validity and necessary universality (for everybody) are equivalent terms, and though we do not know the object in itself, yet when we consider a judgment as universal, and also necessary, we understand it to have objective validity. By this judgment we cognise the object (though it remains unknown as it is in itself) by the universal and necessary connexion of the given perceptions. As this is the case with all objects of sense, judgments of experience take their objective validity not from the immediate cognition of the object (which is impossible), but from the condition of universal validity in empirical judgments, which, as already said, never rests upon empirical, or, in short, sensuous conditions, but upon a pure concept of the understanding. The object always remains unknown in itself; but when by the concept of the understanding the connexion of

the representations of the object, which are given to our sensibility, is determined as universally valid, the object is determined by this relation, and it is the judgment that is objective.

To illustrate the matter: When we say, "the room is warm, sugar sweet, and wormwood bitter"—we have only subjectively valid judgments. I do not at all expect that I or any other person shall always find it as I now do; each of these sentences only expresses a relation of two sensations to the same subject, to myself, and that only in my present state of perception; consequently they are not valid of the object. Such are judgments of perception. Judgments of experience are of quite a different nature. What experience teaches me under certain circumstances, it must always teach me and everybody; and its validity is not limited to the subject nor to its state at a particular time. Hence I pronounce all such judgments as being objectively valid. For instance, when I say the air is elastic, this judgment is as yet a judgment of perception only—I do nothing but refer two of my sensations to one another. But, if I would have it called a judgment of experience, I require this connexion to stand under a condition, which makes it universally valid. I desire therefore that I and everybody else should always connect necessarily the same perceptions under the same circumstances.

20. We must consequently analyse experience in order to see what is contained in this product of the senses and of the understanding, and how the judgment of experience itself is possible. The foundation is the intuition of which I become conscious, i.e., perception (*perceptio*), which pertains merely to the senses. But in the next place, there are acts of judging (which belongs only to the understanding). But this judging may be twofold—first, I may merely compare two perceptions and connect them in a particular state of my consciousness; or, secondly, I may connect them in consciousness generally. The former judgment is merely a judgment of perception, and of subjective validity only: it is merely a connexion of perceptions in my mental state, without reference to the object. Hence it is not, as is commonly imagined, enough for experience to compare perceptions and to connect them in consciousness through judgment; there arises no universality and necessity, for which alone judgments can become objectively valid and be called experience.

Quite another judgment therefore is required before perception can become experience. The given intuition must be subsumed under a concept, which determines the form of judging in
general relatively to the intuition, connects its empirical consciousness in consciousness generally, and thereby procures universal validity for empirical judgments. A concept of this nature
is a pure *a priori* concept of the Understanding, which does nothing but determine for an intuition the general way in which it can
be used for judgments. Let the concept be that of cause, then it
determines the intuition which is subsumed under it, e.g., that of
air, relative to judgments in general, viz., the concept of air serves
with regard to its expansion in the relation of antecedent to consequent in a hypothetical judgment. The concept of cause accordingly is a pure concept of the understanding, which is totally dis-
parate from all possible perception, and only serves to determine
the representation subsumed under it, relatively to judgments in
general, and so to make a universally valid judgment possible.

Before, therefore, a judgment of perception can become a
judgment of experience, it is requisite that the perception be subsumed under some such a concept of the understanding; for
instance, air ranks under the concept of causes, which determines
our judgment about it in regard to its expansion as hypothetical.
Thereby the expansion of the air is represented not as merely
belonging to the perception of the air in my present state or in
several states of mine, or in the state of perception of others, but
as belonging to it necessarily. The judgment, "the air is elastic,"
becomes universally valid, and a judgment of experience, only by
certain judgments preceding it, which subsume the intuition of
air under the concept of cause and effect: and they thereby determine the perceptions not merely as regards one another in me,
but relatively to the form of judging in general, which is here
hypothetical, and in this way they render the empirical judgment
universally valid.

If all our synthetical judgments are analysed so far as they are
objectively valid, it will be found that they never consist of mere
intuitions connected only (as is commonly believed) by comparison into a judgment; but they would be impossible were not a
pure concept of the understanding superadded to the concepts
abstracted from intuition, under which concept these latter are

subsumed, and in this manner only combined into an objectively valid judgment. Even the judgments of pure mathematics in their simplest axioms are not exempt from this condition. The principle, "a straight line is the shortest distance between two points," presupposes that the line is subsumed under the concept of quantity, which certainly is no mere intuition, but has its seat in the understanding alone, and serves to determinedly the intuition (of the line) with regard to the judgments which may be made about it, relatively to their quantity, that is, to plurality (as *judicia plurativa*). For under them it is understood that in a given intuition there is contained a plurality of homogeneous parts.

21. To prove, then, the possibility of experience so far as it rests upon pure concepts of the understanding *a priori*, we must first represent what belongs to judgments in general and the various functions of the understanding, in a complete table. For the pure concepts of the understanding must run parallel to these functions, as such concepts are nothing more than concepts of intuitions in general, so far as these are determined by one or another of these functions of judging, in themselves, that is, necessarily and universally. Hereby also the *a priori* principles of the possibility of all experience, as of an objectively valid empirical cognition, will be precisely determined. For they are nothing but propositions by which all perception is (under certain universal conditions of intuition) subsumed under those pure concepts of the understanding. (See Figure 1.)

21a. In order to comprise the whole matter in one idea, it is first necessary to remind the reader that we are discussing not the origin of experience, but of that which lies in experience. The former pertains to empirical psychology, and would even then never be adequately explained without the latter, which belongs to the Critique of cognition, and particularly of the understanding.

Experience consists of intuitions, which belong to the sensibility, and of judgments, which are entirely a work of the understanding. But the judgments, which the understanding forms alone from sensuous intuitions, are far from being judgments of experience. For in the one case the judgment connects only the perceptions as they are given in the sensuous intuition, while in the other the judgments must express what experience in general, and not what the mere perception (which possesses only subjec-

FIGURE 1

Logical Table of Judgments

1	2
As to Quantity	*As to Quality*
Universal	Affirmative
Particular	Negative
Singular	Infinite

3	4
As to Relation	*As to Modality*
Categorical	Problematical
Hypothetical	Assertoric
Disjunctive	Apodeictical

*Transcendental Table of the Pure
Concepts of the Understanding*

1	2
As to Quantity	*As to Quality*
Unity (Measure)	Reality
Plurality (Quantity)	Negation
Totality (Whole)	Limitation

3	4
As to Relation	*As to Modality*
Substance	Possibility
Cause	Existence
Community	Necessity

*Pure Psychological Table of the Universal Principles
of the Science of Nature*

1	2
Axioms of Intuition	Anticipations of Perception

3	4
Analogies of Experience	Postulates of Empirical Thinking Generally

tive validity) contains. The judgment of experience must therefore add to the sensuous intuition and its logical connexion in a judgment (after it has been rendered universal by comparison) something that determines the synthetical judgment as necessary and therefore as universally valid. This can be nothing else than that concept which represents the intuition as determined in itself with regard to one form of judgment rather than another, viz., a concept of that synthetical unity of intuitions which can only be represented by a given logical function of judgments.

22. The sum of the matter is this: the business of the senses is to intuit — that of the understanding is to think. But thinking is uniting representations in one consciousness. This union originates either merely relative to the subject, and is accidental and subjective, or is absolute, and is necessary or objective. The union of representations in one consciousness is judgment. Thinking therefore is the same as judging, or referring representations to judgments in general. Hence judgments are either merely subjective, when representations are referred to a consciousness in one subject only, and united in it, or objective, when they are united in a consciousness generally, that is, necessarily. The logical functions of all judgments are but various modes of uniting representations in consciousness. But if they serve for concepts, they are concepts of their necessary union in a consciousness, and so principles of objectively valid judgments. This union in a consciousness is either analytical, by identity, or synthetical, by the combination and addition of various representations one to another. Experience consists in the synthetical connexion of phenomena (perceptions) in consciousness, so far as this connexion is necessary. Hence the pure concepts of the understanding are those under which all perceptions must be subsumed ere they can serve for judgments of experience, in which the synthetical unity of the perceptions is represented as necessary and universally valid.

23. Judgments when considered merely as the condition of the union of given representations in a consciousness, are rules. These rules, so far as they represent the union as necessary, are rules a priori, and so far as they cannot be deduced from higher rules, are fundamental principles. But in regard to the possibility

of all experience, merely in the relation to the form of thinking in it, no conditions of judgments of experience are higher than those which bring the phenomena, according to the various forms of their intuition, under pure concepts of the understanding, and render the empirical judgments objectively valid. These concepts are therefore the *a priori* principles of possible experience. The principles of experience are then at the same time universal laws of nature, which can be cognized *a priori*. And thus the problem in our second question, "How is the pure science of nature possible?" is solved. For the system which is required for the form of a science is to be met with in perfection here, because, beyond the above-mentioned formal conditions of all judgments in general offered in logic, no others are possible, and these constitute a logical system. The concepts grounded thereupon, which contain the *a priori* conditions of all synthetical and necessary judgments, accordingly constitute a transcendental system. Finally the principles, by means of which all phenomena are subsumed under these concepts, constitute a physical system, that is, a system of nature, which precedes all empirical cognition of nature, makes it even possible, and hence may in strictness be denominated the universal and pure science of nature.

*   *   *

32. Since the oldest days of philosophy inquirers into pure reason have conceived, besides the things of sense, or appearances (phenomena), which make up the sensible world, certain creations of the understanding (*Verstandeswesen*), called *noumena*, which should constitute an intelligible world. And as appearance and illusion were by those men identified (a thing which we may well excuse in an underdeveloped epoch), actuality was only conceded to the creations of thought.

And we indeed, rightly considering objects of sense as mere appearances, confess thereby that they are based upon a thing in itself, though we know not this thing in its internal constitution, but only know its appearances, viz., the way in which our senses are affected by this unknown something. The understanding therefore, by assuming appearances, grants the existence of things in themselves also, and so far we may say, that the representation of such things as form the basis of phenomena, consequently of mere creations of the understanding, is not only admissible, but unavoidable.

Our critical deduction by no means excludes things of that sort (*noumena*), but rather limits the principles of the Aesthetic (the science of the sensibility) to this, that they shall not extend to all things, as everything would then be turned into mere appearance, but that they shall only hold good of objects of possible experience. Hereby then objects of the understanding are granted, but with the inculcation of this rule which admits of no exception: "that we neither know nor can know anything at all definite of these pure objects of the understanding, because our pure concepts of the understanding as well as our pure intuitions extend to nothing but objects of possible experience, consequently to mere things of sense, and as soon as we leave this sphere these concepts retain no meaning whatever."

33. There is indeed something seductive in our pure concepts of the understanding, which tempts us to a transcendent use—a use which transcends all possible experience. Not only are our concepts of substance, of power, of action, of reality, and others, quite independent of experience, containing nothing of sense appearance, and so apparently applicable to things in themselves, (*noumena*), but what strenthens this conjecture they contain a necessity of determination in themselves which experience never attains. The concept of cause implies a rule, according to which one state follows another necessarily; but experience can only show us that one state of things often, or at most, commonly, follows another, and therefore afford neither strict universality nor necessity.

Hence the Categories seem to have a deeper meaning and import than can be exhausted by their empirical use, and so the understanding inadvertently adds for itself to the house of experience a much more extensive wing, which it fills with nothing but creatures of thought, without ever observing that it has transgressed with its otherwise lawful concepts the bounds of their use.

34. Two important, and even indispensable, though very dry, investigations had therefore become indispensable in the *Critique of Pure Reason*—viz., the two chapters "*Vom Schematismus der*

reinen Verstandsbegriffe," and *"Vom Grunde der Unterscheidung aller Verstandsbegriffe ueberhaupt in Phaenomena und Noumena."* In the former it is shown, that the senses furnish not the pure concepts of the understanding *in concreto,* but only the schedule of their use, and that the object conformable to it occurs only in experience (as the product of the understanding from materials of the sensibility). In the latter it is shown, that, although our pure concepts of the understanding and our principles are independent of experience, and despite the apparently greater sphere of their use, still nothing whatever can be thought by them beyond the field of experience, because they can do nothing but merely determine the logical form of the judgment relatively to given intuitions. But as there is no intuition at all beyond the field of sensibility, these pure concepts, as they cannot possibly be exhibited *in concreto,* are void of all meaning; consequently all these *noumena,* together with their complex, the intelligible world, are nothing but [the] representation of a problem, of which the object in itself is possible, but the solution, from the nature of our understanding, totally impossible. For our understanding is not a faculty of intuition, but of the connexion of given intuitions in experience. Experience must therefore contain all the objects of our concepts; but beyond it no concepts have any significance, as there is no intuition that might offer them a foundation.

35. The imagination may perhaps be forgiven for occasional vagaries, and for not keeping carefully within the limits of experience, since it gains life and vigor by such flights, and since it is always easier to moderate its boldness, than to stimulate its languor. But the understanding which ought to *think* can never be forgiven for indulging in vagaries; for we depend upon it alone for assistance to set bounds, when necessary, to the vagaries of the imagination.

But the understanding begins its aberrations very innocently and modestly. It first elucidates the elementary cognitions, which inhere in it prior to all experience, but yet must always have their application in experience. It gradually drops these limits, and what is there to prevent it, as it has quite freely derived its principles from itself? And when it proceeds first to newly-imagined powers in nature, then to beings outside nature; in short to a world, for whose construction the materials cannot be wanting, because fertile fiction furnishes them abundantly, and though not confirmed, is never refuted, by experience. This is the reason that young thinkers are so partial to metaphysics of the truly dogmatic kind, and often sacrifice to it their time and their talents, which might be otherwise better employed.

But there is no use in trying to moderate these fruitless endeavors of pure reason by all manner of cautions as to the difficulties of solving questions so occult, by complaints of the limits of our reason, and by degrading our assertions into mere conjectures. For if their impossibility is not distinctly shown, and reason's cognition of its own essence does not become a true science, in which the field of its right use is distinguished, so to say, with mathematical certainty from that of its worthless and idle use, these fruitless efforts will never be abandoned for good.

STUDY QUESTIONS

Introduction

1. What is Kant's object in writing the *Prolegomena*?

2. According to Kant, what makes it doubtful that metaphysics is a "science"?

3. According to Kant, what sort of reaction may one expect to the raising of the question whether metaphysics is a science?

4. What does Kant predict will be the independent reader's conclusion in this matter?

5. According to Kant, whose attack on the actual existence of scientific metaphysics has been decisive? What was that attack?

6. How does Kant evaluate Hume's conclusion about causality?

7. According to Kant, what precisely was the issue which Hume raised?

8. According to Kant, what are the proper roles of common sense and of speculative understanding, respectively?

9. How did Kant generalize Hume's objection?

10. What is the general direction of Kant's solution?

Preamble

1. According to Kant, in what possible ways can sciences be distinguished?

2. According to Kant, what characterizes metaphysical cognition as to its source and origin?

3. According to Kant, how are judgments distinguished as to their content? Explain.

4. According to Kant, what principle alone governs analytical judgments? Why does this make them *a priori*?

5. According to Kant, how are synthetical judgments subdivided? Explain.

6. According to Kant, what do empirical judgments and mathematical judgments have in common?

7. According to Kant, what distinguishes mathematical judgments from empirical judgments? Are these judgments *a priori* or *a posteriori*? Explain.

8. How does Kant try to show that $7 + 5 = 12$ is not merely analytic? What is Kant's general conclusion about all mathematical judgments?

9. When Kant denies the existence of a metaphysics which "proves" the existence of God and of a future life, what does he mean by "proof"?

10. On what does Kant blame skepticism?

11. According to Kant, how did Hume conceive of mathematical propositions and why did this have "a decidedly injurious effect upon his [Hume's] whole conception"?

12. What does Kant mean by the distinction between "judgments pertaining to metaphysics" and "metaphysical judgments"?

13. According to Kant, what conclusion is to be drawn from this entire section?

14. What is the question concerning metaphysics which, in Kant's opinion, must be answered?

15. According to Kant, how can mathematics and pure physics help us answer the question about metaphysics?

16. What does Kant mean by "transcendental philosophy"?

17. What, according to Kant, is *the* question which must be answered *before* the question of metaphysics can be answered?

18. What are the steps Kant proposes to take in answering the "transcendental problem"?

How is Pure Science of Nature Possible?

1. Explain what Kant means by "nature."

2. According to Kant, what is the difference between "judgments of experience" and "empirical judgments"?

3. According to Kant, what is the difference between "judgments of experience" and "judgments of perception"?

4. What does Kant understand by the "objective validity" of judgments of experience?

5. If, according to Kant, we can never know the "object in itself," how does he account for "objectively valid" knowledge of the object?

6. According to Kant, what is required for perception to become experience?

7. What, according to Kant, is the function of a pure *a priori* concept of the understanding?

8. Give Kant's analysis of the judgments "Air is elastic" and "A straight line is the shortest distance between two points."

9. Explain Kant's Logical Table of Judgments.

10. How is the Table of Pure Concepts related to the Table of Judgments?

11. What are Kant's Universal Principles of Nature?

12. How does Kant sum up the matter of objectively valid judgments of experience?

13. According to Kant, what are "*a priori* principles of possible experience"?

14. Why does Kant equate principles of possible experience with universal laws of nature known *a priori*?

15. What is Kant's distinction between "noumenon" and "phenomenon"?

16. What limit does Kant put on noumena with regard to their having meaning?

17. What does Kant mean by a "transcendent use" of pure concepts of the understanding?

18. Why, according to Kant, do pure concepts have no meaning outside experience?

19. According to Kant, how does understanding go astray in its use of pure concepts?

20. According to Kant, what must be done to avoid wasting time with dogmatic metaphysics?

From

Critique of Pure Reason

Preface to First Edition

Human reason has this peculiar fate that in one species of its knowledge it is burdened by questions which, as prescribed by the very nature of reason itself, it is not able to ignore, but which, as transcending all its powers, it is also not able to answer.

The perplexity into which it thus falls is not due to any fault of its own. It begins with principles which it has no option save to employ in the course of experience, and which this experience at the same time abundantly justifies it in using. Rising with their aid (since it is determined to this also by its own nature) to ever higher, ever more remote, conditions, it soon becomes aware that in this way—the questions never ceasing—its work must always remain incomplete; and it therefore finds itself compelled to resort to principles which overstep all possible empirical employment, and which yet seem so unobjectionable that even ordinary consciousness readily accepts them. But by this procedure human reason precipitates itself into darkness and contradictions; and while it may indeed conjecture that these must be in some way due to concealed errors, it is not in a position to be able to detect them. For since the principles of which it is making use transcend the limits of experience, they are no longer subject to any empirical test. The battle-field of these endless controversies is called metaphysics.

* * *

Preface to Second Edition

Whether the treatment of such knowledge as lies within the province of reason does or does not follow the secure path of a science, is easily to be determined from the outcome. For if after elaborate preparations, frequently renewed, it is brought to a stop immediately it nears its goal; if often it is compelled to retrace its steps and strike into some new line of approach; or again, if the various participants are unable to agree in any common plan of procedure, then we may rest assured that it is very far from having entered upon the secure path of a science, and is indeed a merely random groping. In these circumstances, we shall be rendering a service to reason should we succeed in discovering the path upon which it can securely travel, even if, as a result of so doing, much that is comprised on our original aims, adopted without reflection, may have to be abandoned as fruitless.

That logic has already, from the earliest times, proceeded upon this sure path is evidenced by the fact that since Aristotle it has not required to retrace a single step, unless, indeed, we care to count as improvements the removal of certain needless subtleties or the clearer exposition of its recognised teachings, features which concern the elegance rather than the certainty of the science. It is remarkable also that to the present day this logic has not been able to advance a single step, and is thus to all appearance a closed and completed body of doctrine. If some of the moderns have thought to enlarge it by introducing *psychological* chapters on the different faculties of knowledge (imagination, wit, etc.), *metaphysical* chapters on the origin of knowledge or on the different kinds of certainty according to difference in the objects (idealism, scepticism, etc.), or *anthropological* chapters on prejudices, their causes and remedies, this could only arise from their ignorance of the peculiar nature of logical science. We do not enlarge but disfigure sciences, if we allow them to trespass upon one another's territory. The sphere of logic is quite precisely delimited; its sole concern is to give an exhaustive exposition and a strict proof of the formal rules of all thought, whether it be *a priori* or empirical, whatever be its origin or its object, and whatever hindrances, accidental or natural, it may encounter in our minds.

That logic should have been thus successful is an advantage which it owes entirely to its limitation, whereby it is justified in abstracting—indeed, it is under obligation to do so—from all objects of knowledge and their differences, leaving the understanding nothing to deal with save itself and its form. But for reason to enter on the sure path of science is, of course, much more difficult, since it has to deal not with itself alone but also with objects. Logic, therefore, as a propaedeutic, forms, as it were, only the vestibule of the sciences; and when we are concerned with specific modes of knowledge, while logic is indeed presupposed in any critical estimate of them, yet for the actual acquiring of them we have to look to the sciences properly so called, that is to the objective sciences.

Now if reason is to be a factor in these sciences, something in them must be known *a priori*, and this knowledge may be related to its object in one or other of two ways, either as merely *determining* it and its concept (which must be supplied from elsewhere) or as also *making it actual*. The former is *theoretical*, the latter *practical* knowledge of reason. In both, that part in which reason determines its object completely *a priori*, namely, the *pure* part—however much or little this part may contain—must be first and separately dealt with, in case it be confounded with what comes from other sources. For it is bad management if we blindly pay out what comes in, and are not able, when the income falls into arrears, to distinguish which part of it can justify expenditure, and in which line we must make reductions.

Mathematics and physics, the two sciences in which reason yields theoretical knowledge, have to determine their objects *a priori*, the former doing so quite purely, the latter having to reckon, at least partially, with sources of knowledge other than reason.

In the earliest times to which the history of human reason extends, *mathematics*, among that wonderful people, the Greeks, had already entered upon the sure path of science. But it must not be supposed that it was as easy for mathematics as it was for logic—in which reason has to deal with itself alone—to light upon, or rather to construct for itself, that royal road. On the contrary I believe that it long remained, especially among the Egyptians, in the groping stage, and that the transformation must have been due to a *revolution* brought about by the happy thought of a single man, the experiment which he devised marking out the path upon which the science must enter, and by following which, secure progress throughout all time and in endless expansion is infallibly secured. The history of this intellectual revolution—far more important than the discovery of the passage round the celebrated Cape of Good Hope—and of its fortunate author, has not been preserved. But the fact that Diogenes Laertius, in handing down an account of these matters, names the reputed author of even the least important among the geometrical demonstrations, even of those which, for ordinary consciousness, stand in need of no such proof, does at least show that the memory of the revolution, brought about by the first glimpse of this new path, must have seemed to mathematicians of such outstanding importance as to cause it to survive the tide of oblivion. A new light flashed upon the mind of the first man (be he Thales or some other) who demonstrated the properties of the isosceles triangle. The true method, so he found, was not to inspect what he discerned either in the figure, or in the bare concept of it, and from this, as it were, to read off its properties; but to bring out what was necessarily implied in the concepts that he had himself formed *a priori*, and had put into the figure in the construction by which he presented it to himself. If he is to know anthing with *a priori* certainty he must not ascribe to the figure anything save what necessarily follows from what he has himself set into it in accordance with his concept.

Natural science was very much longer in entering upon the highway of science. It is, indeed, only about a century and a half since Bacon, by his ingenious proposals, partly initiated this discovery, partly inspired fresh vigour in those who were already on the way to it. In this case also the discovery can be explained as being the sudden outcome of an intellectual revolution. In my present remarks I am referring to natural science only in so far as it is founded on *empirical* principles.

When Galileo caused balls, the weights of which he had himself previously determined, to roll down an inclined plane; when Torricelli made the air carry a weight which he had calculated beforehand to be equal to that of a definite volume of water; or in more recent times, when Stahl changed metals into [oxides], and [oxides] back into metal, by withdrawing something and then restoring it,[1] a light broke upon all students of nature. They learned that reason has insight only into that which it produces

---

[1] I am not, in my choice of examples, tracing the exact course of the history of the experimental method; we have indeed no very precise knowledge of its first beginnings.

after a plan of its own, and that it must not allow itself to be kept, as it were, in nature's leading-strings, but must itself show the way with principles of judgment based upon fixed laws, constraining nature to give answer to questions of reason's own determining. Accidental observations, made in obedience to no previously thought-out plan, can never be made to yield a necessary law, which alone reason is concerned to discover. Reason, holding in one hand its principles, according to which alone concordant appearances can be admitted as equivalent to laws, and in the other hand the experiment which it has devised in conformity with these principles, must approach nature in order to be taught by it. It must not, however, do so in the character of a pupil who listens to everything that the teacher chooses to say, but of an appointed judge who compels the witnesses to answer questions which he has himself formulated. Even physics, therefore, owes the beneficent revolution in its point of view entirely to the happy thought, that while reason must seek in nature, not fictitiously ascribe to it, whatever as not being knowable through reason's own resources has to be learnt, if learnt at all, only from nature, it must adopt as its guide, in so seeking, that which it has itself put into nature. It is thus that the study of nature has entered on the secure path of a science, after having for so many centuries been nothing but a process of merely random groping.

Metaphysics is a completely isolated speculative science of reason, which soars far above the teachings of experience and in which reason is indeed meant to be its own pupil. Metaphysics rests on concepts alone—not, like mathematics, on their application to intuition. But though it is older that all other sciences, and would survive even if all the rest were swallowed up in the abyss of an all-destroying barbarism, it has not yet had the good fortune to enter upon the secure path of a science. For in it reason is perpetually being brought to a stand, even when the laws into which it is seeking to have, as it professes, an *a priori* insight are those that are confirmed by our most common experiences. Ever and again we have to retrace our steps, as not leading us in the direction in which we desire to go. So far, too, are the students of metaphysics from exhibiting any kind of unanimity in their contention, that metaphysics has rather to be regarded as a battleground quite peculiarly suited for those who desire to exercise themselves in mock combats, and in which no participant has ever yet succeeded in gaining even so much as an inch of territory, not at least in such manner as to secure him in its permanent possession. This shows, beyond all questioning, that the procedure of metaphysics has hitherto been a merely random groping, and, what is worst of all, a groping among mere concepts.

What, then, is the reason why, in this field, the sure road to science has not hitherto been found? Is it, perhaps, impossible of discovery? Why, in that case, should nature have visited our reason with the restless endeavour whereby it is ever searching for such a path, as if this were one of its most important concerns? Nay, more, how little cause have we to place trust in our reason, if, in one of the most important domains of which we would fain have knowledge, it does not merely fail us, but lures us on by deceitful promises, and in the end betrays us! Or if it be only that we have thus far failed to find the true path, are there any indications to justify the hope that by renewed efforts we may have better fortune than has fallen to our predecessors?

The examples of mathematics and natural science, which by a single and sudden revolution have become what they now are, seem to me sufficiently remarkable to suggest our considering what may have been the essential features in the changed point of view by which they have so greatly benefited. Their success should incline us, at least by way of experiment, to imitate their procedure, so far as the analogy which, as species of rational knowledge, they bear to metaphysics may permit. Hitherto it has been assumed that all our knowledge must conform to objects. But all attempts to extend our knowledge of objects by establishing something in regard to them *a priori*, by means of concepts, have, on this assumption, ended in failure. We must therefore make trial whether we may not have more success in the tasks of metaphysics, if we suppose that objects must conform to our knowledge. This would agree better with what is desired, namely, that it should be possible to have knowledge of objects *a priori*, determining something in regard to them prior to their being given. We should then be proceeding precisely on the lines of Copernicus' primary hypothesis. Failing of satisfactory progress in explaining the movements of the heavenly bodies on the supposition that they all revolved round the spectator, he tried whether he might not have better success if he made the spectator to revolve and the stars to remain at rest. A similar experiment can be tried in metaphysics, as regards the *intuition* of objects. If intuition must conform to the constitution of the objects, I do not see how we could know anything of the latter *a priori*; but if the object (as object of the senses) must conform to the constitution of our faculty of intuition, I have no difficulty in conceiving such a possibility. Since I cannot rest in these intuitions if they are to become known, but must relate them as representations to something as their object, and determine this latter through them, either I must assume that the *concepts*, by means of which I obtain this determination, conform to the object, or else I assume that the objects, or what is the same thing, that the *experience* in which alone, as given objects, they can be known, conform to the concepts. In the former case, I am again in the same perplexity as to how I can know anything *a priori* in regard to the objects. In the latter case the outlook is more hopeful. For experience is itself a species of knowledge which involves understanding; and understanding has rules which I must presuppose as being in me prior to objects being given to me, and therefore as being *a priori*. They find expression in *a priori* concepts to which all objects of experience necessarily conform, and with which they must agree. As regards objects which are thought solely through reason, and indeed as necessary, but which can never—at least not in the manner in which reason thinks them—be given in experience, the attempts at thinking them (for they must admit of being thought) will furnish an excellent test of what we are adopting as our new method of thought, namely, that we can know *a priori* of things only what we ourselves put into them.²

This experiment succeeds as well as could be desired, and promises to metaphysics, in its first part—the part that is occupied with those concepts *a priori* to which the corresponding objects, commensurate with them, can be given in experience—the secure path of a science. For the new point of view enables us to explain how there can be knowledge *a priori*; and, in addition, to furnish satisfactory proofs of the laws which form the *a priori*

---

²This method, modelled on that of the student of nature, consists in looking for the elements of pure reason in *what admits of confirmation or refutation by*

basis of nature, regarded as the sum of the objects of experience—neither achievement being possible on the procedure hitherto followed. But this deduction of our power of knowing *a priori*, in the first part of metaphysics, has a consequence which is startling, and which has the appearance of being highly prejudicial to the whole purpose of metaphysics, as dealt with in the second part. For we are brought to the conclusion that we can never transcend the limits of possible experience, though that is precisely what this science is concerned, above all else, to achieve. This situation yields, however, just the very experiment by which, indirectly, we are enabled to prove the truth of this first estimate of our *a priori* knowledge of reason, namely, that such knowledge has to do only with appearances, and must leave the thing in itself as indeed real *per se*, but as not known by us. For what necessarily forces us to transcend the limits of experience and of all appearances is the *unconditioned*, which reason, by necessity and by right, demands in things in themselves, as required to complete the series of conditions. If, then, on the supposition that our empirical knowledge conforms to objects as things in themselves, we find that the unconditioned *cannot be thought without contradiction*, and that when, on the other hand, we suppose that our representation of things, as they are given to us, does not conform to these things as they are in themselves, but that these objects, as appearances, conform to our mode of representation, *the contradiction vanishes*; and if, therefore, we thus find that the unconditioned is not to be met with in things, so far as we know them, that is, so far as they are given to us, but only so far as we do not know them, that is, so far as they are things in themselves, we are

---

experiment. Now the propositions of pure reason, especially if they venture out beyond all limits of possible experience, cannot be brought to the test through any experiment with their *objects*, as in natural science. In dealing with those *concepts* and *principles*, which we adopt *a priori*, all that we can do is to contrive that they be used for viewing objects from two different points of view—on the one hand, in connection with experience, as objects of the senses and of the understanding, and on the other hand, for the isolated reason that strives to transcend all limits of experience, as objects which are thought merely. If, when things are viewed from this twofold standpoint, we find that there is agreement with the principle of pure reason, but that when we regard them only from a single point of view reason is involved in unavoidable self-conflict, the experiment decides in favour of the correctness of this distinction.

justified in concluding that what we at first assumed for the purposes of experiment is now definitely confirmed.[3] But when all progress in the field of the supersensible has thus been denied to speculative reason, it is still open to us to enquire whether, in the practical knowledge of reason, data may not be found sufficient to determine reason's transcendent concept of the unconditioned, and so to enable us, in accordance with the wish of metaphysics, and by means of knowledge that is possible *a priori*, though only from a practical point of view, to pass beyond the limits of all possible experience. Speculative reason has thus at least made room for such an extension; and if it must at the same time leave it empty, yet none the less we are at liberty, indeed we are summoned, to take occupation of it, if we can, by practical data of reason.[4]

This attempt to alter the procedure which has hitherto prevailed in metaphysics, by completely revolutionising it in accordance with the example set by the geometers and physicists, forms indeed the main purpose of this critique of pure speculative reason. It is a treatise on the method, not a system of the science itself. But at the same time it marks out the whole plan of the

---

[3]This experiment of pure reason bears a great similarity to what in chemistry is sometimes entitled the experiment of *reduction*, or more usually the *synthetic* process. The *analysis of the metaphysician* separates pure *a priori* knowledge into two very heterogeneous elements, namely, the knowledge of things as appearances, and the knowledge of things in themselves; his *dialectic* combines these two again, in *harmony* with the necessary idea of the *unconditioned* demanded by reason, and finds that this harmony can never be obtained except through the above distinction, which must therefore be accepted.

[4]Similarly, the fundamental laws of the motions of the heavenly bodies gave established certainty to what Copernicus had at first assumed only as an hypothesis, and at the same time yielded proof of the invisible force (the Newtonian attraction) which holds the universe together. The latter would have remained for ever undiscovered if Copernicus had not dared, in a manner contradictory of the senses, but yet true, to seek the observed movements, not in the heavenly bodies, but in the spectator. The change in point of view, analogous to this hypothesis, which is expounded in the *Critique*, I put forward in this preface as an hypothesis only, in order to draw attention to the character of these first attempts at such a change, which are always hypothetical. But in the *Critique* itself it will be proved, apodeictically not hypothetically, from the nature of our representations of space and time and from the elementary concepts of the understanding.

science, both as regards its limits and as regards its entire internal structure. For pure speculative reason has this peculiarity, that it can measure its powers according to the different ways in which it chooses the objects of its thinking, and can also give an exhaustive enumeration of the various ways in which it propounds its problems, and so is able, nay bound, to trace the complete outline of a system of metaphysics. As regards the first point, nothing in *a priori* knowledge can be ascribed to objects save what the thinking subject derives from itself; as regards the second point, pure reason, so far as the principles of its knowledge are concerned, is a quite separate self-subsistent unity, in which, as in an organised body, every member exists for every other, and all for the sake of each, so that no principle can safely be taken in *any one* relation, unless it has been investigated in the *entirety* of its relations to the whole employment of pure reason. Consequently, metaphysics has also this singular advantage, such as falls to the lot of no other science which deals with objects (for *logic* is concerned only with the form of thought in general), that should it, through this critique, be set upon the secure path of a science, it is capable of acquiring exhaustive knowledge of its entire field. Metaphysics has to deal only with principles, and with the limits of their employments as determined by these principles themselves, and it can therefore finish its work and bequeath it to posterity as a capital to which no addition can be made. Since it is a fundamental science, it is under obligation to achieve this completeness. We must be able to say of it: *nil actum reputans, si quid superesset agendum.*

But, it will be asked, what sort of a treasure is this that we propose to bequeath to posterity? What is the value of the metaphysics that is alleged to be thus purified by criticism and established once for all? On a cursory view of the present work it may seem that its results are merely *negative*, warning us that we must never venture with speculative reason beyond the limits of experience. Such is in fact its primary use. But such teaching at once acquires a *positive* value when we recognise that the principles with which speculative reason ventures out beyond its proper limits do not in effect *extend* the employment of reason, but, as we find on closer scrutiny, inevitably *narrow* it. These principles properly belong (not to reason but) to sensibility, and when thus employed they threaten to make the bounds of sensibility coextensive with the real, and so to supplant reason in its pure (practical) employment. So far, therefore, as our Critique limits speculative reason, it is indeed *negative*; but since it thereby removes an obstacle which stands in the way of the employment of practical reason, nay threatens to destroy it, it has in reality a *positive* and very important use. At least this is so, immediately we are convinced that there is an absolutely necessary *practical* employment of pure reason—the *moral*—in which it inevitably goes beyond the limits of sensibility. Though [practical] reason, in thus proceeding, requires no assistance from speculative reason, it must yet be assured against its opposition, that reason may not be brought into conflict with itself. To deny that the service which the Critique renders is *positive* in character, would thus be like saying that the police are of no positive benefit, inasmuch as their main business is merely to prevent the violence of which citizens stand in mutual fear, in order that each may pursue his vocation in peace and security. That space and time are only forms of sensible intuition, and so only conditions of the existence of things as appearances; that, moreover, we have no concepts of understanding, and consequently no elements for the knowledge of things, save in so far as intuition can be given corresponding to these concepts; and that we can therefore have no knowledge of any object as thing in itself, but only in so far as it is an object of sensible intuition, that is, an appearance—all this is proved in the analytical part of the Critique. Thus it does indeed follow that all possible speculative knowledge of reason is limited to mere objects of *experience*. But our further contention must also be duly borne in mind, namely, that though we cannot *know* these objects as things in themselves, we must yet be in position at least to *think* them as things in themselves;[5] otherwise we should be landed in the absurd conclusion that there can be appearance without anything

---

[5]To *know* an object I must be able to prove its possibility, either from its actuality as attested by experience, or *a priori* by means of reason. But I can *think* whatever I please, provided only that I do not contradict myself, that is, provided my concept is a possible thought. This suffices for the possibility of the concept, even though I may not be able to answer for there being, in the sum of all possibilities, an object corresponding to it. But something more is

that appears. Now let us suppose that the distinction, which our Critique has shown to be necessary, between things as objects of experience and those same things as things in themselves, had not been made. In that case all things in general, as far as they are efficient causes, would be determined by the principle of causality, and consequently by the mechanism of nature. I could not, therefore, without palpable contradiction, say of one and the same being, for instance the human soul, that its will is free and yet is subject to natural necessity, that is, is not free. For I have taken the soul in both propositions *in one and the same sense*, namely as a thing in general, that is, as a thing in itself; and save by means of a preceding critique, could not have done otherwise. But if our Critique is not in error in teaching that the object is to be taken *in a twofold sense*, namely as appearance and as thing in itself; if the deduction of the concepts of understanding is valid, and the principle of causality therefore applies only to things taken in the former sense, namely, in so far as they are objects of experience—these same objects, taken in the other sense, not being subject to the principle — then there is no contradiction in supposing that one and the same will is, in the appearance, that is, in its visible acts, necessarily subject to the law of nature, and so far *not free*, while yet, as belonging to a thing in itself, it is not subject to that law, and is therefore *free*. My soul, viewed from the latter standpoint, cannot indeed be known by means of speculative reason (and still less through empirical observation); and freedom as a property of a being to which I attribute effects in the sensible world, is therefore also not knowable in any such fashion. For I should then have to know such a being as determined in its existence, and yet as not determined in time—which is impossible, since I cannot support my concept by any intuition. But though I cannot *know*, I can yet *think* freedom; that is to say, the representation of it is at least not self-contradictory, provided due account be taken of our critical distinction between the two modes of representation, the sensible and the intellectual, and of

---

required before I can ascribe to such a concept objective validity, that is, real possibility; the former possibility is merely logical. This something more need not, however, be sought in the theoretical sources of knowledge; it may lie in those that are practical.

the resulting limitation of the pure concepts of understanding and of the principles which flow from them.

If we grant that morality necessarily presupposes freedom (in the strictest sense) as a property of our will; if, that is to say, we grant that it yields practical principles—original principles, proper to our reason—as *a priori data* of reason, and that this would be absolutely impossible save on the assumption of freedom; and if at the same time we grant the speculative reason has proved that such freedom does not allow of being thought, then the former supposition—that made on behalf of morality—would have to give way to this other contention, the opposite of which involves a palpable contradiction. For since it is only on the assumption of freedom that the negation of morality contains any contradiction, freedom, and with it morality, would have to yield to the mechanism of nature.

Morality does not, indeed, require that freedom should be understood, but only that it should not contradict itself, and so should at least allow of being thought, and that as thus thought it should place no obstacle in the way of a free act (viewed in another relation) likewise conforming to the mechanism of nature. The doctrine of morality and the doctrine of nature may each, therefore, make good its position. This, however, is only possible in so far as criticism has previously established our unavoidable ignorance of things in themselves, and has limited all that we can theoretically *know* to mere appearances.

This discussion as to the positive advantage of critical principles of pure reason can be similarly developed in regard to the concept of *God* and of the *simple nature* of our *soul*; but for the sake of brevity, such further discussion may be omitted. [From what has already been said, it is evident that] even the *assumption*—as made on behalf of the necessary practical employment of my reason—of *God*, *freedom*, and *immortality* is not permissible unless at the same time speculative reason be deprived of its pretensions to transcendent insight. For in order to arrive at such insight it must make use of principles which, in fact, extend only to objects of possible experience, and which, if also applied to what cannot be an object of experience always really change this into an appearance, thus rendering all *practical extension* of pure reason impossible. I have therefore found it necessary to deny *knowledge,* in order to make room for *faith*. The dogmatism of metaphysics, that is, the preconception that it is possible to make headway in metaphysics without a previous criticism of pure reason, is the source of all that unbelief, always very dogmatic, which wars against morality.

Though it may not, then, be very difficult to leave to posterity the bequest of a systematic metaphysic, constructed in conformity with a critique of pure reason, yet such a gift is not to be valued lightly. For not only will reason be enabled to follow the secure path of a science, instead of, as hitherto, groping at random, without circumspection or self-criticism; our enquiring youth will also be in a position to spend their time more profitably than in the ordinary dogmatism by which they are so early and so greatly encouraged to indulge in easy speculation about things of which they understand nothing, and into which neither they nor anyone else will ever have any insight—encouraged, indeed, to invent new ideas and opinions, while neglecting the study of the better-established sciences. But, above all, there is the inestimable benefit, that all objections to morality and religion will be for ever silenced, and this in Socratic fashion, namely, by the clearest proof of the ignorance of the objectors. There has always existed in the world, and there will always continue to exist, some kind of metaphysics, and with it the dialectic that is natural to pure reason. It is therefore the first and most important task of philosophy to deprive metaphysics, once and for all, of its injurious influence, by attacking its errors at their very source.

Notwithstanding this important change in the field of the sciences, and the *loss* of its fancied possessions which speculative reason must suffer, general human interests remain in the same privileged position as hitherto, and the advantages which the world has hitherto derived from the teachings of pure reason are in no way diminished. The loss affects only the *monopoly of the schools*, in no respect the *interests of humanity*. I appeal to the most rigid dogmatist, whether the proof of the continued existence of our soul after death, derived from the simplicity of substance, or of the freedom of the will as opposed to a universal mechanism, arrived at through the subtle but ineffectual distinctions between subjective and objective practical necessity, or of the existence of God as deduced from the concept of an *ens realissimum* (of the contingency of the changeable and of the necessity of a prime mover), have ever, upon passing out from the schools, succeeded in reaching the public mind or in exercising the slightest influence on its convictions? That has never been found to occur, and in view of the unfitness of the common human understanding for such subtle speculation, ought never to have been expected. Such widely held convictions, so far as they rest on rational grounds, are due to quite other considerations. The hope of a *future life* has its source in that notable characteristic of our nature, never to be capable of being satisfied by what is temporal (as insufficient for the capacities of its whole destination); the consciousness of *freedom* rests exclusively on the clear exhibition of duties, in opposition to all claims of the inclinations; the belief in a wise and great *Author of the world* is generated solely by the glorious order, beauty, and providential care everywhere displayed in nature. When the Schools have been brought to recognise that they can lay no claim to higher and fuller insight in a matter of universal human concern than that which is equally within the reach of the great mass of men (ever to be held by us in the highest esteem), and that, as Schools of philosophy, they should limit themselves to the study of those universally comprehensible, and for moral purposes, sufficient grounds of proof, then not only do these latter possessions remain undisturbed, but through this very fact they acquire yet greater authority. The change affects only the arrogant pretensions of the Schools, which would fain be counted the sole authors and possessors of such truths (as, indeed, they can justly claim to be in many other branches of knowledge), reserving the key to themselves, and communicating to the public their use only—*quod mecum nescit, solus vult scire videri*. At the same time due regard is paid to the more moderate claims of the speculative philosopher. He still remains the sole authority in regard to a science which benefits the public without their knowing it, namely, the critique of reason. That critique can never become popular, and indeed there is no need that it should. For just as fine-spun arguments in favour of useful truths make no appeal to the general mind, so neither do the subtle objections that can be raised against them. On the other hand, both inevitably present themselves to everyone who rises to the height of speculation; and it is therefore the duty of the Schools, by means of a thorough investi-

gation of the rights of speculative reason, once for all to prevent
the scandal which, sooner or later, is sure to break out even
among the masses, as the result of the disputes in which metaphysicians (and, as such, finally also the clergy) inevitably
become involved to the consequent perversion of their teaching.
Criticism alone can sever the root to *materialism, fatalism, atheism,
free-thinking, fanaticism,* and *superstition,* which can be injurious
universally; as well as of *idealism* and *scepticism,* which are dangerous chiefly to the Schools, and hardly allow of being handed
on to the public. If governments think proper to interfere with the
affairs of the learned, it would be more consistent with a wise
regard for science as well as for mankind, to favour the freedom
of such criticism, by which alone the labours of reason can be
established on a firm basis, than to support the ridiculous despotism of the Schools, which raise a loud cry of public danger over
the destruction of cobwebs to which the public has never paid
any attention, and the loss of which it can therefore never feel.

This critique is not opposed to the *dogmatic procedure* of reason
in its pure knowledge, as science, for that must always be dogmatic, that is, yield strict proof from sure principles *a priori.* It is
opposed only to *dogmatism,* that is, to the presumption that it is
possible to make progress with pure knowledge, according to
principles, from concepts alone (those that are philosophical), as
reason has long been in the habit of doing; and that it is possible
to do this without having first investigated in what way and by
what right reason has come into possession of these concepts.
Dogmatism is thus the dogmatic procedure of pure reason, *without previous criticism of its own powers.* In withstanding dogmatism
we must not allow ourselves to give free rein to that loquacious
shallowness, which assumes for itself the name of popularity, nor
yet to scepticism, which makes short work with all metaphysics.
On the contrary, such criticism is the necessary preparation for a
throughly grounded metaphysics which, as science, must necessarily be developed dogmatically, according to the strictest
demands of system, in such manner as to satisfy not the general
public but the requirements of the Schools. For that is a demand
to which it stands pledged, and which it may not neglect, namely,
that it carry out its work entirely *a priori,* to the complete satisfaction of speculative reason. In the execution of the plan prescribed

by the critique, that is, in the future system of metaphysics, we have therefore to follow the strict method of the celebrated Wolff, the greatest of all the dogmatic philosophers. He was the first to show by example (and by his example he awakened that spirit of thoroughness which is not extinct in Germany) how the secure progress of a science is to be attained only through orderly establishment of principles, clear determination of concepts, insistence upon strictness of proof, and avoidance of venturesome, non-consecutive steps in our inferences. He was thus peculiarly well fitted to raise metaphysics to the dignity of a science, if only it had occurred to him to prepare the ground beforehand by a critique of the organ, that is, of pure reason itself. The blame for his having failed to do so lies not so much with himself as with the dogmatic way of thinking prevalent in his day, and with which the philosophers of his time, and of all previous times, have no right to reproach one another. Those who reject both the method of Wolff and the procedure of a critique of pure reason can have no other aim than to shake off the fetters of *science* altogether, and thus to change work into play, certainty into opinion, philosophy into philodoxy.

Now, *as regards this second edition,* I have, as is fitting, endeavoured to profit by the opportunity, in order to remove, wherever possible, difficulties and obscurity which, not perhaps without my fault, may have given rise to the many misunderstandings into whichever acute thinkers have fallen in passing judgment upon my book. In the propositions themselves and their proofs, and also in the form and completeness of the [architectonic] plan, I have found nothing to alter. This is due partly to the long examination to which I have subjected them, before offering them to the public, partly to the nature of the subject-matter with which we are dealing. For pure speculative reason has a structure wherein everything is an *organ*, the whole being for the sake of every part, and every part for the sake of all the others, so that even the smallest imperfection, be it a fault (error) or a deficiency, must inevitably betray itself in use. This system will, as I hope, maintain, throughout the future, this unchangeableness. It is not self-conceit which justifies me in this confidence, but the evidence experimentally obtained through the parity of the result, whether we proceed from the smallest elements to the whole of pure reason or reverse-wise from the whole (for this also is presented to reason through its final end in the sphere of the practical) to each part. Any attempt to change even the smallest part at once gives rise to contradictions, not merely in the system but in human reason in general. As to the mode of *exposition*, on the other hand, much still remains to be done; and in this edition I have sought to make improvements which should help in removing, first, the misunderstanding in regard to the Aesthetic, especially concerning the concept of time; secondly, the obscurity of the deduction of the concepts of understanding; thirdly, a supposed want of sufficient evidence in the proofs of the principles of pure understanding; and finally, the false interpretation placed upon the paralogisms charged against rational psychology. Beyond this point, that is, beyond the end of the first chapter of the Transcendental Dialectic, I have made no changes in the mode of exposition.[6] Time was too short to allow of further changes; and besides, I have not found among competent and impartial critics any misapprehension in regard to the remaining sections. Though I shall not venture to name these critics with the praise that is their due, the attention which I have paid to their comments will easily be recognised in the [new] passages [above mentioned]. These improvements involve, however, a small loss, not to be prevented save by making the book too voluminous, namely, that I have had

---

[6]The only addition, strictly so called, though one affecting the method of proof only, is the new refutation of psychological *idealism* . . . , and a strict (also, as I believe, the only possible) proof of the objective reality of outer intuition. However harmless idealism may be considered in respect of the essential aims of metaphysics (though, in fact, it is not thus harmless), it still remains a scandal to philosophy and to human reason in general that the existence of things outside us (from which we derive the whole material of knowledge, even for our inner sense) must be accepted merely on *faith*, and that if anyone thinks good to doubt their existence, we are unable to counter his doubts by any satisfactory proof. Since there is some obscurity in the expressions used in the proof, from the third line to the sixth line, I beg to alter the passage as follows: *"But this permanent cannot be an intuition in me. For all grounds of determination of my existence which are to be met with in me are representations; and as representation themselves require a permanent distinct from them, in relation to which their change, and so my existence in the time wherein they change, may be determined.* To this proof it will probably be objected, that I am immediately conscious only of that which is in me, that is, of my *representation* of outer things; and consequently that it must still remain uncertain whether outside me there is anything corresponding to it, or not. But through inner *experience* I am conscious of *my existence* in time (conse-

to omit or abridge certain passages which, though not indeed essential to the completeness of the whole, may yet be missed by many readers as otherwise helpful. Only so could I obtain space for what, as I hope, is now a more intelligible exposition, which, though altering absolutely nothing in the fundamentals of the

---

quently also of its determinability in time), and this is more than to be conscious merely of my representation. It is identical with the *empirical consciousness of my existence*, which is determinable only through relation to something which, while bound up with my existence, is outside me. This consciousness of my existence in time is bound up in the way of identity with the consciousness of a relation to something outside me, and it is therefore experience not invention, sense not imagination, which inseparably connects this outside something with my inner sense. For outer sense is already in itself a relation of intuition to something actual outside me, and the reality of outer sense, in its distinction from imagination, rests simply on that which is here found to take place, namely, its being inseparably bound up with inner experience, as the condition of its possibility. If, with the *intellectual consciousness* of my existence, in the representation 'I am,' which accompanies all my judgements and acts of understanding, I could at the same time connect a determination of my existence through *intellectual intuition*, the consciousness of a relation to something outside me would not be required. But though that intellectual consciousness does indeed come first, the inner intuition, in which my existence can alone be determined, is sensible and is bound up with the condition of time. This determination, however, and therefore the inner experience itself, depends upon something permanent which is not in me, and consequently can be only in something outside me, to which I must regard myself as standing in relation. The reality of outer sense is thus necessarily bound up with inner sense, if experience in general is to be possible at all; that is, I am just as certainly conscious that there are things outside me, which are in relation to my sense, as I am conscious that I myself exist as determined in time. In order to determine to which given intuitions objects outside me actually correspond, and which therefore belong to outer *sense* (to which, and not to the faculty of imagination, they are to be ascribed), we must in each single case appeal to the rules according to which experience in general, even inner experience, is distinguished from imagination—the proposition that there is such a thing as outer experience being always presupposed. This further remark may be added. The representation of something *permanent* in existence is not the same as *permanent representation*. For though the representation of [something permanent] may be very transitory and variable like all our other representations, not excepting those of matter, it yet refers to something permanent. This latter must therefore be an external thing distinct from all my representations, and its existence must be included in the *determination* of my own existence, constituting with it but a single experience such as would not take place even inwardly if it were not also at the same time, in part, outer. How this should be possible we are as little capable of explaining further as we are of accounting for out being able to think the abiding in time, the coexistence of which with the changing generates the concept of alteration.

propositions put forward or even in their proofs, yet here and there departs so far from the previous method of treatment, that mere interpolations could not be made to suffice. This loss, which is small and can be remedied by consulting the first edition, will, I hope, be compensated by the greater clearness of the new text. I have observed, with pleasure and thankfulness, in various published works—alike in critical reviews and in independent treatises—that the spirit of thoroughness is not extinct in Germany, but has only been temporarily overshadowed by the prevalence of a pretentiously free manner of thinking; and that the thorny paths of the Critique have not discouraged courageous and clear heads from setting themselves to master my book—a work which leads to a methodical, and as such alone and enduring, and therefore most necessary, science of pure reason. To these worthy men, who so happily combine thoroughness of insight with a talent for lucid exposition—which I cannot regard myself as possessing—I leave the task of perfecting what, here and there, in its exposition, is still somewhat defective; for in this regard the danger is not that of being refuted, but of not being understood. From now on, though I cannot allow myself to enter into controversy, I shall take careful note of all suggestions, be they from friends or from opponents, for use, in accordance with this propaedeutic, in the further elaboration of the system. In the course of these labours I have advanced somewhat far in years (this month I reach my sixty-fourth year), and I must be careful with my time if I am to succeed in my proposed scheme of providing a metaphysic of nature and of morals which will confirm the truth of my Critique in the two fields, of speculative and of practical reason. The clearing up of the obscurities in the present work—they are hardly to be avoided in a new enterprise—and the defence of it as a whole, I must therefore leave to those worthy men who have made my teaching their own. A philosophical work cannot be armed at all points, like a mathematical treatise, and may therefore be open to objection in this or that respect, while yet the structure of the system, taken in its unity, is not in the least endangered. Few have the versatility of mind to familiarise themselves with a new system; and owing to the general distaste for all innovation, still fewer have the inclination to do so. If we take single passages, torn from their contexts, and compare them with one another, apparent contradictions are not likely to be lacking, especially in a work that is written with any freedom of expression. In the eyes of those who rely on the judgment of others, such contradictions have the effect of placing the work in an unfavourable light; but they are easily resolved by those who have mastered the idea of a whole. If a theory has in itself stability, the stresses and strains which may at first have seemed very threatening to it serve only, in the course of time, to smooth away its inequalities; and if men of impartiality, insight, and true popularity devote themselves to its exposition, it may also, in a short time, secure for itself the necessary elegance of statement.

Study Questions

Preface to the First Edition

1. According to Kant, what sort of questions does Reason find itself compelled to ask but to which it has no answers?
2. What traditional discipline is Kant talking about?

Preface to Second Edition

1. How can we determine whether a branch of learning is following the secure path of a science?
2. What specific science has proceeded on this path from the earliest times?
3. What does it mean to call a discipline "the vestibule of the sciences"? What discipline, in particular, occupies this position?
4. What two sciences yield theoretical knowledge?
5. What is the main difference noted by Kant in this context between these two theoretical sciences?
6. How does Kant characterize or describe the state of metaphysics?
7. What revolution did Copernicus achieve in astronomy?
8. What revolution does Kant propose in epistemology? In what respect is this revolution analogous to or significantly like the Copernican revolution in astronomy?
9. What does Kant mean by "pure reason"? by "pure speculative reason"?
10. What is the twofold sense in which "object" is understood by Kant?

11. What are the three main topics of traditional metaphysics? What is Kant's position regarding our knowledge of these?

12. What does Kant mean by "dogmatism"?

13. How does Kant understand or depict the nature of his own projects?

14. What metaphor does Kant use to illuminate the "territory of pure understanding"?

15. What is the function played by the principles of pure understanding? (By "function," what is meant here is simply the role played by these principles in the acquisition of knowledge.)

Transcendental Doctrine of Judgement
(Analytic of Principles)

CHAPTER III

THE GROUND OF THE DISTINCTION
OF ALL OBJECTS IN GENERAL
INTO PHENOMENA AND NOUMENA

We have now not merely explored the territory of pure understanding, and carefully surveyed every part of it, but have also
measured its extent, and assigned to everything in it its rightful
place. This domain is an island, enclosed by nature itself within
unalterable limits. It is the land of truth—enchanting name!—surrounded by a wide and stormy ocean, the native home of illusion,
where many a fog bank and many a swiftly melting iceberg give
the deceptive appearance of farther shores, deluding the adven-
turous seafarer ever anew with empty hopes, and engaging him
in enterprises which he can never abandon and yet is unable to
carry to completion. Before we venture in this sea, to explore it in
all directions and to obtain assurance whether there be any
ground for such hopes, it will be well to begin by casting a glance
upon the map of the land which we are about to leave, and to
enquire, first, whether we cannot in any case be satisfied with
what it contains—are not, indeed, under compulsion to be satisfied, inasmuch as there may be no other territory upon which we
can settle; and, secondly, by what title we possess even this
domain, and can consider ourselves as secured against all oppos-
ing claims. Although we have already given a sufficient answer
to these questions in the course of the Analytic, a summary statement of its solutions may nevertheless help to strengthen our conviction, by focussing the various considerations in their bearing
on the questions now before us.

We have seen that everything which the understanding
derives from itself is, though not borrowed from experience, at
the disposal of the understanding solely for use in experience.
The principles of pure understanding, whether constitutive *a pri-*

ori, like the mathematical principles, or merely regulative, like the dynamical, contain nothing but what may be called the pure schema of possible experience. For experience obtains its unity only from the synthetic unity which the understanding originally and of itself confers upon the synthesis of imagination in its relation to apperception; and the appearances, as data for a possible knowledge, must already stand *a priori* in relation to, and in agreement with, that synthetic unity. But although these rules of understanding are not only true *a priori*, but are indeed the source of all truth (that is, of the agreement of our knowledge with objects), inasmuch as they contain in themselves the ground of the possibility of experience viewed as the sum of all knowledge wherein objects can be given to us, we are not satisfied with the exposition merely of that which is true, but likewise demand that account be taken of that which we desire to know. If, therefore, from this critical enquiry we learn nothing more than what, in the merely empirical employment of understanding, we should in any case have practised without any such subtle enquiry, it would seem as if the advantage derived from it by no means repays the labour expended. The reply may certainly be made that in the endeavour to extend our knowledge a meddlesome curiosity is far less injurious than the habit of always insisting, before entering on any enquiries, upon antecedent proof of the utility of the enquiries—an absurd demand, since prior to completion of the enquires we are not in a position to form the least conception of this utility, even if it were placed before our eyes. There is, however, one advantage which may be made comprehensible and of interest even to the most refractory and reluctant learner, the advantage, that while the understanding, occupied merely with its empirical employment, and not reflecting upon the sources of its own knowledge, may indeed get along quite satisfactorily, there is yet one task to which it is not equal, that, namely, of determining the limits of its employment, and of knowing what it is that may lie within and what it is that lies without its own proper sphere. This demands just those deep enquiries which we have instituted. If the understanding in its empirical employment cannot distinguish whether certain questions lie within its horizon or not, it can never be assured of its claims or of its possessions, but must be prepared for many a humiliating disillusionment, whenever, as must unavoidably and constantly happen, it oversteps the limits of its own domain, and loses itself in opinions that are baseless and misleading.

If the assertion, that the understanding can employ its various principles, and its various concepts solely in an empirical and never in a transcendental manner, is a proposition which can be known with certainty, it will yield important consequences. The transcendental employment of a concept in any principle is its application to things *in general and in themselves*; the empirical employment is its application *merely to appearances*; that is, to objects of a possible experience. That the latter application of concepts is alone feasible is evident from the following considerations. We demand in every concept, first, the logical form of the concept (of thought) in general, and secondly, the possibility of giving it an object to which it may be applied. In the absence of such object, it has no meaning and is completely lacking in content, though it may still contain the logical function which is required for making a concept out of any data that may be presented. Now the object cannot be given to a concept otherwise than in intuition; for though a pure intuition can indeed precede the object *a priori*, even this intuition can acquire its object, and therefore objective validity, only through the empirical intuition of which it is the mere form. Therefore all concepts, and with them all principles, even such as are possible *a priori*, relate to empirical intuitions, that is, to the data for a possible experience. Apart from this relation they have no objective validity, and in respect of their representations are a mere play of imagination or of understanding.

*   *   *

Transcendental Doctrine of Method

CHAPTER II
THE CANON OF PURE REASON

SECTION 3

Opining, Knowing, and Believing

The holding of a thing to be true is an occurrence in our understanding which, though it may rest on objective grounds, also requires subjective causes in the mind of the individual who makes the judgment. If the judgment is valid for everyone, provided only he is in possession of reason, its ground is objectively sufficient, and the holding of it to be true is entitled *conviction*. If it has its ground only in the special character of the subject, it is entitled *persuasion*.

Persuasion is a mere illusion, because the ground of the judgment, which lies solely in the subject, is regarded as objective. Such a judgment has only private validity, and the holding of it to be true does not allow of being communicated. But truth depends upon agreement with the object, and in respect of it the judgments of each and every understanding must therefore be in agreement with each other (*consentientia uni tertio, consentiunt inter se*). The criterion whereby we decide whether our holding a thing to be true is conviction or mere persuasion is therefore external, namely, the possibility of communicating it and of finding it to be valid for all human reason. For there is then at least a presumption that the ground of the agreement of all judgments with each other, notwithstanding the differing characters of individuals, rests upon the common ground, namely, upon the object, and that it is for this reason that they are all in agreement with the object—the truth of the judgment being thereby proved.

So long, therefore, as the subject views the judgment merely as an appearance of his mind, persuasion cannot be subjectively distinguished from conviction. The experiment, however, whereby we test upon the understanding of others whether those grounds of the judgment which are valid for us have the same effect on the reason of others as on our own, is a means, although only a subjective means, not indeed of producing conviction, but of detecting any merely private validity in the judgement, that is, anything in it which is mere persuasion.

If, in addition, we can specify the subjective *causes* of the judgement, which we have taken as being its objective *grounds*, and can thus explain the deceptive judgment as an event in our mind, and can do so without having to take account of the character of the object, we expose the illusion and are no longer deceived by it, although always still in some degree liable to come under its influence, in so far as the subjective cause of the illusion is inherent in our nature.

I cannot *assert* anything, that is, declare it to be a judgement necessarily valid for everyone, save as it gives rise to conviction. Persuasion I can hold to on my own account, if it so pleases me, but I cannot, and ought not to, profess to impose it as binding on anyone but myself.

The holding of a thing to be true, or the subjective validity of the judgement, in its relation to conviction (which is at the same time objectively valid), has the following three degrees: *opining*, *believing*, and *knowing*. *Opining* is such holding of a judgment as is consciously insufficient, not only objectively, but also subjectively. If our holding of the judgment be only subjectively sufficient, and is at the same time taken as being objectively insufficient, we have what is termed *believing*. Lastly, when the holding of a thing to be true is sufficient both subjectively and objectively, it is *knowledge*. The subjective sufficiency is termed *conviction* (for myself), the objective sufficiency is termed *certainty* (for everyone). There is no call for me to spend further time on the explanation of such easily understood terms.

I must never presume to *opine*, without *knowing at least something* by means of which the judgment, in itself merely problematic, secures connection with truth, a connection which, although not complete, is yet more than arbitrary fiction. Moreover, the law of such a connection must be certain. For if, in respect of this law also, I have nothing but opinion, it is all merely a play of the imagination, without the least relation to truth. Again, *opining* is not in any way permissible in judging by means of pure reason. For since such judging is not based on grounds of experience, but being in every case necessary has all to be arrived at *a priori*, the principle of the connection requires universality and necessity, and therefore complete certainty; otherwise we should have no guidance as to truth. Hence it is absurd to have an opinion in pure mathematics; either we must know, or we must abstain from all acts of judgment. It is so likewise in the case of the principles of morality, since we must not venture upon an action on the mere opinion that it is *allowed*, but must know it to be so.

In the transcendental employment of reason, on the other hand, while opining is doubtless too weak a term to be applicable, the term knowing is too strong. In the merely speculative sphere we cannot therefore make any judgments whatsoever. For the subjective grounds upon which we may hold something to be true, such as those which are able to produce belief, are not permissible in speculative questions, inasmuch as they do not hold independently of all empirical support, and do not allow of being communicated in equal measure to others.

But it is only from a *practical point of view* that the theoretically insufficient holding of a thing to be true can be termed believing. This practical point of view is either in reference to *skill* or in reference to *morality*, the former being concerned with optional and contingent ends, the latter with ends that are absolutely necessary.

Once an end is accepted, the conditions of its attainment are hypothetically necessary. This necessity is subjectively, but still only comparatively, sufficient, if I know of no other conditions under which the end can be attained. On the other hand, it is sufficient, absolutely and for everyone, if I know with certainty that no one can have knowledge of any other conditions which lead to the proposed end. In the former case my assumption and the holding of certain conditions to be true is a merely contingent belief; in the latter case it is a necessary belief. The physician must do something for a patient in danger, but does not know the nature of his illness. He observes the symptoms, and if he can find no more likely alternative, judges it to be a case of phthisis. Now even in his own estimation his belief is contingent only; another observer might perhaps come to a sounder conclusion. Such contingent belief, which yet forms the ground for the actual employment of means to certain actions, I entitle *pragmatic belief.*

The usual touchstone, whether that which someone asserts is merely his persuasion—or at least his subjective conviction, that is, his firm belief—is *betting*. It often happens that someone propounds his views with such positive and uncompromising assurance that he seems to have entirely set aside all thought of possible error. A bet disconcerts him. Sometimes it turns out that he has a conviction which can be estimated at a value of one ducat, but not of ten. For he is very willing to venture one ducat, but when it is a question of ten he becomes aware, as he had not previously been, that it may very well be that he is in error. If, in a given case, we represent ourselves as staking the happiness of our whole life, the triumphant tone of our judgment is greatly abated; we become extremely diffident, and discover for the first time that our belief does not reach so far. Thus pragmatic belief always exists in some specific degree, which, according to differences in the interests at stake, may be large or may be small.

But in many cases, when we are dealing with an object about which nothing can be done by us, and in regard to which our judgment is therefore purely theoretical, we can conceive and picture to ourselves an attitude for which we regard ourselves as having sufficient grounds, while yet there is no existing means of arriving at certainty in the matter. Thus even in purely theoretical judgments there is an *analogon of practical* judgments, to the mental entertaining of which the term *"belief"* is appropriate, and which we may entitle *doctrinal belief.* I should be ready to stake my all on the contention—were it possible by means of any experience to settle the question—that at least one of the planets which we see is inhabited. Hence I say that it is not merely opinion, but a strong belief, on the correctness of which I should be prepared to run great risks, that other worlds are inhabited.

Now we must admit that the doctrine of the existence of God belongs to doctrinal belief. For as regards theoretical knowledge of the world, I can *cite* nothing which necessarily presupposes this thought as the condition of my explanations of the appearances exhibited by the world, but rather am bound so to employ my reason as if everything were mere nature. Purposive unity is, however, so important a condition of the application of reason to nature that I cannot ignore it, especially as experience supplies me so richly with examples of it. But I know no other condition under which this unity can supply me with guidance in the investigation of nature, save only the postulate that a supreme intelligence has ordered all things in accordance with the wisest ends. Consequently, as a condition of what is indeed a contingent, but still not unimportant purpose, namely, to have guidance in the investigation of nature, we must postulate a wise Author of the world. Moreover, the outcome of my attempts [in explanation of nature] so frequently confirms the usefulness of this postulate, while nothing decisive can be cited against it, that I am saying much too little if I proceed to declare that I hold it merely as an opinion. Even in this theoretical relation it can be said that I firmly believe in God. This belief is not, therefore, strictly speaking, practical; it must be entitled a doctrinal belief, to which the *theology* of nature (physico-theology) must always necessarily give rise. In view of the magnificent equipment of our human nature, and the shortness of life so ill-suited to the full exercise of our powers, we can find in this same divine wisdom a no less sufficient ground for a doctrinal belief in the future life of the human soul.

In such cases the expression of belief is, from the *objective* point of view, an expression of modesty, and yet at the same time, from the *subjective* point of view, an expression of the firmness of our confidence. Were I even to go the length of describing the merely theoretical holding of the belief as an hypothesis which I am justified in assuming, I should thereby be pledging myself to have a more adequate concept of the character of a cause of the world and of the character of another world than I am really in a position to supply. For if I assume anything, even merely as an hypothesis, I must at least know so much of its properties that I require to assume, *not its concept*, but *only its existence*. The term "belief" refers only to the guidance which an idea gives me, and to its subjective influence in that furthering of the activities of my reason which confirms me in the idea, and which yet does so without my being in a position to give a speculative account of it.

But merely doctrinal belief is somewhat lacking in stability; we often lose hold of it, owing to the speculative difficulties which we encounter, although in the end we always inevitably return to it.

It is quite otherwise with moral belief. For here it is absolutely necessary that something must happen, namely, that I must in all points conform to the moral law. The end is here irrefragably established, and according to such insight as I can have, there is only one possible condition under which this end can connect with all other ends, and thereby have practical validity, namely, that there be a God and a future world. I also know with complete certainty that no one can be acquainted with any other conditions which lead to the same unity of ends under the moral law. Since, therefore, the moral precept is at the same time my maxim (reason prescribing that it should be so), I inevitably believe in the existence of God and in a future life, and I am certain that nothing can shake this belief, since my moral principles would thereby be themselves overthrown, and I cannot disclaim them without becoming abhorrent in my own eyes.

Thus even after reason has failed in all its ambitious attempts to pass beyond the limits of all experience, there is still enough left to satisfy us, so far as our practical standpoint is concerned. No one, indeed, will be able to boast that he *knows* that there is a God, and a future life; if he knows this, he is the very man for whom I have long [and vainly] sought. All knowledge, if it concerns an object of mere reason, can be communicated; and I might therefore hope that under his instruction my own knowledge would be extended in this wonderful fashion. No, my conviction is not *logical*, but *moral* certainty; and since it rests on subjective grounds (of moral sentiment), I must not even say, "*It is* morally certain that there is a God, etc.," but "*I am* morally certain, etc." In other words, belief in a God and in another world is so interwoven with my moral sentiment that as there is little danger of my losing the latter, there is equally little cause for fear that the former can ever be taken from me.

The only point that may seem questionable is the basing of this rational belief on the assumption of moral sentiments. If we leave these aside, and take a man who is completely indifferent with regard to moral laws, the question propounded by reason then becomes merely a problem for speculation, and can, indeed, be supported by strong grounds of analogy, but not by such as must compel the most stubborn scepticism to give way.[1] But in

---

[1]The human mind (as, I likewise believe, must necessarily be the case with every rational being) takes a natural interest in morality, although this interest is

these questions no man is free from all interest. For although, through lack of good sentiments, he may be cut off from moral interest, still even in this case enough remains to make him *fear* the existence of a God and a future life. Nothing more is required for this than that he at least cannot pretend that there is any *certainty* that there is *no* such being and *no* such life. Since that would have to be proved by mere reason, and therefore apodeictically, he would have to prove the impossiblility of both, which assuredly no one can reasonably undertake to do. This may serve as a *negative* belief, which may not, indeed, give rise to morality and good sentiments, but may still give rise to an analogon of these, namely, a powerful check upon the outbreak of evil sentiments.

But, it will be said, is this all that pure reason achieves in opening up prospects beyond the limits of experience? Nothing more than two articles of belief? Surely the common understanding could have achieved as much, without appealing to philosophers for counsel in the matter.

I shall not here dwell upon the service which philosophy has done to human reason through the laborious efforts of its criticism, granting even that in the end it should turn out to be merely negative; something more will be said on this point in the next section. But I may at once reply: Do you really require that a mode of knowledge which concerns all men should transcend the common understanding, and should only be revealed to you by philosophers? Precisely what you find fault with is the best confirmation of the correctness of the above assertions. For we have thereby revealed to us, what could not at the start have been foreseen, namely, that in matters which concern all men without distinction nature is not guilty of any partial distribution of her gifts, and that in regard to the essential ends of human nature the highest philosophy cannot advance further than is possible under the guidance which nature has bestowed even upon the most ordinary understanding.

---

not undivided and practically preponderant. If we confirm and increase this interest, we shall find reason very teachable and in itself more enlightened as regards the uniting of the speculative with the practical interest. But if we do not take care that we first make men good, at least in some measure good, we shall never make honest believers of them.

* * *

STUDY QUESTIONS

Phenomena and Noumena

1. What does Kant mean by saying that all principles of pure understanding, whether constitutive or regulative, contain nothing but pure schema of possible experience?

2. What, according to Kant, is the one task which the understanding in its merely empirical employment can not do?

3. How does Kant show that the empirical employment of a concept is confined to appearances alone?

4. In your own words, what does Kant mean by phenomena? by noumena? by constitutive principle? by regulative principle?

Opining, Knowing, and Believing

1. What is the difference between a conviction and a persuasion?

2. What is the touchstone whereby we can distinguish the one from the other?

3. What are the three degrees of holding a thing to be true? What are the principal differences among these degrees? Explain these terms.

4. What different types of belief does Kant distinguish? Explain each of these.

5. What does pure reason achieve in opening up prospects beyond the limits of experience?

6. What service has philosophy done for human reason?

From

An Answer to the Question: What is Enlightenment? (1784)

Enlightenment is man's emergence from his self-imposed immaturity. Immaturity is the inability to use one's understanding without guidance from another. This immaturity is *self-imposed* when its cause lies not in lack of understanding, but in lack of resolve and courage to use it without guidance from another. *Sapere Aude!*[1] "Have courage to use your own understanding!"—that is the motto of enlightenment.

Laziness and cowardice are the reasons why so great a proportion of men, long after nature has released them from alien guidance (*naturaliter maiorennes*[2]), nonetheless gladly remain in lifelong immaturity, and why it is so easy for others to establish themselves as their guardians. It is so easy to be immature. If I have a book to serve as my understanding, a pastor to serve as my conscience, a physician to determine my diet for me, and so on, I need not exert myself at all. I need not think, if only I can pay: others will readily undertake the irksome work for me. The guardians who have so benevolently taken over the supervision of men have carefully seen to it that the far greatest part of them (including the entire fair sex) regard taking the step to maturity as very dangerous, not to mention difficult. Having first made their domestic livestock dumb, and having carefully made sure that these docile creatures will not take a single step without the go-cart to which they are harnessed, these guardians then show them the danger that threatens them, should they attempt to walk alone. Now this danger is not actually so great, for after falling a few times they would in the end certainly learn to walk; but an example of this kind makes men timid and usually frightens them out of all further attempts.

---

[1]Horace, *Epodes*, 1, 2, 40.
[2]"Those who have come of age by virtue of nature."

Thus, it is difficult for any individual man to work himself out of the immaturity that has all but become his nature. He has even become fond of this state and for the time being is actually incapable of using his own understanding, for no one has ever allowed him to attempt it. Rules and formulas, those mechanical aids to the rational use, or rather misuse, of his natural gifts, are the shackles of a permanent immaturity. Whoever threw them off would still make only an uncertain leap over the smallest ditch, since he is unaccustomed to this kind of free movement. Consequently, only a few have succeeded, by cultivating their own minds, in freeing themselves from immaturity and pursuing a secure course.

But that the public should enlighten itself is more likely; indeed, if it is only allowed freedom, enlightenment is almost inevitable. For even among the entrenched guardians of the great masses a few will always think for themselves, a few who, after having themselves thrown off the yoke of immaturity, will spread the spirit of a rational appreciation for both their own worth and for each person's calling to think for himself. But it should be particularly noted that if a public that was first placed in this yoke by the guardians is suitably aroused by some of those who are altogether incapable of enlightenment, it may force the guardians themselves to remain under the yoke—so pernicious is it to instill prejudices, for they finally take revenge upon their originators, or on their descendants. Thus a public can only attain enlightenment slowly. Perhaps a revolution can overthrow autocratic despotism and profiteering or power-grabbing oppression, but it can never truly reform a manner of thinking; instead, new prejudices, just like the old ones they replace, will serve as a leash for the great unthinking mass.

Nothing is required for this enlightenment, however, except *freedom*; and the freedom in question is the least harmful of all, namely, the freedom to use reason *publicly* in all matters. But on all sides I hear: *"Do not argue!"* The officer says, "Do not argue, drill!" The taxman says, "Do not argue, pay!" The pastor says, "Do not argue, believe!" (Only one ruler in the world [Frederick the Great of Prussia] says, "*Argue* as much as you want and about what you want, *but obey!"*) In this we have (examples of) pervasive restrictions on freedom. But which restriction hinders enlightenment and which does not, but instead actually advances it? I reply: The *public* use of one's reason must always be free, and it alone can bring about enlightenment among mankind; the *private use* of reason may, however, often be very narrowly restricted, without otherwise hindering the progress of enlightenment. By the public use of one's own reason I understand the use that anyone as a *scholar* makes of reason before the entire *literate world*. I call the private use of reason that which a person may make in *civic post* or office that has been entrusted to him. Now in many affairs conducted in the interests of a community, a certain mechanism is required by means of which some of its members must conduct themselves in an entirely passive manner so that through an artificial unanimity the government may guide them toward public ends, or at least prevent them from destroying such ends. Here one certainly must not argue, instead one must obey. However, insofar as this part of the machine also regards himself as a member of the community as a whole, or even of the world community, and as a consequence addresses the public in the role of a scholar, in the proper sense of that term, he can most certainly argue, without thereby harming the affairs for which as a passive member he is partly responsible. Thus it would be disastrous if an officer on duty who was given a command by his superior were to question the appropriateness or utility of the order. He must obey. But as a scholar he cannot be justly constrained from making comments about errors in military service, or from placing them before the public for its judgment. The citizen cannot refuse to pay the taxes imposed on him; indeed, impertinent criticism of such levies, when they should be paid by him, can be punished as a scandal (since it can lead to widespread insubordination). But the same person does not act contrary to civic duty when, as a scholar, he publicly expresses his thoughts regarding the impropriety or even injustice of such taxes. Likewise a pastor is bound to instruct his catecumens and congregation in accordance with the symbol of the church he serves, for he was appointed on that condition. But as a scholar he has complete freedom, indeed even the calling, to impart to the public all of his carefully considered and well-intentioned thoughts concerning mistaken aspects of that symbol, as well as his suggestions for the better arrangement of religious and church matters. Nothing in this can weigh on his conscience. What he teaches in consequence of his office as a servant of the church he sets out as something with regard to which he has no discretion to teach in accord with his own lights; rather, he offers it under the direction and in the name of another. He will say, "Our church teaches this or that and these are the demonstrations it uses." He thereby extracts for his congregation all practical uses from precepts to which he would not himself subscribe with complete conviction, but whose presentation he can nonetheless undertake, since it is not entirely impossible that truth lies hidden in them, and, in any case, nothing contrary to the very nature of religion is to be found in them. If he believed he could find anything of the latter sort in them, he could not in good conscience serve in his position; he would have to resign. Thus an appointed teacher's use of his reason for the sake of his congregation is merely *private*, because, however large the congregation is, this use is always only domestic; in this regard, as a priest, he is not free and cannot be such because he is acting under instructions from someone else. By contrast, the cleric—as a scholar who speaks through his writings to the public as such, i.e., the world—enjoys in this *public use* of reason an unrestricted freedom to use his own rational capacities and to speak his own mind. For that the (spiritual) guardians of a people should themselves be immature is an absurdity that would insure the perpetuation of absurdities.

But would a society of pastors, perhaps a church assembly or venerable presbytery (as those among the Dutch call themselves), not be justified in binding itself by oath to a certain unalterable symbol in order to secure a constant guardianship over each of its members and through them over the people, and this for all time: I say that this is wholly impossible. Such a contract, whose intention is to preclude forever all further enlightenment of the human race, is absolutely null and void, even if it should be ratified by the supreme power, by parliaments, and by the most solemn peace treaties. One age cannot bind itself, and thus conspire, to place a succeeding one in a condition whereby it would be impossible for the later age to expand its knowledge (particularly where it is so very important), to rid itself of errors, and generally to increase its enlightenment. That would be a crime against human nature, whose essential destiny lies precisely in such progress; subsequent generations are thus completely justified in dismissing such agreements as unauthorized and criminal. The criterion of everything that can be agreed upon as a law by a people lies in this question: Can a people impose such a law on itself? Now it might be possible, in anticipation of a better state of affairs, to introduce a provisional order for a specific, short time, all the while giving all citizens, especially clergy, in their role as scholars, the freedom to comment publicly, i.e., in writing, on the present institution's shortcomings. The provisional order might last until insight into the nature of these matters had become so widespread and obvious that the combined (if not unanimous) voices of the populace could propose to the crown that it take under its protection those congregations that, in accord with their newly gained insight, had organized themselves under altered religious institutions, but without interfering with those wishing to allow matters to remain as before. However, it is absolutely forbidden that they unite into a religious organization that nobody may for the duration of a man's lifetime publicly question, for so doing would deny, render fruitless, and make detrimental to succeeding generations an era in man's progress toward improvement. A man may put off enlightenment with regard to what he ought to know, though only for a short time and for his own person; but to renounce it for himself, or, even more, for subsequent generations, is to violate and trample man's divine rights underfoot. And what a people may not decree for itself may still less be imposed on it by a monarch, for his lawgiving authority rests on his unification of the people's collective will in his own. If he only sees to it that all genuine or purported improvement is consonant with civil order, he can allow his subjects to do what they find necessary to their spiritual well-being, which is not his affair. However, he must prevent anyone from forcibly interfering with another's working as best he can to determine and promote his well-being. It detracts from his own majesty when he interferes in these matters, since the writings in which his subjects attempt to clarify their insights lend value to his conception of governance. This holds whether he acts from his own highest insight—whereby he calls upon himself the reproach, *"Caesar non est supra grammaticos"*—as well as, indeed even more, when he despoils his highest authority by supporting the spiritual despotism of some tyrants in his state over his other subjects.

If it is now asked, "Do we presently live in an *enlightened age?*" the answer is, "No, but we do live in an age of *enlightenment.*" As matters now stand, a great deal is still lacking in order for men as a whole to be, or even to put themselves into a position to be able without external guidance to apply understanding confidently to religious issues. But we do have clear indications that the way is now being opened for men to proceed freely in this direction and that the obstacles to general enlightenment—to their release from their self-imposed immaturity—are gradually diminishing. In this regard, this age is the age of enlightenment, the century of Frederick.

A prince who does not find it beneath him to say that he takes it to be his *duty* to prescribe nothing, but rather to allow men complete freedom in religious matters—who thereby renounces the arrogant title of *tolerance*—is himself enlightened and deserves to be praised by a grateful present and by posterity as the first, at least where the government is concerned, to release the human race from immaturity and to leave everyone free to use his own reason in all matters of conscience. Under his rule, venerable pastors, in their role as scholars and without prejudice to their official duties, may freely and openly set out for the world's scrutiny their judgments and views, even where these occasionally differ from the accepted symbol. Still greater freedom is afforded to those who are not restricted by an official post. This spirit of freedom is expanding even where it must struggle against the external obstacles of governments that misunderstand their own function. Such governments are illuminated by the example that the existence of freedom need not give cause for the least concern regarding public order and harmony in the commonwealth. If only they refrain from inventing artifices to keep themselves in it, men will gradually raise themselves from barbarism.

I have focused on religious matters in setting out my main point concerning enlightenment, i.e., man's emergence from self-imposed immaturity, first because our rulers have no interest in assuming the role of their subjects' guardians with respect to the arts and sciences, and secondly because that form of immaturity is both the most pernicious and disgraceful of all. But the manner of thinking of a head of state who favors religious enlightenment goes even further, for he realizes that there is no danger to his *legislation* in allowing his subjects to use reason *publicly* and to set before the world their thoughts concerning better formulations of his laws, even if this involves frank criticism of legislation currently in effect. We have before us a shining example, with respect to which no monarch surpasses the one whom we honor.

But only a ruler who is himself enlightened and has no dread of shadows, yet who likewise has a well-disciplined, numerous army to guarantee public peace, can say what no republic may dare, namely: *"Argue as much as you want and about what you want, but obey!"* Here as elsewhere, when things are considered in broad perspective, a strange, unexpected pattern in human affairs reveals itself, one in which almost everything is paradoxical. A greater degree of civil freedom seems advantageous to a people's *spiritual* freedom; yet the former established impassable boundaries for the latter; conversely, a lesser degree of civil freedom provides enough room for all fully to expand their abilities. Thus, once nature had removed the hard shell from this kernel for which she has most fondly cared, namely, the inclination to and vocation for free *thinking*, the kernel gradually reacts on a people's mentality (whereby they become increasingly able to *act freely*), and it finally even influences the principles of *government*, which finds that it can profit by treating men, *who are now more than machines*, in accord with their dignity.

Koenigsberg in Prussia, 30 September 1784

I. KANT

STUDY QUESTIONS

1. Paraphrase (in your own words) Kant's definition of "Enlightenment." Be careful not to lose anything in the translation!

2. What are the two principal causes of our lack of enlightenment?

3. What does Kant suppose is the sufficient condition for enlightenment in his sense? What is your assessment of this supposition?

4. What restrictions does Kant suggest hinder enlightenment? Which one(s) actually advance the cause of enlightenment?

5. What is the difference between an "enlightened age" and "an age of enlightenment"?

6. What is the criterion of anything that can agreed upon as law?

7. What is the difference between the public and the private use of reason? Be careful to look very closely at what the text actually says regarding this distinction.

Appendix

St. Thomas Aquinas
(1224–1274)

AT THE END OF 1224 or the beginning of 1225, outside of Naples, in the castle of Roccasecca, Thomas Aquinas was born, the seventh and youngest son of Landulf, Count of Aquino, and Theodora of Theate. In 1230, at the age of about five he was sent to the Benedictine abbey of Monte Cassino for his scholarly and religious education. His father hoped that Thomas would become a monk and eventually succeed to the post of abbot of Monte Cassino.

Because of political events Thomas had to leave the abbey in 1239 and return to his parents. This turn of events was providential since it would bring young Thomas in contact with members of the newly founded Dominican Order to which he would devote his life. It happened this way: Thomas was sent for further studies to the University in Naples in which city the Dominican Friars had a convent. Thomas was very much impressed with these men and in 1244 joined the Order to share in their work of preaching and teaching.

His family was very much opposed to Thomas' plan, so much so that while he was on his way from Naples to Paris, where he was to study at the Dominican house at the University of Paris, his brothers kidnapped him and held him at Aquino for almost a year. The family failed to dissuade Thomas, and in 1245 he escaped and this time successfully made his way to Paris.

In 1248, Thomas left Paris for Cologne in the company of his fellow Dominican and teacher, Albert the Great, who was to open there a house of studies for the Order. Thomas remained there under Albert's tutelage until 1252. During this period Albert, recognizing Thomas' talent, encouraged him to take up theological research and teaching as a career. Albert also introduced Thomas to the "new" philosophy, Aristotelianism, which was so to shape Thomas' philosophical and theological writings. And thus, Thomism, as it came to be known, acquired its Aristotelian flavor.

In 1252 Thomas returned to Paris, where he continued his course of studies. In 1256 he received his Licentiate (that is, permission to teach as a member of the theology faculty) and in the same year was awarded the title Magister, a degree equivalent to our Doctorate. He continued to

teach until 1259 when he left Paris for Italy, where he taught theology at
the Papal court for nine years.

He was summoned back to Paris in 1268 to offset the influence of
the Latin Averroists whose chief spokesman was Siger of Brabant. The
Averroists were so called because they followed the Muslim philosopher Ibn Rushd's (Averroës) understanding of Aristotle. Averroës was
called the "Commentator" because of his copious writings interpreting
Aristotle's views. Some of these interpretations were incompatible with
Christianity, and these were espoused by the Latin Averroists. Perhaps
the major point contrary to Christian belief held by this group was the
thesis that there was only one single spiritual intellect common to all
men and that this agent intellect, as it was called, resided in one of the
divine heavenly bodies, perhaps the moon. Such a doctrine would have
rendered personal immortality impossible, and this of course was contrary to Christian doctrine. Thomas combated that view with his accustomed vigor and thoroughness.

In 1272 his Order sent him to Naples to establish a house of studies
for his brother Dominicans. Two years later he was summoned by Pope
Gregory X to take part in a church Council to be held at Lyons. On the
journey to that place Thomas died at the Cistercian monastery of
Fossanuova between Naples and Rome. He was just 50 years old.

The number of works produced during that short lifetime is truly
prodigious. To cite only some of the better-known works I mention the
following: the *Summa theologiae* (a "summary" of theology which runs to
four or five volumes depending on which edition one uses); the *Summa
contra Gentes* (a treatise written to respond to Muslim attacks on
Christian belief); numerous commentaries on the books of Aristotle; and
short pieces on a variety of philosophical and theological topics.

The selection reproduced here is taken from the *Summa theologiae*
and deals with a key consideration in any philosophical reflection on
human knowing: that is, the role of formal signs in that activity. The for-
mat of this article illustrates what is sometimes called the "scholastic"
method of presentation: namely, a question is posed; an opinion is
given, along with arguments and authorities to support it, then the
author's opinion is given and argued for; and, finally, the objections
posed by the first position are answered.

The point to look for in this piece is that in knowing, we do not
know ideas, but things by means of ideas. "Ideas" in this sense are
sometimes called pure or "formal" signs. Scholastic philosophers have
often referred to such a formal sign as a principle by which something is
known (*principium quo*) in the case of sensation, or as a principle in

which something is known (*principium in quo*) in the case of intellection, but never as *that which* is known in either case. If we become aware of these formal signs or ideas, it is only indirectly and by reflection.

SUGGESTED READING

Chesterton, G. K. *St. Thomas Aquinas*. New York: Sheed & Ward, 1933.

Copleston, F., S.J. *Aquinas*. Harmondworth, Middlesex: Penguin, 1955.

——. *A History of Philosophy*. II. *Mediaeval Philosophy: Augustine to Scotus*. Westminster, Md.: Newman, 1955.

Gilson, E. *A History of Christian Philosophy in the Middle Ages*. New York: Random House, 1955.

Maritain, J. *St. Thomas Aquinas*. 3rd. ed. London, 1946.

Pieper, J. *Guide to Thomas Aquinas*. Notre Dame: University of Notre Dame Press, 1987.

Weisheipl, J. A., O.P. *Friar Thomas D'Aquino: His Life, Thought and Works*. Garden City, N.Y.: Doubleday, 1974.

From

Summa Theologiae

Part I, Question 85

Second Article

Whether the intelligible species abstracted from phantasms are related to our intellect as that which is understood?

We proceed thus to the second article:—

Objection 1. It would seem that the intelligible species abstracted from phantasms are related to our intellect as that which is understood. For the understood in act is the one who understands: since the understood in act is the intellect itself in act. But nothing of what is understood is in the actually understanding intellect save the abstracted intelligible species. Therefore this species is what is actually understood.

Obj. 2. Further, what is actually understood must be in something; or else it would be nothing. But it is not in something outside the soul; for, since what is outside the soul is material, nothing therein can be actually understood. Therefore what is actually understood is in the intellect. Consequently it can be nothing else than the aforesaid intelligible species.

Obj. 3. Further, the Philosopher says that *words are signs of the passions in the soul.* But words signify the things understood, for we express by word what we understand. Therefore these passions of the soul, viz., the intelligible species, are what is actually understood.

On the contrary, the intelligible species is to the intellect what the sensible species is to the sense. But the sensible species is not *what* is perceived, but rather that *by which* the sense perceives. Therefore the intelligible species is not what is actually understood, but that by which the intellect understands.

I answer that, Some have asserted that our intellectual powers know only the impressions made on them; as, for example, that sense is cognizant only of the impression made on its organ. According to this theory, the intellect understands only its own impressions, namely, the intelligible species which it has received.

This is, however, manifestly false for two reasons. First, because the things we understand are also objects of science. Therefore, if what we understand is merely the intelligible species in the soul, it would follow that every science would be concerned, not with things outside the soul, but only with the intelligible species within the soul; just as, according to the teaching of the Platonists, all the sciences are about Ideas, which they held to be that which is actually understood. Secondly, it is untrue, because it would lead to the opinion of the ancients who maintained *whatever seems, is true,* and that consequently contradictories are true simultaneously. For if a power knows only its own impressions, it can judge only of them. Now a thing *seems* according to the impression made on the cognitive power. Consequently the cognitive power will always judge of its own impression as such; and so every judgment will be true. For instance, if taste perceived only its own impression, when anyone with a healthy taste perceives that honey is sweet, he would judge truly, and if anyone with a corrupt taste perceives that honey is bitter, this would be equally true; for each would judge according to the impression of his taste. Thus every opinion, in fact, every sort of apprehension, would be equally true.

Therefore it must be said that the intelligible species is related to the intellect as that by which it understands. Which is proved thus. Now action is twofold, as it is said in *Metaph.* ix: one which remains in the agent (for instance, to see and to understand), and another which passes into an external object (for instance, to heat and to cut). Each of these actions proceeds in virtue of some form. And just as the form from which proceeds an act tending to something external is the likeness of the object of the action, as heat in the heater is a likeness of the thing heated, so the form from which proceeds an action remaining in the agent is a likeness of the object. Hence that by which the sight sees is the likeness of the visible thing: and the likeness of the thing understood, that is, the intelligible species, is the form by which the intellect understands. But since the intellect reflects upon itself, by such reflection it understands both its own act of understanding, and the species by which it understands. Thus the intelligible species is secondarily that which is understood; but that which is primarily understood is the thing, of which the species is the likeness.

This also appears from the opinion of the ancient philosophers, who said that *like is known by like* [Empedocles]. For they said that the soul knows the earth outside itself by the earth within itself; and so of the rest. If, therefore, we take the species of the earth instead of the earth, in accord with Aristotle who says that *a stone is not in the soul, but only the likeness of the stone*, it follows that by means of its intelligible species the soul knows the things which are outside it.

Reply Obj. 1. The thing understood is in the knower by its own likeness. It is in this sense that we say that the thing actually understood is in the intellect in act, because the likeness of the thing understood is the form of the intellect, just as the likeness of a sensible thing is the form of the sense in act. Hence it does not follow that the abstracted intelligible species is what is actually understood; but rather that it is the likeness thereof.

Reply Obj. 2. In these words *the thing actually understood* there is a double meaning:—the thing which is understood, and the fact that it is understood. In like manner, the words *abstract universal* mean two things, the nature of a thing and its abstraction or universality. Therefore the nature itself which suffers the act of being understood, or the act of being abstracted, or the intention of universality, exists only in individuals; but that it is understood, abstracted or considered as universal is in the intellect. We see something similar to this in the senses. For the sight sees the color of the apple apart from its smell. If therefore it be asked where is the color which is seen apart from the smell, it is quite clear that the color which is seen is only in the apple; but that it be perceived apart from the smell, this is owing to the sight. inasmuch as sight receives the likeness of color and not of smell. In like manner, the humanity which is understood exists only in this or that man; but that humanity be apprehended without the conditions of individuality, that is, that it be abstracted and consequently considered as universal, befalls humanity inasmuch as it is perceived by the intellect, in which there is a likeness of the specific nature, but not of the individual principles.

Reply Obj. 3. There are two operations in the sensitive part. One is limited to immutation, and thus the operation of the senses takes place when the senses are impressed by the sensible. The other is formation, inasmuch as the imagination forms for itself an image of an absent thing, or even of something never seen. Both of these operations are found in the intellect. For in the first place there is the passion of the possible intellect as informed by the intelligible species; and then the possible intellect, as thus informed, then forms a definition, or a division, or a composition which is expressed by language. And so, the notion signified by a *term* is a definition; and a *proposition* signifies the intellect's division or composition. Words do not therefore signify the intelligible species themselves; but that which the intellect forms for itself for the purpose of judging of external things.

STUDY QUESTIONS

1. What two reasons does St. Thomas give to show that our concepts or ideas (in his terminology "intelligible species") are *not* the objects of our intellectual powers?

2. How are ideas or "intelligible species" related to the human intellect if they are not the object of the intellect?

3. How are "things" understood?

4. What two meanings of the expression "the thing actually understood" does St. Thomas distinguish?

5. What two operations in the sensitive part of the soul does St. Thomas distinguish? How does this distinction help meet the third objection?